D0345848

University of
Chester

CHESTER CAMPUS
LIBRARY
01244 513301

This book is to be returned on or before the last date stamped
below. Overdue charges will be incurred by the late return of
books.

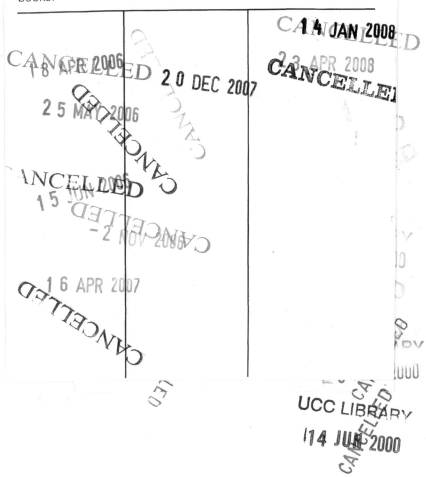

CANCELLED
1 8 APR 2006

2 5 MAY 2006

CANCELLED
1 5 JUN

16 APR 2007

2 0 DEC 2007

CANCELLED
-2 NOV 2007

CANCELLED

14 JAN 2008

23 APR 2008
CANCELLED

UCC LIBRARY
14 JUN 2000

Teaching and learning geography

Edited by Daniella Tilbury and
Michael Williams

LIBRARY

ACC. No.
0100973

DEPT.

CLASS No.
375 91 TIL

UNIVERSITY
COLLEGE CHESTER

1044308

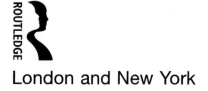

London and New York

First published 1997
by Routledge
11 New Fetter Lane, London EC4P 4EE

Simultaneously published in the USA and Canada
by Routledge
29 West 35th Street, New York, NY 10001

Selection and editorial material © 1997 Daniella Tilbury and Michael Williams;
individual chapters © the contributors

Typeset in Garamond by J&L Composition Ltd, Filey, North Yorkshire
Printed and bound in Great Britain by TJ Press (Padstow) Ltd, Padstow, Cornwall

All rights reserved. No part of this book may be reprinted or
reproduced or utilized in any form or by any electronic,
mechanical, or other means, now known or hereafter
invented, including photocopying and recording, or in any
information storage or retrieval system, without permission in
writing from the publishers.

British Library Cataloguing in Publication Data

A catalogue record for this book is available from the British Library

Library of Congress Cataloguing in Publication Data

Teaching and learning geography / edited by Daniella Tilbury and
Michael Williams.
  p. cm.
  Includes bibliographical references and index.
  1. Geography – Study and teaching (Primary) 2. Geography – Study and
teaching (Secondary) I. Tilbury, Daniella, Ph.D. II. Williams, Michael.
G73. T415 1997
910'.71'173–dc20   96–22402

ISBN 0–415–14244–X

Contents

List of figures   viii
List of tables   x
Notes on contributors   xi
List of abbreviations   xv

1 Introduction   1
  Daniella Tilbury and Michael Williams

Part I

⊀ 2 The place of geography in the school curriculum: an historical
      overview 1886–1976   7
      Bill Marsden

⊀ 3 The great debate and 1988   15
      Rex Walford

⊀ 4 Geographical education in the 1990s   25
      Norman Graves

Part II

  5 Curriculum planning and course development: a matter of
      professional judgement   35
      Margaret Roberts

  6 The scope of school geography: a medium for education   49
      Michael Naish

  7 Progression and transition in a coherent geography curriculum   59
      Michael Williams

  8 Differentiation in teaching and learning geography   69
      Jeff Battersby

9 Cross-curricular concerns in geography: Earth science and
    physical geography   80
    Duncan Hawley

10 Cross-curricular concerns in geography: citizenship and economic
    and industrial understanding   93
    Daniella Tilbury

11 Environmental education and development education: teaching
    geography for a sustainable world   105
    Daniella Tilbury

12 Equal opportunity and the teaching of geography   117
    Brian Gonzalez and Elizabeth Gonzalez

Part III

13 Instructional design   133
    Michael Williams

14 Cognitive acceleration in geographical education   143
    David Leat

15 Language and learning in geography   154
    Graham Butt

16 Learning through maps   168
    Paul Weeden

17 Ethnocentric bias in geography textbooks: a framework for
    reconstruction   180
    Christine Winter

18 Teaching and learning through fieldwork   189
    Nick Foskett

19 Using information technology and new technologies in
    geography   202
    Diana Freeman

20 Teaching about the local community: using first-hand
    experience   218
    Rachel Bowles

21 The European dimension in primary education   231
    John Halocha

22 Towards a critical school geography   241
    John Huckle

Part IV

23 Principles of pupil assessment   255
    David Lambert

24 Assessment in the primary school   266
    Patrick Wiegand

25 Teacher assessment in the National Curriculum   275
    David Lambert

26 Geography and the GCSE   287
    Sheila King

27 Student assessment in geography post-16   298
    Graham Butt

    Index   310

List of figures

3.1 Combining the attainment targets   19
5.1 Two models of curriculum planning in geography   37
6.1 A caricature of Advanced level geography (1974)   52
7.1 The curriculum staircase   61
7.2 Proposals for progression at each of Key Stages 1 to 3   63
7.3 Contrasts in curriculum culture between upper primary and lower secondary schools   65
8.1 Differentiation strategies   73
9.1 The Earth science component of the Science National Curriculum   84
9.2 Inductive and deductive routes to explanation   85
9.3 Cross-curricular co-ordination in science and geography   87
9.4 Science curriculum concepts that are useful in geography   89
12.1 Book evaluation matrix   126
13.1 Instructional design as a system   134
15.1 Two dimensions of questioning   156
15.2 Analyses of questions   157
15.3 Example of a sequencing DART: tea   165
16.1 A simplified map communication system   169
16.2 A map showing a range of symbols and information   172
19.1 How IT supports enquiry learning in geography   206
19.2 Information- and data-handling skills used for enquiry learning   208
19.3 Data collected by an automatic data-logging weather station   209
19.4 Satellite images   209
19.5 Results of an environmental assessment survey   210
19.6 World map indicating life expectancy   210
19.7 Some contexts for introducing IT into geography activities   212–13
20.1 Regular journeys of children in their locality   222–3
20.2 Questions to be asked about a locality   228–9
23.1 Part of a marking policy which distinguishes purpose   262
23.2 Records at the disposal of a teacher   263

25.1 Looking inside a level description   279
25.2 Progression in knowledge and understanding of places and
     themes   280–1
25.3 Identifying progression in geographical skills   283
25.4 Assessment in the Geography National Curriculum   285
26.1 Comparable examination grades   289
26.2 Aims of geography GCSE syllabuses   291
26.3 Grade C grade description   295
27.1 'No golden age of A-levels'   300
27.2 National Qualifications Framework   306
27.3 National targets for education and training by 2000   307

List of tables

12.1 Gender bias of KS3 textbooks published 1991/1992   127
18.1 A spectrum of fieldwork locations for geography   192
18.2 A continuum of teaching and learning strategies for fieldwork   194
18.3 Outline planning checklist for fieldwork organization   196
18.4 A geography fieldwork plan for a secondary school   199
23.1 A glossary of the principal features of educational assessment   256
25.1 Checklist of quality criteria in Teacher Assessment (TA)   277
27.1 A/AS approved syllabuses (as of 30 June 1995)   303
27.2 Comparisons between A/AS levels, GNVQs and NVQs   305

Notes on contributors

Jeff Battersby has taught in secondary schools for over twenty-five years. He is now a Lecturer in Geography and Environmental Education at the University of East Anglia, where he is also responsible for the Secondary PGCE course. He was a member of the SCAA Geography Advisory Group and a consultant developing optional tasks for Key Stage 3 assessment. He is a consultative and coursework moderator for Avery Hill Geography. He is a member of The Geographical Association's Education Standing Committee.

Rachel Bowles lectures and tutors in education and environmental sciences at the University of Greenwich and is an INSET consultant for geography and environmental education. A regular contributor to Geographical Association and other publications for primary teachers, she has recently produced three locality studies and is now compiling a register on primary children's geographical perceptions.

Graham Butt is a Lecturer in Geography Education at the University of Birmingham. He is a member of The Geographical Association and has been involved with its Assessment and Examinations Working Group for many years. His research and writing has largely focused on different aspects of both the teaching and examining of geography courses.

Nick Foskett is Deputy Head of the School of Education, University of Southampton. He has taught geography in schools and 16–19 colleges and has been Head of Geography. His research interests are in the areas of fieldwork practice and in the links between international/national environmental policy and the practice of geography teachers in schools and colleges.

Diana Freeman is a founder and director of The Advisory Unit: Computers in Education. She has been closely involved in developing educational software and associated curriculum materials to support teaching and learning geography with information technology. She is a member of the

IT Working Group of The Geographical Association, chairs the GIS subgroup, and is on the Education Sub-Committee of the Royal Geographical Society.

Brian Gonzalez is head of Geography at Westside School for Girls in Gibraltar. He is a graduate of the University of Aberdeen. His M.Ed. focused on the changing role of the teacher. He is now carrying out doctoral research on the problems of geographical education in Gibraltar.

Elizabeth Gonzalez is head of the sixth form at Bayside School, a boys' comprehensive school in Gibraltar. She was born and educated in Aberdeen, where she took a degree in geography. She has taught geography at Cults Academy in Aberdeen and at Bayside since 1978. At present she is working on an M.Ed. on the transition of students from the sixth form to university.

Norman Graves is Professor Emeritus of Geography Education at the Institute of Education, University of London, formerly Director of Professional Studies and Holder of the Royal Geographical Society's Victoria Medal for services to geographical education. He is the author of several books and many articles on education generally, and on geographical education in particular, and is working at the moment on a handbook for doctoral students (to be published by Routledge).

John Halocha is Principal Lecturer in Geography Education and Teaching Studies and Co-ordinator of Professional Studies on the B.Ed. course at Westminster College, University of Oxford. He has taught in primary and middle schools and was Deputy Head Teacher of two schools. He is engaged in partnership work with schools in initial teacher education.

Duncan Hawley has taught geography and earth sciences in comprehensive schools, field centres and a city technology college. He has worked as an Advisory Teacher for geography and earth sciences in Gloucestershire, is co-tutor of the geography PGCE course at the University of Wales Swansea and chairman of the Earth Sciences Teachers' Association.

John Huckle is a Principal Lecturer in Geographical and Environmental Education at De Montfort University Bedford. He is a consultant to the World Wide Fund for Nature's education department and is the main author of *Reaching Out: Education for Sustainability*, the department's programme of professional development for teachers.

Sheila King taught geography in a variety of schools for seventeen years and was Head of Humanities in one of the largest comprehensive schools in west London. She is now a geography lecturer in initial teacher training at the University of London Institute of Education. She is also co-ordinator of the south-east region of The Geographical Association.

David Lambert is Senior Lecturer in Geography Education at the University of London Institute of Education where he is co-ordinating tutor for the geography PGCE. He is also involved in the teaching of INSET, various short courses and the MA in Geography Education. His research interests include assessment policy and practice, and the concept of prejudice in Geography Education. He also has an interest in textbooks and produced the Cambridge Geography Project which won the 1992 *TES* Schoolbook of the Year Award.

David Leat taught for twelve years, including four years at an LEA field centre. He is now a geography PGCE tutor at the University of Newcastle, and his research interests lie in teachers' thinking and professional development. He works with a group of teachers on a project entitled 'Thinking Through Geography', preparing a series of books on how to make geography more challenging to pupils. He is engaged in two curriculum development projects in Northumberland (humanities) and Cleveland (science) focusing on the barriers to implementing thinking skills approaches, with a view to devising more powerful in-service education models.

Bill Marsden is Emeritus Professor of Education at the University of Liverpool. He is the author of many publications in geographical education and in the history of education, including *Evaluating the Geography Curriculum* (Oliver and Boyd 1976) and *Geography 11–16; Rekindling Good Practice* (David Fulton 1995). He edited *Historical Perspectives on Geographical Education* (IGU 1980) and *Primary School Geography* (David Fulton 1994).

Michael Naish is Reader in Education at the Institute of Education, University of London. His main interests are curriculum development and teacher education. He was director of the Geography 16–19 Project and has written school-books as well as works for teachers.

Margaret Roberts is Lecturer in Education at the University of Sheffield Division of Education, where she has been centrally involved in the development of the University's partnership in teacher education with schools. She is responsible for co-ordinating the geography curriculum element of the PGCE course. Her main research interest is the implementation of the Geography National Curriculum in secondary schools.

Daniella Tilbury is a Lecturer in Geography Education at the University of Wales Swansea, where she is responsible for the geography PGCE course. She has taught geography in English, Gibraltarian and Australian schools and has been involved with in-service teacher education in several European countries. Her doctoral research focused on environmental education. She has been an environmental education consultant to a number of organizations, including the European Educational Regional Partnership.

Rex Walford is University Lecturer in Geography and Education at the University of Cambridge and a Fellow of Wolfson College. He was a member of the National Curriculum Geography Working Group, is a past President of The Geographical Association and is currently a Vice-President of the Royal Geographical Society.

Paul Weeden is Lecturer in Education (Geography) at the University of Bristol. He previously taught in a Bristol comprehensive school and was Advisory Teacher in both Somerset and Avon. Current research interests include Key Stage 3 assessment and assessing locational knowledge.

Patrick Wiegand is Senior Lecturer in Geography Education at the University of Leeds. His research interests are in educational cartography, including electronic atlases, and children's understanding of distant places. He has edited several atlases for schools.

Michael Williams is Professor of Education and Dean of the Faculty of Education and Health Studies at the University of Wales Swansea. He has written many articles and books on aspects of geographical education and his special interests are in curriculum design and evaluation. His most recent book is *Understanding Geographical and Environmental Education: The Role of Research* (Cassell 1995).

Christine Winter is a lecturer at the University of Sheffield Division of Education. She teaches geography on the PGCE course and educational studies at Masters degree level. She is joint author of the National Curriculum textbook series *Enquiry Geography* (Hodder and Stoughton 1991). From 1991 to 1992 she was involved in an ESRC research project which explored cognitive and social processes in secondary schools. She is at present carrying out research which focuses on changes in the humanities curriculum.

List of abbreviations

ACAC	*Awdurdod Cwricwlwm ac Asesu Cymru*
AT	Attainment Target
CAAW	Curriculum and Assessment Authority for Wales
CASE	Cognitive Acceleration in Science Education
CCTH	Cross-curricular theme
CCW	Curriculum Council for Wales
CoRT	Cognitive Research Trust
DARTS	Directed Activities Related to Texts
DES	Department of Education and Science
DFE	Department for Education
EFC	Education for Citizenship
EFS	Education for Sustainability
EIU	Economic and Industrial Understanding
ERA	Education Reform Act
GA	The Geographical Association
GCSE	General Certificate of Secondary Education
GEON	Geography and Equal Opportunities Network
GIS	Geographic Information Systems
GNC	Geography National Curriculum
GNVQ	General National Vocational Qualification
GSIP	Geography Schools and Industry Project
GWG	Geography Working Group
HMI	Her Majesty's Inspectorate
HMSO	Her Majesty's Stationery Office
IGU	International Geographical Union
INSET	In-Service Education and Training
IT	Information Technology
IUCN	International Union for the Conservation of Nature
KS	Key Stage
LEA	Local Education Authority
LINC	Language in the National Curriculum

NCC	National Curriculum Council
NCE	National Commission on Education
NEAB	Northern Examinations and Assessment Board
NFER	National Foundation for Educational Research
OFSTED	Office for Standards in Education
OS	Ordnance Survey
PGCE	Post-Graduate Certificate in Education
PoS	Programme of Study
RGS	Royal Geographical Society
SCAA	School Curriculum and Assessment Authority
SEC	Secondary Examination Council
SoA	Statement of Attainment
TA	Teacher Assessment
TGAT	Task Group on Assessment and Training
TTG	Thinking Through Geography
UNEP	United Nations Environment Programme
UNESCO	United Nations Educational, Scientific and Cultural Organization
WCED	World Commission on Environment and Development
WJEC	Welsh Joint Education Committee
WOED	Welsh Office Education Department

Chapter 1

Introduction

Daniella Tilbury and Michael Williams

Unlike the core subjects of language, mathematics and science the place of geography in the curriculum of primary and secondary schools is relatively uncertain. In some countries the separate identity of the subject is not recognized while in others it is often squeezed into elective structures as pressures mount on the limited amount of curriculum time. In elementary and primary schools geography is sometimes included as one component of topics studied there while in secondary schools it may be integrated into courses labelled humanities, social studies or environmental education.

The focus in this book is predominantly on geography identified as a separate subject, largely within the context of schools in England and Wales. Our overall aim is to provide a clear and thorough overview of contemporary concerns in the teaching and learning of geography and to offer pointers for future developments in the subject. The National Curriculum introduced by legislation in 1988 is the obvious backcloth for the chapters and we have sought to take into account any variations which have emerged in curriculum provision between England and Wales. Even in the short period since 1988 changes have been made in the statutory requirements for curriculum content and pupil assessment. As part of a slimming-down process the status of geography has been modified, particularly for pupils aged 14–16 in Key Stage 4, and the amount of content in each of the four Key Stages has been reduced. Major alterations are also being implemented in the whole 16–19 curriculum in response to the pressure to develop vocational courses and examinations. Despite the many changes taking place in geography teaching, however, central principles and practices in teaching and learning continue to be relevant. We have sought to concentrate on the continuities while placing them within the context of the changing curriculum environment.

The historical context is the subject of the first three chapters. Initially, the focus is upon the broad sweep of the changing nature of school geography in the twentieth century. This takes into account the reorganization of state schools and the legislation and official reports which have had a major influence on geography teaching. The next chapter discusses the period since 1976, which marked the start of the 'great debate' about the curriculum, and emphasizes the significance of the 1988 Education Reform Act which made geography a mandatory foundation subject for pupils aged 5–16 in state schools. The tensions encountered in seeking to define the nature of the subject and the achievements in implementing the Act are considered. The final chapter in this section brings the history up to date. While, at one stage, it appeared that the Education Reform Act marked the end of a developmental process, it is now clear that further refinements are necessary. It is one thing to define mandatory subjects, but it is quite another to implement centrally defined innovations in school classrooms. Further, it must be acknowledged that the framework provided by legislation is only a framework and that there is scope for schools to design their own courses which take account of local circumstances and the special interests of pupils and teachers. Contemporary trends in primary and secondary geographical education are reviewed in the framework of aims, content, teaching methods and modes of assessment, and suggestions are made for likely changes in the future.

In Part II the authors address issues of course planning and design. The nature of school geography, distinct in many ways from geography in other sectors of education, is examined from the perspectives of its scope and of the way it is structured to take account of the developing pupil and student. It includes consideration of how courses can be designed to meet the needs of pupils with different abilities and interests. That geography should not be considered in isolation from other subjects lies at the heart of the concept of the entire curriculum. The search for coherence and continuity both in the whole curriculum and in the geography curriculum continues. A key to this is cross-curricularity. Geography teachers have been particularly active in seeking to identify the links between geography and other subjects – for example, history and science – and, indeed, there have been transfers in content between these subjects. Cross-curricularity also embraces a number of themes, dimensions and skills. These are explored in chapters about environmental and development education, economic and industrial understanding and citizenship (community understanding in Wales) and equal opportunities.

From a concern with course design, syllabuses and programmes of study we move in Part III to classroom concerns. An attempt is made to strike a balance between emphases on learning and teaching. Learning theories and teaching theories are introduced and the centrality of language in facilitating pupil learning is explored. School geography is especially concerned with mapwork, fieldwork and the use of new technologies. Each of these is given separate treatment. That geography can be studied at a number of different levels is self-evident to geographers and approaches to teaching about the local community, on the one hand, and the international community, on the other, are discussed. As contemporary political debates highlight, studying other countries and, indeed, any environmental issues is laden with controversy. Bias and propaganda, stereotyping and misinformation, are dangers of which geography teachers need always to be aware. There is also a danger in promoting a bland and uncritical neutrality. Part III concludes with an exploration of the implications of adopting a radical perspective for defining course aims, content, teaching methods and pupil assessment.

Just as the content and teaching methods associated with geography will vary as pupils and students move through the stages of schooling so do the purposes and modes of pupil assessment. Although there are certain key principles underpinning assessment in general, it is important to distinguish between the way pupils are assessed in the topic-based courses characteristic in primary schools and the subject-specialist courses typical in secondary schools and colleges. Similarly, there are fundamental distinctions between, for example, external examinations and teacher assessments and between summative and formative assessment. Recent years have witnessed the reform of assessment at all levels – statutory standard attainment tests, General Certificate of Secondary Education (GCSE), General Certificate of Education (GCE) Advanced (A) and Advanced Supplementary (AS) levels, and General National Vocational Qualifications (GNVQs) – and these issues are reviewed in Part IV from the perspective of the geography teacher.

It is obvious from the chapters in this book that nothing in the school geographical curriculum is stable. Indeed, there never has been a period of stability in geographical education: reform and innovation are the buzz words rather than consolidation and entrenchment. Through all the changes, whether they are external or internal to the school in origin, the professionalism of individual teachers and groups of teachers in primary and secondary schools is crucial if an appropriate blend between the continuing principles underpinning good geographical education and innovations is to be achieved. It is our hope that this book will make a contribution to sustaining this professionalism and will offer some guidance to both new and experienced teachers who are charged with the task of modernizing the subject in the interest of future students and citizens.

Part I

Chapter 2

The place of geography in the school curriculum

An historical overview 1886–1976

Bill Marsden

SOME GEOGRAPHICAL ROOTS

The 1880s were an important time in the development of geography as a secondary school and university subject. In 1886, the Royal Geographical Society (RGS) commissioned the Keltie Report, the *Proceedings of the Royal Geographical Society in Reference to the Improvement of Geographical Education*. A second key publication was Halford Mackinder's 'On the scope and methods of geography' (1887), published in the RGS's journal, in which he sought to resolve the great schism between geography's physical and political components. Both publications made it clear that geography would not establish itself in universities and secondary schools unless it acquired the status of a genuine academic discipline, which meant forsaking its previous image as a mere repository of world knowledge.

Another major authority at this time was Archibald Geikie, a Scottish geologist of commanding intellectual stature. He took a keen interest in geography, especially as a school subject. His paper to the RGS in 1879 on 'Geographical evolution' preceded and matched Mackinder's in its grasp of the issues at stake. In his superb *The Teaching of Geography* (1887), Geikie infused his methodology with the best principles of progressive primary practice. Mackinder reviewed the book respectfully but was critical of Geikie's incorporation of a whole range of environmental sciences into geography. More damaging for Geikie's future influence with the geographical establishment was his refusal publicly to support justifications for geography as a separate discipline in the universities.

A critical event of the 1890s was the establishment of the Geographical Association (GA) (Balchin 1993) as a result of a group of secondary teachers joining together to exchange lantern slides. The new organization in effect took over the educational functions of the RGS, leaving the latter to concentrate on its support for world exploration and empire building. The GA was soon to produce a journal, *The Geographical Teacher*, which helped to seal the success of geography in establishing a place in secondary schools, and to disseminate a knowledge and understanding of the subject.

Thus Mackinder's pioneering endeavours in this quest were reinforced and achieved ultimate success. Geikie was almost forgotten and it was a Mackinder disciple, A.J. Herbertson, who was credited with establishing a new and important paradigm in geography, the regional principle. This was outlined in his famous paper of 1905 and transmitted into schools through his amazingly successful textbook *Senior Geography*, first appearing in 1907 and still in print in the early 1950s.

This regional paradigm represented on the face of it a great leap forward, but it was not an uncontested innovation. Two major arguments were raised against it, one academic and one pedagogic. First, it was recognized early on that the systematization of the world's natural regions and their climatic characteristics as they affected human occupance often led to blatant determinism. During the 1920s, for example, the geographical educationist, James Fairgrieve rejected the 'geographic control' argument (Fairgrieve 1936: 6–7). The thesis also had racist undertones, for writers were widely prone to accept the idea that climate served to determine not only human economic activity, but also human energies, attitudes and intelligence. Second, educational experts pointed out that the abstractions of the regional paradigm were unsuited to younger children, who required more vivid and smaller-scale place-based study. Herbertson himself conceded that 'the best logical order is not necessarily the best pedagogical order' (Herbertson 1906: 281).

Another outcome, regarded then positively rather than negatively, was that the regional paradigm emerged in the heyday of imperialism. It was instantly recognized by Newbigin (1914) and others of her generation that one great advantage of the climatic regions approach was that there was a bit of the British Empire in each major region. Thus in restricting the selection of areas to be covered in order to avoid excessive pressure on the timetable, priority could be given to imperial places. Textbooks focusing on the British Empire and, after World War II, on the Commonwealth, appeared in large numbers. Many of the great names in British geography also, such as Freshfield (1886), Mackinder (1911) and Fairgrieve (1924), were unashamed imperialists, averring that it was not only the right but also the duty of geography, even at the cost of scientific distortion, to give priority to the study of Britain and its Empire.

EXTERNAL SUPPORT FOR GEOGRAPHY IN THE SCHOOL CURRICULUM

This section will draw on official reports and consultative documents, and on generic texts in educational methodology which, like geographical sources, generally justified the subject's claims for a place in primary and secondary curricula.

Let us begin with two key progressive figures in primary education. One was the former HMI Edmond Holmes, who, after his retirement, launched a contemptuous attack on mechanical teaching, as practised in subjects such as elementary geography. But the attack was not, as later progressive disciples were to infer, on subject-teaching as such. Genuine knowledge, as he conceived it, was above all conceptual, something very different from factual recall. The memorization of geographical information 'is easily converted into knowledge of these facts, but it is not easily converted into knowledge of geography' (Holmes 1911: 90).

John Dewey similarly stressed that the key issue in promoting a progressive primary education was not through the polarization of child- and subject-centredness as incompatibles, but was much more to do with ensuring that the valuable and distinctive contributions of subjects such as geography and history were not polluted by didactic and mechanical teaching (Dewey 1916: 211).

In general, official reports on both primary and secondary curricula subsequently supported the case for geography (see Williams 1976). The Hadow Reports, for example, made cogent pleas for a well-taught geography. Thus, *The Education of the Adolescent* (Board of Education 1926) urged that the case for geography in post-primary education needed 'little arguing'. The subject should 'occupy no subsidiary or doubtful place', whether on utilitarian grounds, as 'an instrument of education', or as being appealing to children. The main objective should not be merely to accumulate information, but to develop 'an attitude of mind and a mode of thought characteristic of the subject' (ibid. 203–4).

The Primary School (Board of Education 1931) was subsequently hijacked and misused by progressive ideologues, who claimed that in its support for progressive methods it argued against the use of subject approaches in the primary school. The essence of Hadow's thesis, however, was that it was the traditional, didactic, grammar school-type methods of teaching subjects that were not appropriate, rather than the subject inputs themselves. While subjects as such should not be given priority, especially in the early years, and while the qualification was made that such work should not be merely a preparation for stages yet to come, Hadow included a three-and-a-half-page section on geography which began, 'Work in the primary school in geography, as in other subjects, must be thought of in terms of activity and experience, rather than of knowledge to be acquired and facts to be stored' (ibid. 171).

The Spens Report of 1938 on *Secondary Education* would seem to have accepted as read the case for geography. It was more concerned with the actual nature of the offering, which it saw as giving:

a conception of the world and of its diverse environments and peoples, which should enable boys and girls to see social and political problems in a truer perspective, and give them sympathetic understanding of other

peoples. For the older pupils a comprehensive scheme of world-study
. . . can offer scope for the consideration of vital problems bearing on
social, economic and political life.

(Board of Education 1938: 174)

The Norwood Report of 1943 on *Curriculum and Examinations in Secondary
Schools* offered fuller and equally positive support for geography in the
secondary school, noting its potential as a cementing subject in the curriculum, through studies of the environment. It stressed the pedagogic
principle of starting with the familiar and proceeding out into the wider
world, the importance of fieldwork, the interdependence of the world's
regions, and geography's function as a foundation subject for enlightened
citizenship. Without a firm basis in geography 'we cannot proceed with
confidence to the planning of the economic or the political design of the
future world' (Board of Education 1943: 102–4).

Post-war consultative documents and official statements were equally
supportive of the case for geography in both primary and secondary
curricula. The Ministry of Education advice in *The Primary School* of 1959
included a long résumé of what it saw as a suitable geography for use in
that phase. Its subheadings retain contemporary currency: the study of the
locality, involving a lively and intimate acquaintance with their own immediate environment; the study of other parts of the world using – in the case of
more distant places – 'illustrative material made alive with vivid detail' and
– in the case of other parts of the country perhaps school journeys or
holiday visits; stories and travellers' tales; the use of globe, maps and books;
recording the results of observations; and the scheme of work and the
outcomes of the course. Behind it all:

transcending national and geographical differences, is the idea of common humanity which has given rise to the various specialised agencies –
Food and Agriculture Organisation (FAO), United Nations Children's
Fund (UNICEF), World Health Organisation (WHO), etc. – which exist
to help all who need it and which embody man's concern for man.

(Ministry of Education 1959: 304)

Discussion of the Plowden Report, *Children and their Primary Schools*
(Ministry of Education 1967), is particularly significant and interesting
because this is the source used above all by progressives as clinching the
argument that subjects like geography are inappropriate in the primary
school (see, for example, Kelly 1986). In turn, of course, the Plowden
Report had been condemned by élitist commentators as 'mere ideology'
(see, for example, Peters 1969). Following Hadow, the Plowden Report
predictably suggested that work in the primary school should lay emphasis
on discovery and first-hand experience. But while it made abundantly clear
its view that formal subject categories did not fit in with younger children's

learning styles, it accepted that a subject input was increasingly appropriate as progress was made through the junior department. The Report included a four-page section on geography in the primary school, and offered differentiated advice on how it should be used – information that die-hard progressives chose either to ignore or suppress. Plowden supported not only local study but also the idea of sample studies which 'carry much of the authenticity of local geography and permit comparisons to be made with the home region' (Ministry of Education 1967, 1: 231). In content terms, there was not a great deal of difference between Plowden's conception of how geography was appropriate in the junior school and that of the National Curriculum (see Marsden 1991: 42–3).

The attack on geography as a subject was by no means confined to progressive primary supporters. The move to comprehensive schooling provoked similar conflict. Perhaps understandably, subjects were associated with traditional teaching methods, but the assault was on subjects as such, not merely on the methods by which they were taught.

The reactions of geographical lobbies, and most notably that of the RGS (1950), to such early attempts at promoting curriculum integration as the post-war social studies movement, were narrow-minded, rabble-rousing and even chauvinist, citing, among other things, American experience as a dubious parentage. In general, however, this resistance to the social studies movement of the 1950s achieved its goals, and the dream faded. After all, it was not too difficult to pinpoint a lack of coherence and rigour, but these deficiencies were recognized and acted upon by the next generation, and the 'new' social studies movement of the 1960s and 1970s (Lawton and Dufour 1973) was more carefully thought out. It was promoted, like other cross-curricular endeavours, under the label of inter-disciplinary enquiry, a tighter concept than curriculum integration. Graves' critique of interdisciplinary enquiry (1968) concentrated on the complexities resulting from the tensions between a wide-ranging conceptual offering, and the achievement of curriculum balance, sequence and focus, of building in progression, and not least of coping with the logistics of organization. It concluded, however, with the contradictory proposition that the more complex frameworks of social studies were more useful for less able children 'where traditional class teaching has failed' (Graves 1968: 394).

The later work of the Schools Council's Avery Hill Project also promoted the idea that to motivate less able children the work should be issues-based and related to everyday concerns within their own, mostly urban, localities. Drawing sustenance both from the increasing disenchantment with quantitative geography and from the promotion of welfare geography at the academic frontiers, and conducting its dissemination procedures with great skill, the Project was one of the most powerful forces in providing a foundation for the issues-based geography that was to come in the late 1970s and 1980s.

There were, however, a number of flaws in this reasoning. The first was that there has long been powerful psychological evidence that the attention of less able and certainly less motivated children is not necessarily captured by the immediacy and topicality of issues-based work. One of the most trenchant advocates of this view during the 1960s was Ausubel (Ausubel and Robinson 1969), arguing that the best way of motivating an unmotivated pupil was to bypass the tactic of direct motivation, and to establish instead motivational beach-heads by ensuring the reinforcement of success. Motivation he saw as developing 'retroactively from successful educational achievement'. Wall (1968) and Marland (1973) also argued in their different ways that relying for motivation by drawing on perceived pupil interests was of doubtful value in itself.

Issues-based work is also by definition interdisciplinary. It is difficult to think of any major world issue, whether economic, political, social or environmental, that can successfully be addressed purely by distinctive geographical methods. Issues-based work is demonstrably more effectively approached through integrated schemes. Thus geographers should be clear about their objectives in the broader sphere of social education. If they see their work as issues-based, or even as issues-dominated (see Marsden 1995), they can hardly at the same time deny that a more appropriate strategy is through an interdisciplinary approach in an integrated curriculum. That is not, however, the preferred route for this writer, whose reasoning is heavily based on the historical record. While subjects in the curriculum, like geography, can and have been politicized (Marsden 1989), there is at least at the same time an academic counter-culture in the foreground to remind us that we are in the business of education and not of indoctrination (Marsden 1992, 1993).

CONCLUSIONS

The political context of educational discussion has become one of increasing polarization and confrontation, no longer one of differentiated intellectual debate. The curricular interchanges of the 1980s and 1990s have been disfigured by the overstated and often malicious cross-fire of the far right and the far left. The cross-curricular productions of the National Curriculum, in principle contained by and large a stronger element of politicization than all the subject areas of the National Curriculum, with the possible exceptions of history and religion. This is in line with previous historical experience. As an agent of social education, the subject must strive to ensure that in the development of geographical meanings and of social commitments, pupils, as partners in this endeavour, are equipped to recognize and resist what were once called 'the hidden persuaders'. Such forces, thirty years on, have emerged more tangibly and influentially in the form of self-appointed gatekeepers of official standards and as promoters of traditional instruction, whether in quangos and so-called think-tanks, in the often vindictive, ill-informed and Pavlovian effluent of the press – tabloid or broadsheet – or in official political pronouncement.

The historical record makes clear to us that instruction has exercised its controlling grip through inculcation (the process of impressing on the mind through frequent and intense repetition) and indoctrination (the content to be studied, i.e. the associated doctrines or ideologies being inculcated). From whatever source, it has perennially been designed to exercise thought control over a docile and compliant population, offering a curriculum for passive future subjects rather than one for autonomous, independently thinking and constructively active future citizens (see Machon 1991). While the evidence is not watertight, curriculum history suggests that a permeation of issues into geography and other subjects may be a safer bet for avoiding indoctrination in an interventionist political climate than an integrated, issue-dominated curriculum into which subjects may (or may not) be permeated. It is perhaps a source of hope that the government does not see it this way round.

REFERENCES

Ausubel, D.P. and Robinson, F.G. (1969) *School Learning: an Introduction to Educational Psychology*, New York: Holt, Rinehart and Winston.
Balchin, W.G. (1993) *The Geographical Association: the First Hundred Years, 1893–1993*, Sheffield: The Geographical Association.
Board of Education (1926) *The Education of the Adolescent* (Hadow Report), London: HMSO.
Board of Education (1931) *The Primary School* (Hadow Report), London: HMSO.
Board of Education (1938) *Secondary Education* (Spens Report), London: HMSO.
Board of Education (1943) *Curriculum and Examinations in Secondary Schools* (Norwood Report), London: HMSO.
Dewey, J. (1916) *Democracy and Education: an Introduction to the Philosophy of Education*, New York: The Free Press.
Fairgrieve, J. (1924) *Geography and World Power*, London: University Tutorial Press.
Fairgrieve, J. (1926) *Geography in School*, London: University of London Press.
Fairgrieve, J. (1936) 'Can we teach geography better?', *Geography* 21: 1–17.
Freshfield, D.W. (1886) 'The place of geography in education', *Proceedings of the Royal Geographical Society, New Series* 8: 698–718.
Geikie, A. (1879) 'Geographical evolution', *Proceedings of the Royal Geographical Society, New Series* 1: 422–44.
Geikie, A. (1887) *The Teaching of Geography*, London: Macmillan.
Graves, N.J. (1968) 'Geography, social science and inter-disciplinary enquiry', *Geographical Journal* 134: 390–4.
Herbertson, A.J. (1905) 'The major natural regions of the world', *Geographical Journal* 25: 300–10.
Herbertson, A.J. (1906) 'Recent regulations and syllabuses in geography affecting schools', *Geographical Journal* 27: 279–88.

Hirst, P.H. (1974) *Knowledge and the Curriculum*, London: Routledge and Kegan Paul.

Holmes, E. (1911) *What Is and What Might Be: a Study of Education in General and Elementary Education in Particular*, London: Constable.

Kelly, A.V. (1986) *Knowledge and Curriculum Planning*, London: Harper Row.

Lawton, D. and Dufour, B. (1973) *The New Social Studies*, London: Heinemann.

Machon, P. (1991) 'Subject or citizen?', *Teaching Geography* 16: 128.

Mackinder, H.J. (1887) 'On the scope and methods of geography', *Proceedings of the Royal Geographical Society, New Series* 9: 141–73.

Mackinder, H.J. (1911) 'The teaching of geography from the imperial point of view, and the use which could and should be made of visual instruction', *The Geographical Teacher* 6: 79–86.

Mackinder, H.J. (1921) 'Geography as a pivotal subject in education', *Geographical Journal* 57: 376–84.

Marland, M. (1973) 'Preference Shares', *Education Guardian*, 11 September 1973: 18.

Marsden, W.E. (1986) 'The Royal Geographical Society and geography in secondary education', in M.H. Price (ed.) *The Development of the Secondary Curriculum*, London: Croom Helm, 182–213.

Marsden, W.E. (1989) ' "All in a Good Cause": geography, history and the politicization of the curriculum in nineteenth- and twentieth-century England', *Journal of Curriculum Studies* 21: 509–26.

Marsden, W.E. (1991) 'Primary geography and the National Curriculum', in B.T. Gorwood (ed.) *Changing Primary Schools*, University of Hull: *Aspects of Education* 45: 38–54.

Marsden, W.E. (1992) 'W(h)ither international understanding?', in G. Hall (ed.) *Themes and Dimensions of the National Curriculum*, London: Kogan Page, 101–15.

Marsden, W.E. (1993) 'Recycling religious instruction?: historical perspectives on contemporary cross-curricular issues', *History of Education* 22: 321–33.

Marsden, W.E. (1995) *Geography 11–16: Rekindling Good Practice*, London: David Fulton Publishers.

Ministry of Education (1959) *Primary Education*, London: HMSO.

Ministry of Education (1967) *Children and their Primary Schools*, vol. 1 (Plowden Report), London: HMSO.

Newbigin, M. (1914) *The British Empire Beyond the Sea: an Introduction to World Geography*, London: G. Bell and Sons.

Peters, R. (ed.) (1969) *Perspectives on Plowden*, London: Routledge and Kegan Paul.

Royal Geographical Society (1886) *Report in Reference to the Improvement of Geographical Education* (Keltie Report), London: John Murray.

Royal Geographical Society (1950) 'Geography and "Social Studies" in schools', *Geographical Journal* 116: 181–5.

Wall, W.D. (1968) *Adolescents in School and Society*, Slough: National Foundation for Educational Research.

Williams, M. (ed.) (1976) *Geography and the Integrated Curriculum: a Reader*, London: Heinemann.

Chapter 3

The great debate and 1988

Rex Walford

INTRODUCTION

The so-called 'great debate' about education followed Prime Minister Callaghan's speech at Ruskin College, Oxford in 1976 which questioned the success of the work which British schools were doing in meeting the needs of a modern society. It was hardly a 'debate' at all, since it involved a number of public meetings around the country at which most contributors came from established positions and reiterated their present point of view, but it did have the effect of further opening the door to the 'secret garden' of the curriculum which had been in the hands of schoolteachers rather than of administrators for almost the whole of the century. The idea of a National Curriculum was born.

In the next few years, the Department of Education edged its way towards implementation of this idea with a series of discussion documents (DES 1980, 1981). The position of geography within these publications was marginal. In *A Framework for the Curriculum* (1980) most of the text was about English, maths, science and modern languages. Geography merited a single mention in the thirty-second paragraph of a 35-paragraph document, along with a brief and glancing reference to a group of subjects named as 'also important for the preparation for adult life'. A corresponding set of documents from Her Majesty's Inspectors (HMI 1977) had floated the idea of the curriculum being demarcated by 'areas of experience' rather than by subjects, and for a time other more radical formulations (Hargreaves 1982), in which geography figured hardly at all, were the focus of discussion.

During this period the Geographical Association (GA) had to revive the role it had played in various campaigns to increase the status of the subject at the start of the century. It became again a politically active body as well as one which offered professional support to schoolteachers. It learnt quickly from events and experience and developed a variety of campaigns and strategies to mobilize support for the subject and to emphasize its potential contribution to a general curriculum (Daugherty and Walford 1980; GA 1981, 1982; Williams 1985). As a result the Secretary of State for Education,

Sir Keith Joseph, was persuaded to make the first ever major ministerial speech about geographical education at a special conference organized by the GA at King's College London in 1985 (Joseph 1985). Joseph, demonstrating his characteristically deep reflection about curriculum matters, acknowledged the value of geography as a school subject, while making no commitments about whether it should be studied by all pupils, and left geographers with a provocative list of 'seven questions'. If this was a rhetorical flourish, its bluff was soon called, since the GA quickly mobilized a 'Task Force' to provide an initial answer to the questions (Bailey and Binns 1987a). Following conferences around the country in 1986, the GA produced a book called *A Case for Geography*, a more weighty and measured response (Bailey and Binns 1987b) which, with astute timing, was laid on the desk of the incoming Secretary of State after Sir Keith Joseph retired from office early in 1987.

THE BAKER INITIATIVE

Joseph's successor, Kenneth Baker, favoured a more active and robust approach to curriculum reform and quickly determined 'that there was no chance of a voluntary agreement'. He first announced proposals in outline for a National Curriculum while being interviewed on a weekend television programme in December 1986 and then amplified this at the North of England Education Conference a few weeks later. The matter was discussed in detail by the Government in the following spring. Prime Minister Margaret Thatcher favoured a core of specified subjects restricted to English, maths and science but in one of her rare Cabinet defeats, she was forced to back down in the face of Baker's bold insistence on a 'broad and balanced curriculum' (Baker 1993: 189).

Thus, when a GA delegation went to meet Baker in his Elizabeth House headquarters in June 1987, he greeted them with a broad smile and an assurance that geography would have a place in the proposals which he would shortly put to Parliament. How far this was due to the GA's campaigning it is difficult to judge, though an appendix to *A Case for Geography* outlining 'expectations' at various ages certainly found favour with him and was in tune with his plans for assessment at the end of Key Stages. There were, however, other factors which came into the reckoning.

Baker, previously Minister for Technology and responsible for encouraging the introduction of computers into schools, had been impressed by the use that geographers were making of the new technology. As an Oxford historian by first degree, he was keen to ensure that teaching about Britain's heritage was a prominent part of the curriculum and he saw 'a structured body of geographical knowledge' (1993: 193) as complementary to that. He was also disturbed about the lack of rigour in 'integrated humanities', and the apparent political bias of such hybrids as 'peace studies' and 'world studies' then being developed in some schools, and wanted to return to the supposed safety of traditional subjects. Thus, although many geography teachers and office-holders in the GA held views about the nature of the subject rather different to those of the Minister, they basked in the satisfaction of seeing it included in the proposed ten-subject National Curriculum when only a few years before they had been resigned to seeing it outside any proposed core. It would take the actual discussion of the detail of the proposed geography curriculum to expose these differences.

The proposals for a National Curriculum to be composed of ten 'traditional' subjects was disappointing to some educational philosophers (White 1988, Hirst 1993), who had been disseminating ideas of 'forms and fields' of knowledge in the years previous, but commanded much more general assent from the public and from most teachers. It is not clear how Baker arrived at his final list, but we know from his political memoirs that he was 'given much help in developing the idea of the National Curriculum by Eric Bolton, the Chief Inspector for Schools' (Baker 1993: 191). A format to reflect a conservative consensus was, in the circumstances, not surprising, though Baker's own views had been instrumental in providing a wider frame than expected. There was inevitably some skirmishing around the edges of the formulation by representatives of those who had been excluded (notably classics and home economics) but in the event only the powerful House of Lords lobby for religious education introduced any change to the original plan. Religious education was added as an eleventh 'basic' subject to the three 'core' subjects (English, maths, science) and the other seven 'foundation' subjects (technology, modern languages, history, geography, music, art and physical education).

Agreement about the desirability of introducing a subject-based National Curriculum and its constituent parts stretched, somewhat surprisingly, across all parties in the House of Commons in the debates on the 1988 Education Bill and it was in the House of Lords that the more discerning and individual views were put forward. Geography survived one 'dangerous corner' when an amendment to the main Bill was put down suggesting that history should be made a core subject. A small group of peers sympathetic to geography's interests gathered anxiously to protect geography's comparability with history, but their efforts were not needed. By the time the amendment was called, it was late at night and the peer due to speak to it failed to rise, presumably having either fallen asleep somewhere or gone home.

Thus by September 1988, the Education Act was on the statute book and details of an eleven-subject 5–16 National Curriculum in which geography figured as statutory were due to be worked out. The Government proposed to do this by the setting up of Subject Working Groups who were given about a twelve-month period (working in the time that could be spared from their normal working lives) to come up with proposals. The composition of the groups was determined by the Secretary of State, and in each case he took good care to ensure that there was strong lay representation to match that of the professionals drawn from various parts of the education system. The Geography Working Group was set up in December 1988, with Sir Leslie Fielding, Vice-Chancellor of the University of Sussex, but for much of his life a British diplomat in various countries around the world, being appointed Chairman. Five of the twelve members were lay people.

This was soon to be of some significance as it became clear that advising DES civil servants, acting as the Group's secretariat, had no wish for it to endorse the status quo. The Group began by considering the nature of geography itself and its role in schools and it was soon clear that no easy consensus was going to be reached. On the one hand there was a spectrum of views among the professionals concerning the balance and health of the subject in relation to both content and pedagogy; on the other was some trenchant criticism of the present state of geographical education from those who, as parents or employers, were the receivers of its fruits. Members of the Group have offered their perceptions of what happened in the twelve months (Rawling 1993, Walford 1992), but there is little doubt that among the 'blood spilt all over the floor' (a phrase used by one of the secretariat to describe one important late-night argument) there were some fundamental re-examinations of cherished beliefs and supposed basic principles on all sides. The document eventually produced by the Group (Fielding *et al.* 1990) attracted both praise and criticism, but it represented (almost) consensus on major curriculum issues hammered out in a very educating way. It is revealing to see how, five years on, despite numerous adjustments, revisions and reductions (the most significant of which were those wrought by a committee set up by Sir Ron Dearing in 1994), many of the broad major principles worked out by the Group have become the touchstone for future curriculum development.

The key image developed by the group to encapsulate the nature of school geography was the 'cube' (Fig. 3.1) of areas, themes and skills.

The three elements were seen as being of equal importance and as interactive with each other. Such an apparently basic assertion served to begin the restoration and rehabilitation of place and area studies which, in previous decades, had fallen out of favour as organizing frameworks in many schools. A previous influential revolution in school geography in the 1960s and 1970s had helped to explore spatial patterns and to emphasize similarities rather than differences in geographical studies, but it had led almost to the dismissal of place as a significant factor.

Another important principle arrived at by the Group was the belief that physical geographical studies were as important as human ones and should be given as much curriculum prominence – a matter of moment in some

Figure 3.1 Combining the attainment targets

schools where geography has become subsumed under a social studies or 'humanities' umbrella, and where its scientific and landscape aspects were played down as a result. Following on from this (and strongly supported by DES advice), the notion of 'environmental geography' was developed (a tautology in the strict sense, but necessary to avoid using the politically dangerous term 'environmental issues'). One of the five Attainment Targets in the original Final Orders set before Parliament in 1991 was given this name (the other four were Geographical Skills, the Knowledge and Understanding of Places, Human Geography, and Physical Geography) and the key role of the subject recognized in the rising concern about environmental education. It also provided, importantly, a rationale for the subject in terms of future citizenship, a suitable replacement for the old Imperial imperative which had enthused the pioneers of the subject in the period from 1870 to 1939.

Content was a much safer base on which to secure the distinctiveness of the subject in curriculum (and political) terms than the pedagogic thrust of 'enquiry learning' favoured by some. But the Group became divided and 'hung up' on this and various other technical curriculum matters during its life because a hidden (and sometimes not-so-hidden) agenda from the DES was also playing its part in determining the shape of the new National Curriculum.

By 1990, the approach being favoured by government was a curriculum which would be assessment-led and there emerged a plan to have the statutory curriculum formulations subject to national tests which could be regularly administered and schools and teachers then held accountable. This overriding emphasis on assessment was not part of Kenneth Baker's original plan (Taylor 1995) which probably accounted for the fact that he excluded the task of considering assessment matters from the agendas of the Subject Working Groups. This latter action was well-intentioned in its context but, given the change of policy, was ultimately to prove catastrophic when the linkage of syllabus and testing came to be worked out in more detail.

There was, moreover, a fatal lack of guidance from the centre about the realities of school-curriculum time to which Subject Groups should tailor their proposals. When pressed, the DES gave benignly optimistic figures about how many hours per year might be available for each subject, and all the Groups (geography included), anxious to do their subject justice, over-weighted the curriculum content in their desire not to leave basic or interesting parts of the subject unstatutory. As well as this, another problem arose from the restricted time given to the Working Groups for their work, and the inability to institute any pilot trials. Baker's successors as Secretary of State for Education (and there were quite a number in a short time – MacGregor, Clarke, Patten, Shephard) never quite emulated his full grasp of the National Curriculum plan despite their individual differences and initiatives.

THE CLARKE INTERVENTION

The geography formulation, in particular, suffered from another fickle finger of fate in December 1990. Just after the Draft Orders of the curriculum had been published, a new Secretary of State came into office. Kenneth Clarke, while at the Ministry of Health, had just been involved in bruising battles with the doctors, and seemed anxious to take up a similar stance at Education. (It was widely believed that his predecessor, John MacGregor, had been moved on because in the Prime Minister's eye it seemed as if he was 'going native' and siding too much with the teachers' lobby on educational reforms.) The Draft Statutory Orders for both History and Geography were at the top of the in-tray as the new Minister began his work and over the Christmas holiday, working with the aid only of his personal political adviser, he took a correcting pencil to the carefully balanced documents and worked them over.

His justifications afterwards, in Parliament, in media interviews and in a speech at the Royal Geographical Society (Clarke 1992), hinged around the vexed issue of 'attitudes and values'. The Geography Subject Group had sought to retain the possibility of handling issues of controversy (particularly in Key Stage 4, the 14–16 age-range) by inserting them discreetly into some of the Statements of Attainment which formed the basis of the curriculum, and by agreeing that this would be balanced by a reassuring inclusion of a base of factual information. (The Group reached a surprising degree of unanimity about this and was never as nervous as the History Working Group about specifying an overall basic framework of facts which everyone should learn.) Clarke fastened on to this and commented:

> The Secretary of State recognises that geography lessons will sometimes deal with conflicting points of view on important geographical issues. However, he considers that the main emphasis in the statutory requirements should be on teaching a knowledge and understanding of geography rather than on the study of people's attitudes and opinions. Some statements of attainment which appear to concentrate on attitudes and opinions rather than geographical knowledge and understanding have therefore been removed.
>
> (DES 1991 Annexe B: 2)

Thus a Statement of Attainment such as 'Pupils should discuss how people's attitudes can affect the exploitation of natural resources' (Environmental Geography, Level 4) was struck out, along with nearly forty others. This was beneficial in reducing overload, but unfortunate in wrecking the carefully constructed web of 'strands' in each Attainment Target as constructed by the Geography Working Group and in taking away some of the most interesting, relevant and topical issues which had been included in the proposed Geography Orders.

THE DEARING REFORMS

In the event it was a nugatory battle since, at a later stage, the whole of geography at Key Stage 4 was removed from the statutory requirement of the National Curriculum, and the possibility of studying issues of controversy now depends on whether or not pupils opt for the subject post-14, and which GCSE examination their schools choose to take.

Clarke did not stay long at the Ministry of Education, but moved onwards and upwards to the Chancellorship. Geography teachers expected more satisfaction from his successor, John Patten, who had been a don in the subject at Oxford and had edited one of its major academic journals. Patten had many interesting and radical ideas, but ran into heavy storms in his inability to temporize either with teachers' unions (who were complaining about the chronic overload of timetables and mounting National Curriculum bureaucracy) or with parents (whose representatives he unwisely accused of holding Neanderthal views early in his ministry).

Thus the possibility of successful compromise was soon exhausted and Patten had to call in an industrialist as a 'fixer' before he relinquished office in 1994. The 'fixer' was Sir Ron Dearing, who had formerly run the Post Office but whose knowledge of education was avowedly as a layman.

Dearing appointed committees to reduce the perceived overload of the subject curricula and also to try and bring order from the chaotic and fast-spreading jungle of the proposed assessment system. Geography's position and status suffered on both accounts. The loss of geography and history as statutory subjects in the 14–16 age-group was pushed through relatively easily, both in the interests of lightening the load and as Dearing espoused and restored to prominence the Thatcherian view that the really important National Curriculum was a core of English, maths and science (Dearing 1994).

The nature of the curriculum formulation was also changed, with 'level descriptors' now replacing Statements of Attainment at different levels. This incidentally reduced the amount of material within each subject specification, though it has yet to be proved that it will be any easier to understand, unpack or assess. The number of Attainment Targets was reduced in most subjects and geography's original five became one. The number of standard national tests was reduced, and these were now restricted to the 'core' subjects. The general view has quickly emerged that those subjects (including geography) without a national testing pro-gramme are perceived to have less 'status' than those which are annually examined in this way. This has been buttressed by a similar concentration of emphasis in the inspection and reporting programmes of OFSTED since 1994.

An additional Dearing proposal was to open up the possibility of separate pathways for academic, vocational and occupational education post-14, a proposal which has startling echoes of the tripartite system of education espoused in the 1944 Education Act and abandoned in the 1960s. Eric Bolton, Chief Inspector (and perhaps a key influence) when Kenneth Baker introduced the concept of the 'broad and balanced' curriculum which underpinned the 1988 Act, remonstrated in vain (Bolton 1994).

CONCLUSIONS

Thus, at the end of a period of great curriculum turbulence, the position of geography in schools appears to have returned largely to what it was before the Education Act of 1988 was ever mooted.

But it is not quite the same. If there is again to be the familiar 'beauty contest' of optional subjects from which pupils may choose at the end of their ninth year of study, there is now stiffer competition at the post-14 stage. Whether GCSE numbers in geography will hold up under the competition of other subjects and alternative pathways is an open question.

Conversely, however, the introduction of a National Curriculum at Key Stages 1 and 2 is providing a much-needed fillip for primary geography. Teachers are rediscovering the value of subject-focused study after decades of experiment with amorphous topic work and the 'integrated day'. The reintroduction of such requirements as studies of a contrasting locality and of a basic framework of locational knowledge will eventually assist secondary school teachers to work from a higher and firmer baseline.

The turmoil in curriculum politics between 1976 and 1995 has, at least, helped geography begin to re-examine its own practice and principles. Of necessity there has been a thorough public debate about its purposes and nature in schools, and a structure and those key elements which command common assent within and beyond the discipline have been identified. A backwash of this has spread into post-16 and higher education. In the 'period of calm' promised by Sir Ron Dearing, there may be a chance to take this on in more measured, reflective and, ultimately, discerning fashion.

REFERENCES

Bailey, P. and Binns, J.A. (1987a) 'A case for geography: a response to Sir Keith Joseph', *Geography* 72 (4): 327–31.

Bailey, P. and Binns, J.A. (1987b) *A Case for Geography*, Sheffield: The Geographical Association.

Baker, K. (1993) *The Turbulent Years: My Life in Politics*, London: Faber and Faber.

Bolton, E. (1994) 'Divided we fall', *Times Educational Supplement*, 21 January 1994: 17.

Callaghan, J. (1987) *Time and Chance*, London: Collins.

Clarke, K. (1992) 'Geography in the National Curriculum', *The Geographical Journal* 158 (1): 75–8.

Daugherty, R. and Walford, R. (1980) 'A framework for the school curriculum', *Geography* 65 (3): 232–5.

Dearing, R. (1994) *The National Curriculum and its Assessment: A Final Report*, London: SCAA.

Department of Education and Science (1980) *A Framework for the National Curriculum*, London: HMSO.

Department of Education and Science (1981) *The School Curriculum*, London: HMSO.

Department of Education and Science (1991) *Geography in the National Curriculum: Draft Orders* (typescript), London: DES.

Fielding, L. *et al.* (1990) *Geography for Ages 5 to 16: Final Report of the Geography Working Group*, London: HMSO.

Geographical Association (1981) *Geography in the School Curriculum 5–16*, Sheffield: Geographical Association.

Geographical Association (1982) *Geography in the Curriculum 16–19*, Sheffield: Geographical Association.

Hargreaves, D.H. (1982) *The Challenge of the Comprehensive School*, London: Routledge and Kegan Paul.

Her Majesty's Inspectors (1977) *Curriculum 11–16*, London: HMSO.

Hirst, P. (1993) 'The foundations of the National Curriculum: why subjects?', in P.

O'Hear and J. White (eds) *Assessing the National Curriculum*, London: Paul Chapman.

Joseph, K. (1985) 'Geography and the school curriculum', *Geography* 70 (4): 290–7.

Rawling, E. (1993) 'The making of a national curriculum', *Geography* 77 (4): 292–309.

Taylor, T. (1995) 'Movers and shakers: high politics and the origins of the National Curriculum', *The Curriculum Journal* 6 (2): 161–84.

Walford, R. (1992) 'Creating a National Curriculum: a view from the inside', in Hill, D. (ed.) *International Perspectives in Geographic Education*, Boulder, USA: Centre for Geographic Education.

Walford, R. (1995) 'Geography in the National Curriculum of England and Wales: rise and fall?' *The Geographical Journal* 161 (2): 192–8.

White, J. (1988) 'An unconstitutional National Curriculum', in Lawton, D. and Chitty, C. (eds) *The National Curriculum, Bedford Way Papers* 33, London: Institute of Education.

Williams, M. (1985) 'The Geographical Association and the Great Debate', *Geography* 70 (2): 129–37.

Chapter 4

Geographical education in the 1990s

Norman Graves

INTRODUCTION

Geographical education in the state primary and secondary schools of England and Wales in the 1990s is dominated by the contents of a series of reports emanating from the Geography Working Group (GWG) set up under the 1988 Education Reform Act (ERA). Each report has been modified either by the GWG itself, by the Secretaries of State for Education, or as a result of the Dearing Report. The Final Report (June 1990) proposed seven Attainment Targets (ATs) while the wording of the Programmes of Study (PoS) was modified to show how these could contribute to geographical enquiry, geographical skills, and places and themes, within each Key Stage. However, the National Curriculum Council decided to reduce the ATs to five by combining three area studies targets into one called 'Knowledge and Understanding of Places'.

Meanwhile, the position of geography in the whole curriculum was changing. Under the 1988 ERA, geography was part of a ten-subject (eleven-subject in Wales with the addition of Welsh) compulsory National Curriculum for all pupils from 5 to 16 years of age and would be tested at each Key Stage (KS). In January 1990, the then Secretary of State (John MacGregor) announced that it would be permissible for schools to run half-size courses in geography for 14- to 16-year-olds. By February 1991, Kenneth Clarke decreed that such pupils need not take both history and geography, but could choose either one or the other or a combined course taking up the same time as a single subject.

Teachers found that teaching and testing the curriculum was proving increasingly stressful. Consequently John Patten, the new Secretary of State following the 1992 General Election, appointed the chairman of the School Curriculum and Assessment Authority (SCAA), Sir Ron Dearing, to review the National Curriculum and its assessment (April 1993).

THE DEARING REPORT AND ITS SEQUEL

The Final Report of the Dearing enquiry (1994) broadly stipulated that:

- the total content required to be taught by law should be substantially reduced;
- the Programmes of Study (PoS) should be simplified and allow teachers more scope to exercise their professional judgement;
- the Orders in Parliament should be drafted in such a way that they offer as much support as possible to classroom teachers (Battersby 1995).

Since the Dearing Report suggested that some 20 per cent of teaching time be used in ways the schools saw as appropriate to their own situation, this resulted in a reduced amount of teaching time being available to the subjects of the National Curriculum. In the case of geography, this meant that approximately one hour per week would be available for KS1 and one and a quarter hours for KS2 and KS3. At KS4, the time allocation could vary according to the choices made of subjects studied for the General Certificate of Secondary Education (GCSE) or for the General National Vocational Qualification (GNVQ), since the latter may be taken alongside GCSE. This stems from the recommendation of the Dearing Report that at KS4 there should be both an academic and a vocational pathway, each linking up at a later stage with courses for the 16–19 age-group.

The Dearing Report was accepted by the Government and, consequently, the SCAA set up a Geography Working Group that published its Final Report in January 1995 (Department for Education 1995). It deals only with the geography curriculum in KS1, 2 and 3 since geography is no longer compulsory in KS4. The detailed curriculum and assessment for KS4 became the responsibility of the various examining groups. The Statutory Orders were published as *Geography in the National Curriculum*, the main feature of which is that at each Key Stage the Programme of Study is divided into three sections: geographical skills; places; and thematic study.

The Attainment Targets (ATs) and Statements of Attainments (SoAs) have virtually disappeared, having been replaced by a description of the kind of performance that might be expected from pupils at each of eight levels, and a description of what might be an exceptional performance above Level 8. The concept that pupils' performance might be classified as belonging to various levels is derived from the TGAT (Task Group on Assessment and Testing) Report (1987) that suggested, *inter alia*, that in order to ensure progression in the National Curriculum from Year 1 to Year 11, it would be necessary to assess pupils' performances as belonging to one of ten levels in each subject area.

WHAT ARE WE TRYING TO DO IN THE 1990s?

Geography in the National Curriculum is silent on the overall aims of geographical education, though clearly these can be inferred from the Programmes of Study. Each Key Stage begins with statements of what 'pupils should be given an opportunity to' learn. These may be summarized as:

- the investigation of places and themes at a variety of scales;
- the posing of such geographical questions as 'What is it?', 'What is it like?', 'How did it get like this?', 'How and why is it changing?', 'What are the implications?';
- The development of fieldwork skills and the ability to find out relevant information from documentary, map sources, and from data stored in computer files and disks;
- the understanding of and ability to explain physical and human processes and the interaction between them;
- the consideration of issues arising from peoples' interaction with their environment;
- the understanding of how places are set in a global context and how different areas have become interdependent and are therefore affected by processes in other parts of the world.

While these give certain medium-term objectives for geography teachers, they do not explain why these objectives are considered worth pursuing. Here one enters the realm of values. One of the most significant shifts to have occurred in the curriculum in the 1990s is the shift towards the instrumental aims of education. This does not mean that the intrinsic aims, i.e. those that state that education is worthwhile because it broadens and deepens the mind, are abandoned, but that these are no longer considered sufficient. Thus, geography's position in the National Curriculum cannot be justified solely because it is a discipline of knowledge; it must also be justified because it has a function in contemporary society. What is that function?

First, it is evident that geography, as part of the total curriculum, helps to reinforce all those communications skills which most curriculum subjects attempt to get pupils to acquire and which are of growing importance in the evolving world economy. Geography puts a special emphasis on graphical skills (ability to read and interpret maps, graphs and charts, photographs and tabular information). This is closely related to the development of an ability to orient oneself, to develop mental maps of an environment and to plan routes, abilities which are at a premium in a world in which people are often on the move. Second, most economic and social problems have a spatial aspect – whether one is dealing on the small scale with planning the layout of one's garden, or the medium scale with the location of a hypermarket or industrial works, or on the large scale with planning air-routes, it is important to be aware of the way decisions are made and the factors that influence those decisions. Third, geography, with its long tradition of examining the manner in which different influences play their part in giving a place its character, is well placed to investigate the nature of an environmental problem and to suggest a solution, though as in all value-laden decisions there will probably be alternatives. This is one area in which geography has to inculcate a substantive value: the need to care for the environment (Fien and Gerber 1986).

Thus, to answer the question which heads this section, in teaching geography teachers could be said to be developing spatial skills in their pupils, to be getting them used to analysing the spatial aspects of economic and social problems and to be making them aware of the nature of environmental issues and developing in their minds the concept of an environmental ethic. Each teacher, however, may also have his or her own agenda according to the circumstances in which he or she is teaching.

TEACHING–LEARNING STRATEGIES AND MODES OF ASSESSMENT

Most teachers continue to adopt an essentially pragmatic attitude to teaching methods. A good teaching method is one that works in the circumstances in which one is teaching, i.e. one that enables pupils to learn what they are supposed to learn. Since the main objective in any lesson or series of lessons is to get the pupils to learn a skill, a concept or principle which they can later apply, the proof that a particular teaching strategy has worked lies in the pupils' ability to apply what they have learned in a new situation. Hence the importance of assessment in the sense of monitoring pupils' progress. Can one, therefore, say anything of general validity about teaching strategies? While one can point to research that has validated particular teaching strategies, one can never be sure that with another teacher, with another group of pupils, in other circumstances, the methods used will always yield the same results. Thus one can only point to the possibilities offered by certain teaching strategies, but never offer the guarantee that they will always be successful.

Perhaps the first thing that can be said about teaching strategies is that they must be in harmony with one's aims and objectives. If you as a teacher aim to produce pupils who can think things out for themselves, then they must be given the opportunity to do so. This means that to feed them continually with information that they must learn to reproduce is not conducive to achieving this aim. Second, it is common experience that, if one particular strategy is repeated too often, then pupils get bored with it. So a variety of approaches and activities is necessary. Thus, whole-class teaching can include question and answer oral work followed by worksheet completion, or it can involve the class in attempting to solve a problem, documents having been provided to enable pupils to arrive at some solution. Group work may involve groups in attempting to answer a series of questions, for example, on environmental pollution, each group concentrating on one sort of pollution and bringing their knowledge to the whole class at the end of the teaching unit. Much of the variety in pupil activity comes not only from the tasks set, but also from the kind of teaching aids used: from textbooks through large-scale maps and tabulated statistics to information technology, videos and satellite photographs. Later chapters in this book (Chapters 13 to 22) deal in detail with various teaching-learning strategies.

The formative monitoring of pupil progress needs to be done by individual teachers and should be based on decisions taken at departmental or school level about the nature of the assessment to be undertaken. Because the experience in the early stages of implementing the National Curriculum showed that too much formal testing was unmanageable, it is likely that much of this monitoring will be based on the informal assessment of pupils' work, though occasional formal tests may be given as appropriate. SCAA (1995a) has issued guidance on how to ensure consistency in teacher assessment. This suggests that teachers need to develop a common understanding about standards of work and that that may be helped by collecting together in a 'portfolio' examples of pupils' work in geography to illustrate a particular standard.

The summative aspect involves being able to classify the work of a pupil as belonging to one of the eight levels described in *Geography in the National Curriculum*. Little experience is yet available on how this may be done but some suggestions are contained in a helpful article by Digby and Lambert (1996). Further, the Geographical Association has published a booklet entitled *Assessment Works* (Butt, Lambert and Telfer 1995) which helps teachers to understand the system of assessment based on level descriptions and indicates what teachers should look out for in pupils' work. It usefully unpacks two level descriptions, to show what a pupil's work should reveal at a particular level. Essentially a judgement has to be made, given a range of a pupil's work, as to the level to which the work should be assigned. In the case of GCSE work at Key Stage 4, SCAA (1995b) has also published a document giving both general regulations for the GCSE and specific criteria for each subject area, guidance on syllabus content, schemes of assessment and grade descriptions. To a large extent this repeats much that is in *Geography in the National Curriculum*, but it does specify that in any scheme of assessment:

1   The weightings for the assessment objectives must be in the following range:

(i) knowledge of places and themes at a range of scales: 30–40 per cent;

(ii) understanding of geographical ideas and the application of knowledge and understanding in a variety of physical and human contexts: 30–40 per cent;

(iii) selection and use of skills appropriate to geographical enquiry: 30–40 per cent.

2 Each scheme of assessment has to incorporate a terminal examination with a minimum weighting of 75 per cent in non-modular schemes and 50 per cent in modular schemes.

3 The weighting allocated to coursework must be not less than 20 per cent but not more than 25 per cent. This coursework must include a geographical investigation supported by fieldwork.

4 Candidates must be given opportunities to demonstrate their graphical ability through practical work and their ability to write extended prose.

More detailed consideration of assessment will be given in Chapters 23 to 27.

TOWARDS THE MILLENNIUM?

Given the educational turmoil of the past decade it is hazardous to predict what is likely to happen to school geography in the next ten years. However, following the promise of the Dearing Report that no substantial changes would be made to the National Curriculum for at least five years, teachers can expect a period of relative stability in geographical education which they can put to good use by consolidating their work in schools. Consolidation does not mean stagnation, though, but being able to organize the smooth running of their teaching while at the same time having the professional freedom to undertake some experimentation – within the limits set by the National Curriculum – with content, teaching strategies and assessment, in order to meet the particular needs of their pupils. More than ever, teachers need to bear in mind that the curriculum is a means to an end and not an end in itself. The end is the development of those competencies and qualities of mind that will produce a citizen able to earn his or her living as well as being capable of critical thought.

REFERENCES

Battersby, J. (1995) 'Rationale for the revised curriculum', *Teaching Geography* 20 (2): 57–8.

Butt, G., Lambert, D. and Telfer, S. (eds) (1995) *Assessment Works*, Sheffield; Geographical Association.

Dearing, R. (1994) *The National Curriculum and its Assessment: Final Report*, London: HMSO.

Department for Education (1995) *Geography in the National Curriculum*, London: HMSO.

Department of Education and Science (1987) *National Curriculum. Taskgroup on Assessment and Testing: A Report*, London and Cardiff: DES and Welsh Office.

Department of Education and Science/Welsh Office (1990) *Geography for Ages 5 to 16*, London: HMSO.

Digby, R. and Lambert, D. (1996) 'Using level descriptions in the classroom at Key Stage 3', *Teaching Geography* 21 (1): 40–3.

Fien, J. and Gerber, R. (1986) *Teaching Geography for a Better World*, Sydney: Jacaranda.

SCAA (1995a) *Consistency in Teacher Assessment, Guidance for Schools, Key Stages 1 to 3*, London: School Curriculum and Assessment Authority.

SCAA (1995b) *GCSE Regulations and Criteria*, London: School Curriculum and Assessment Authority.

Part II

Chapter 5

Curriculum planning and course development
A matter of professional judgement

Margaret Roberts

There is a dilemma in describing a course of study . . . it is only in a trivial sense that one gives a course to 'get something across', merely to impart information. There are better means to that end than teaching. Unless the learner also masters himself, disciplines his taste, deepens his view of the world, the 'something' that is got across is hardly worth the effort of transmission.

(Bruner 1966: 73)

INTRODUCTION

Now that there is a geography national curriculum (GNC) for pupils aged 5 to 14 and detailed syllabuses for GCSE and A Level, teachers might wonder whether their role in curriculum planning has been taken away from them. Clearly, the existence or nature of statutory requirements and examination syllabuses could be challenged. However, this chapter does not enter that debate but focuses on what teachers might do within the current educational context to plan the geography curriculum in their schools and to develop their own geography courses.

The terms 'curriculum planning' and 'course development' encompass the thinking and documentation that occurs before, during and after teaching and learning takes place in the classroom. Teachers approach the task of planning in different ways, being influenced, consciously or subconsciously, by the models of planning they have encountered, by the GNC, by examination syllabuses, by textbooks, by colleagues and by experience. The way a curriculum is planned is a matter of debate and ultimately a matter of professional judgement. This chapter focuses on two models of curriculum development: an objectives model and a process model. It outlines the basic features and origins of each model, gives examples of their impact on geographical education and looks at the merits and criticisms of each approach. Finally, it highlights the dilemmas teachers face in adapting these models to their own use. Before looking at these s, however, it is worth distinguishing between a syllabus and a curriculum plan.

FROM SYLLABUS TO CURRICULUM

Before the impact of the Schools Council's curriculum development projects in the 1970s most geography teachers in England and Wales planned their courses by deciding what should be taught, and in what order. The documentation resulting from this simplest of planning models was a syllabus, i.e. a concise list of content stating what should be taught and when. The starting point for planning was the subject itself. It was taken for granted that planning the geography curriculum meant thinking primarily about content. Issues of contention were largely limited to debates about what should be included and about the best ways to transmit the selected content.

A possible legacy of the syllabus model of curriculum planning is the tendency of most geography teachers to begin their planning, not with the kinds of considerations on which theoretical models are based, but with a rough plotting of content onto a grid. If the only consideration taken into account in completing the grid is the content of geography then the result is a syllabus rather than a curriculum plan. From such a framework it is, however, possible to develop the geography curriculum.

While a syllabus is about content, a curriculum plan is concerned with transforming that content into a course. To do this it has to take into account the complexity of the total educational experience in schools, its purposes, its content, its processes and its outcomes, and it must evaluate all of these. Further, it is concerned with the way in which these various elements of education are inter-related.

There are different views on how the curriculum should be planned and where the emphasis should be, as is evident in the models outlined below. Whichever model of curriculum planning is adopted by a geography department, there are two valuable preliminary stages which can be used in both models of planning. First, it has to be decided what general considerations need to be taken into account and, second, a rough outline of the course has to be drafted. Although these stages are shown at the top of the curriculum plan in Fig. 5.1, general considerations need to be taken into account throughout the planning process and, moreover, the results of the initial drafting may be modified during the planning process.

GENERAL CONSIDERATIONS

The general considerations are represented below in the form of questions. The order in which they are considered and their relative importance are matters of judgement.

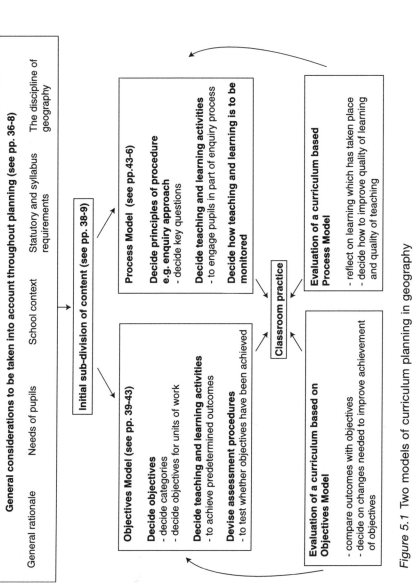

Figure 5.1 Two models of curriculum planning in geography

General considerations to be taken into account throughout planning (see pp. 36-8)

General rationale   Needs of pupils   School context   Statutory and syllabus requirements   The discipline of geography

Initial sub-division of content (see pp. 38-9)

Objectives Model (see pp. 39-43)

Decide objectives
- decide categories
- decide objectives for units of work

Decide teaching and learning activities
- to achieve predetermined outcomes

Devise assessment procedures
- to test whether objectives have been achieved

Evaluation of a curriculum based on Objectives Model
- compare outcomes with objectives
- decide on changes needed to improve achievement of objectives

Process Model (see pp.43-6)

Decide principles of procedure e.g. enquiry approach
- decide key questions

Decide teaching and learning activities
- to engage pupils in part of enquiry process

Decide how teaching and learning is to be monitored

Evaluation of a curriculum based Process Model
- reflect on learning which has taken place
- decide how to improve quality of learning and quality of teaching

Classroom practice

)nale
- What is the overall purpose of education in the school?
- What implications do these aims have for the geography curriculum?
- In what ways can the geography curriculum contribute to the school's general aims?

The pupils
- What experiences of learning geography (from feeder schools and from outside school) do pupils bring with them and how can these be used?
- How can the interests and enthusiasms brought by pupils be used?
- What individual needs do pupils have in relation to their learning of geography?

The school context
- What opportunities and constraints are provided by the economic, social and environmental context in which the school is situated?
- What opportunities are there for making use of the local and regional context, e.g. visits, fieldwork, links with the local community?
- What are the opportunities and constraints of the school buildings, the school grounds, and the school's resources?
- What links does the school have with other places in Britain and abroad?
- How can links with the feeder schools be built in to curriculum planning?

Statutory and syllabus requirements
- What are the requirements of the GNC and the selected examination syllabuses?
- To what extent can geography courses contribute to statutory and examination requirements in other parts of the curriculum, e.g. through integrated courses, in developing literacy, IT skills and numeracy?

The subject of geography
- Within the constraints of the GNC and examination syllabuses, what aspects of geography and approaches to geography does the department want to emphasize, e.g. people/environment approach, a scientific approach, a geography of social concern?

INITIAL DRAFTING

What is prescribed for schools now in the GNC and examination syllabuses is prescribed for long periods of time: two years (examination syllabuses); three years (Key Stage 1 and Key Stage 3) and four years (Key Stage 2). A useful initial task in curriculum planning is to divide these long courses into more manageable units, possibly varying from two weeks to one term in length. This process is similar to syllabus construction in its focus on what should be taught and when. It differs in that it takes into account the general considerations outlined above. It also takes into account the model of curriculum planning which will subsequently be used. Initial drafting involves consideration of the following questions.

- What units of work have been used previously in the school?
- Should these be maintained, modified or scrapped?
- What resources does the school have, in terms of staffing and physical resources?
- What should be the focus of the units: themes, places, issues, particular experiences (e.g. individual investigations) or a mixture of all four?
- What opportunities arise from the general considerations (pp. 36–8)?
- What opportunities are there for incorporating the use of information technology and fieldwork?
- What opportunities are there for liasing with work done in other subjects?
- What scope is there for progression in the units of work?

Initial decisions can be marked on a two-, three- or four-year plan depending on course length. Examples of such frameworks are found in several publications (e.g. Grimwade 1995).

THE OBJECTIVES MODEL OF PLANNING

Characteristics

There are three essential characteristics of the objectives model of planning. First, decisions are made at the start of a course of study about the intended outcomes. These decisions are expressed first as broad aims and then as more detailed objectives, i.e. statements of what pupils are expected to learn. Second, teaching and learning activities are designed so that the chosen objectives can be achieved. Third, the success of the course is determined by the extent to which the objectives have been achieved.

Origins

The objectives model of planning had its origins in the United States of America (Bobbit 1918; Tyler 1949; Taba 1962) where ideas related to behavioural psychology were applied to curriculum planning. There has been considerable debate about how specific objectives have to be. Some (e.g. Mager 1962) have argued that an objective must describe what a pupil has to be able to do in relation to a particular area of content, e.g. identify symbols on a weather map. This has been termed a 'behavioural objective' on the grounds that it indicates the intended behaviour. Other advocates of the objectives model of planning would argue against such detailed specification, saying that it would lead to proliferation of statements, but see value in general statements of objectives, e.g. the understanding of weather maps.

The use of objectives in curriculum planning in the USA encouraged thinking about different types of learning outcomes. The most influential categorization of learning outcomes was devised by Bloom (1956). He published a taxonomy of education objectives in two parts: the cognitive domain in which learning outcomes were defined by different types of thinking, and the affective domain in which learning outcomes were defined by different types of response and attitude. He subdivided each domain into a hierarchy of levels of achievement. Thus, for example, he subdivided the cognitive domain into knowledge (with emphasis on recall), comprehension, analysis, synthesis and evaluation.

Influence of the objectives model of curriculum planning on geographical education

Geographical education has been influenced by the objectives model of planning in several ways – in the use of both behavioural and more general objectives as a framework for planning, in the use of Bloom's 'categories' of objectives, and in the accountability of courses.

Examples of objectives taken from geography curriculum documents, shown in the list below, range from one which could be easily transformed into a behavioural objective to one which gives no indication of what the pupil has to do in order to achieve the objective. In geographical education more general statements about learning outcomes have been used more frequently than highly specific behavioural objectives.

1   To draw an accurate cross-section from measurements taken outside the classroom (GNC. DES 1991: 5).
2   To analyse the effect on the environment of the development of two energy sources (GNC. DES 1991: 26).
3   To recall specific facts relating to the syllabus content and demonstrate locational knowledge within the range of small, regional, national, international and world scales (GCSE syllabuses. NEAB 1995).
4   To recognize alternative value positions and to relate these to the ideologies with which they are associated (Geography Avery Hill GCSE syllabus. WJEC 1995).
5   Key idea: Leisure activities often involve extensive use of land, sometimes in competition with other users (GYSL 1974).

Bloom's categorization of objectives has been very influential. The following are examples of different categorizations used in geography.

1   Key ideas; skills; values (GYSL 1974).
2   Knowledge; understanding; skills; values (National Criteria for GCSE Geography. HMSO 1985).

3 Knowledge; understanding; application; skills and techniques (Core Criteria for GCSE. SCAA 1995).
4 Knowledge; skills; attitudes and values (NCC 1991).
5 Concepts; skills and techniques; values and attitudes; cross-curricular themes (Currie *et al.* 1994).

In geographical education, the categorization of objectives has focused attention on the relative importance of different types of learning in relation to an area of content. If, for example, a teacher is teaching a unit of work about the Lower Don Valley in Sheffield, what is the main purpose? Is it to enable pupils to recall specific facts, to increase understanding of the concepts of urban decay and regeneration, to increase understanding of the political processes involved in change, to teach skills in map-reading and resource interpretation, or a combination of all of these? There could be valid reasons for any of these purposes, but the teaching and learning activities would be different. Clarification of objectives provides some guidelines in deciding which teaching and learning activities should be used.

Categorization of objectives, as well as helping to clarify teachers' thinking, has enabled examination boards to give different weighting in assessing different types of learning. For example, the NEAB Geography GCSE syllabus D for 1996/7 has the following weighting: recall 20 per cent; understanding, application and skills 45 per cent; practical skills 24 per cent; values 11 per cent. Over the last twenty years the emphasis on recall has decreased while that on understanding, skills and values has increased.

Objectives have also become important in geographical education as a means of accountability. The success of a course of geographical education is for the most part measured publicly by the achievement of predetermined objectives. Examination results of geography at GCSE and A Level are fed into national league tables. The Education Reform Act of 1988 emphasized the outcomes of learning. The terms of reference to the Geography Working Group stated that: 'There should be clear objectives, attainment targets, for the knowledge, skills and understanding which pupils of different abilities and maturities should be expected to have acquired by the end of the academic year in which they reach the ages of 7, 11, 14, and 16' (DES 1990: 93). The expectation that curriculum planning involves the specification of objectives is reinforced by OFSTED inspection guidelines – 'purpose is demonstrated by effective planning, including the clarity of objectives' (OFSTED 1993: Section 4.7.1. p. 49).

If the objectives model of planning is adopted the following questions need to be considered:

● What categories of objectives should be included in the curriculum plan (taking into account what is prescribed and the department's professional judgements)?

- Using these categories, what should the objectives be for each unit of work?
- What teaching and learning activities would lead to an achievement of these objectives?
- What resources are available to support these teaching and learning activities?
- What means of assessment will the department use to assess the achievement of these objectives for each unit of work?
- What criteria will be used to establish levels of achievement?
- What degree of precision is needed in defining objectives for individual lessons?
- How can the objectives provide for progression throughout the course?

The answers to these questions are likely to result in the use of a planning framework for each unit of work, with different categories of objectives used as headings.

The merits of the objectives model

The objectives model encourages systematic thinking about outcomes of learning, types of learning, and the emphasis given in assessment to different types of learning. This can encourage activities which are deemed to be more worthwhile. The categories of knowledge and understanding, skills and values, have provided a useful and supportive framework for organizing geography courses, textbooks and syllabuses during the last twenty-five years. The inclusion of objectives in a curriculum plan can provide a sense of purpose to the teaching and learning. The extent to which objectives have been achieved can be used in external accountability to parents and to society generally.

Criticisms of the objectives model

The objectives model has been criticized on several grounds. It is much easier to prescribe outcomes and define outcomes for the learning of simple skills than for the understanding of ideas or complex situations. Understanding develops rather than being reached. The fact that some objectives are more easily defined than others could lead to greater emphasis being given to these outcomes of learning which are easily defined and assessed, but which are not necessarily more worthwhile.

Pursuit of clarity in defining objectives can lead to proliferation of statements. For example, the 1991 GNC was criticized for the large number of Statements of Attainment, while being at the same time found fault with because some of these statements needed to be broken down into separate statements in order to clarify what was needed. It is burdensome to write the number of objectives needed for clarity and impractical to assess the achievement of them all. Yet general objectives used in geography, such as statements of key ideas, are open to criticism for failing to state what pupils need to do to achieve them.

There have been objections to the emphasis on predetermined outcomes because there is little role for the pupils, apart from complying with the teacher's plans. If one of the aims of education is to encourage pupils to think, how can all the outcomes be predetermined? As Stenhouse wrote: 'Education as induction into knowledge is successful to the extent that it makes the behavioural outcomes of the students unpredictable' (Stenhouse 1975: 82).

The objectives model might focus too much attention on the final products of learning. This could encourage teaching to the test, leading to closed, limited activities rather than to activities with unpredictable outcomes. It could also discourage teachers from using the unpredictable opportunities for learning which may arise from topical events, or from opportunities which may emerge during the course of a lesson.

A strong focus on objectives can act as a blinker to what is really happening in a classroom, so that the teacher is unaware of learning taking place which is unrelated to the objectives.

A curriculum plan tends to have common objectives for all pupils. This tends to overlook individual differences and needs.

A PROCESS MODEL OF CURRICULUM DEVELOPMENT

Characteristics

There are three essential features of the process model of curriculum development. First, decisions are made about the principles of procedure which should guide teaching and learning activities before detailed planning takes place. Second, teaching and learning activities are designed which are underpinned by the principles of procedure and, third, the course is evaluated by monitoring the processes as well as the outcomes of learning.

Origins

The process model of curriculum development grew out of a belief in the intrinsic value of the education process, and from criticisms of the objectives model of planning (Peters 1959; Bruner 1966; Raths 1971; Stenhouse 1975).

One of the first examples of curriculum development based on a process model was an American social science course, developed by Jerome Bruner in the 1960s. The course, 'Man: A Course of Study', expressed its aims as principles instead of objectives. The first of the seven principles was: 'To initiate and develop in youngsters a process of question-posing'. The principles were intended to underpin all classroom activity, instead of representing end points of learning. The first principle was built into the course by using a framework of questions: What is human about human beings? How did they get that way? How can they be made more so?

Another notable example of the use of the process model was the Schools Council Humanities Curriculum Project, directed by Lawrence Stenhouse in the 1970s. One of its principles was 'that the mode of enquiry in controversial areas should have discussion rather than instruction as its core' (Ruddock 1983: 8). The project applied this principle in the provision of resources and devising of strategies to promote discussion. Raths, writing generally about curriculum development, advocated using criteria for identifying worthwhile activities. An example of his criteria is: 'All other things being equal, one activity is more worthwhile than another if it asks students to engage in inquiry into ideas, applications of intellectual processes, or current problems, either personal or social' (Raths 1971: 716).

As the process model of the curriculum was developed, new ways of evaluating teaching and learning developed, including action research in which teachers investigated the processes taking place in their own classrooms. The process model is associated with types of evaluation which depend on teachers 'reflecting in action', i.e. while they are teaching (Schon 1983), and after action, considering different types of evidence collected during classroom experience. Planning and developing a curriculum using the process model became not only a means of providing a curriculum for pupils, but also a means of continuous professional development.

Application of the process model of curriculum planning to geographical education

The impact of the process model of curriculum development in geography can be seen in the development of the enquiry approach and on research into classroom processes.

The principles of procedure implicit in the enquiry approach would emphasize first, the importance of both teachers and pupils asking questions and, second, the importance of the active involvement of pupils in the processes necessary to answer them.

The importance given to questioning in geography has led to the use of key questions at an early stage of curriculum planning. Instead of starting curriculum planning by defining the end products of learning it has become common to start at the beginning point of learning, i.e. with questions. Examples include the Schools Council 16–19 Project and the 1995 GNC.

The Schools Council 16–19 Geography Project produced a sequence of questions to be answered in investigating any geographical issue, in its route to geographical enquiry: what? where? how? why? what might? what will?

with what impact? what decision? what do I think? why? what next? what shall I do? (Naish *et al.* 1987). These questions were to provide a framework for use in any area of content.

The 1995 GNC also has a series of questions in the Programmes of Study: what/where is it? what is it like? how did it get like this? how and why is it changing? what are the implications?

Many examination syllabuses are now set out as a series of questions, e.g. 'What is quality of life and how can it be measured?' (WJEC. Geography, Avery Hill. GCSE 1995).

The second implicit principle of the enquiry approach is the involvement of pupils in the processes needed to answer those questions, rather than being provided with answers by the teacher. The impact of this principle on geographical education is seen in the emphasis on the skills needed to process geographical information in the GNC and in some examination syllabuses.

The 1995 GNC lists the investigative processes in Section 2 of each Programme of Study. Furthermore, the Level Descriptors in the Statement of Attainment for Geography in GNC emphasize process skills rather than terminal points in learning.

Examination Boards encourage the development of enquiry processes by setting decision-making examination papers and by assessing the ability to construct and process geographical knowledge from given data. Individual coursework investigations required for some external examinations engage pupils in the process of constructing geography for themselves. Marking schemes for such investigations attempt to assess engagement in different parts of the process, albeit from a final product.

The process model of thinking about curriculum has encouraged research into the processes of teaching and learning taking place in the classroom, focusing particularly on teachers' and pupils' use of language to learn geography. Research on oracy (Carter 1991), written work (Barnes 1976) and reading (Davies 1986) has revealed the role that pupils can play in developing their own understanding of geography. The increase in the use of small group work, role play, simulations, different genres of writing, and learning diaries are all evidence of the acknowledgement of the pupils' role in the construction of geographical knowledge and their contribution to the curriculum.

If the process model of curriculum planning is adopted, then the following questions need to be considered.

- What key questions need to be asked to enable pupils to engage with this area of subject-matter?
- Which questions should be asked initially by the teacher?
- How can teaching and learning activities be devised to encourage pupils to ask their own questions?

LIBRARY, UNIVERSITY COLLEGE CHESTER

- What resources are needed to enable pupils to answer these questions?
- How are these resources collected and selected?
- What geographical techniques and procedures could be used to answer these questions?
- How can these techniques and procedures be incorporated into pupil activities?
- Which parts of the enquiry process will pupils be engaged in during the course unit and which during individual lessons?
- How can the processes in which the pupils are engaged be evaluated during and after lessons?
- How can what has been learned from the evaluation be built into subsequent lessons and units of work?

Merits of the process model

The process model of curriculum development focuses on learning. It recognizes the role of pupils in shaping what they learn and in constructing geography for themselves. It recognizes the complexity of classroom inter-action. It values the learning that takes place, whether it is intended, unintended or unexpected. It takes account of individual differences. It is based on the intrinsic value of education. The professional judgement of teachers is valued in evaluating courses and assessing individuals.

Criticisms of the process model

The principles underpinning courses planned using the process model are not sufficiently precise to be used objectively in evaluation or assessment. The understanding of what takes place during a course is a matter for personal interpretation and professional judgement. Such judgements are less valuable than those based on a curriculum plan which follows the objectives model when comparisons are needed for purposes of public accountability and national assessment.

PROFESSIONAL DILEMMAS IN CURRICULUM PLANNING

How teachers plan the geography curriculum and develop courses is a matter of professional judgement. The current educational context is pulling them in two different directions.

The 1995 GNC encourages the use of the process model in curriculum development, with its focus on questions, processes of learning, and professional judgement in making holistic assessments of the pupils' levels of learning. Yet OFSTED inspections expect every unit of work and every lesson to have 'clearly formulated objectives'. Should open-ended questions or predetermined outcomes be the starting-point for planning for the GNC? Should key questions be interpreted as not being open-ended but just another form of expressing content? If a department wants to use a process model, how can objectives be defined to satisfy OFSTED? How much scope is there in the GNC to allow for the unexpected and the unpredictable, and to value the variety of response from individuals and schools? If a department wants to use an objectives model, what categories should be used for the GNC? How can the general statements in the level descriptors be developed into more precise statements of objectives? What should the balance be between openness and prescription in departmental GNC plans?

In the examination years the dilemmas for teachers are different. External examinations inevitably have to state the end products of learning which they are going to assess. Objectives are clearly stated. Yet some examinations place emphasis on individual enquiries, and frame the syllabus with key questions. What emphasis should geography departments give during the development and teaching of examination courses to the processes of learning geography compared to the end products of learning? League tables and OFSTED inspections encourage geography teachers to teach to the test, to what is required at the end, and to what will achieve high grades for the pupils. There may well be a conflict between the aims of enabling pupils to achieve the highest possible grades in public examinations and enabling pupils to become critical, enquiring people.

We seem to have reached a point in geographical education when both the objectives model and the process model have to be taken into account in curriculum planning and course design. This is because both models have had an influence on present-day geographical education. It is important to be aware of their influence and of some of the dilemmas they present. Inevitably, there will be compromises. This may mean using different models for different units of work, having some units emphasizing questioning and the enquiry process, and others concentrating on the product of learning. It may mean modifying the process model so that enquiry is rarely open-ended but is to a large extent controlled by the teacher. It may mean attempting to define objectives which would assess, formatively, a pupil's ability to engage in the enquiry process.

Geography teachers have to make professional judgements about how to work within the current context. Curriculum planning models, objectives, principles, approaches, etc. are not given by law but have been devised to meet needs. They are ideas which teachers have used for support in the challenging task of developing a worthwhile curriculum. It is up to teachers and departments to decide how to use these ideas, and what decisions to make, in the best interests of the pupils, the school and, ultimately, society. Within the current context, there are still many important decisions to be made about the geography curriculum.

REFERENCES

Barnes, D. (1976) *From Communication to Curriculum*. Harmondsworth: Penguin.

Bloom, B.S. (1956) *Taxonomy of Educational Objectives*, New York: David McKay Co.

Bobbitt, J.F. (1918) *The Curriculum*, Boston: Houghton Mifflin.

Bruner, J.S. (1966) *Towards a Theory of Instruction*, New York: W.W. Norton and Company Inc.

Carter, R. (1991) *Talking about Geography: The Work of Geography Teachers in the National Oracy Project*, Sheffield: Geographical Association.

Currie, S., Battersby, J., Bowden, D., Webster, A. and Whittal, R. (1994) *Landscape and Water Resources*, Glasgow: Collins Educational.

Davies, F. (1986) *Books in the School Curriculum*, London: Educational Publishers Council and National Book League.

DES (1990) *Geography for Ages 5 to 16*, London: HMSO.

DES (1991) *Geography in the National Curriculum*, London: HMSO.

Grimwade, K. (1995) 'Revising courses', *Teaching Geography* 20 (2): 62–6.

Geography for the Young School Leaver Project (1974) *Man, Land and Leisure: Teachers' Guide*, London: Schools Council Publications.

Mager, R.F. (1962) *Preparing Instructional Objectives*, Belmont, California: Fearon Publishers.

Naish, M., Rawling, E. and Hart, M. (1987) *The Contribution of a Curriculum Project to 16–19 Education*, London: Longman.

NCC (1991) *Geography Non-statutory Guidance (England)*, York: National Curriculum Council.

OFSTED (1993) *Handbook for the Inspection of Schools*, London: HMSO.

Peters, R.S. (1959) *Authority, Responsibility and Education*, London: Allen and Unwin.

Raths, J.D. (1971) 'Teaching without specific objectives', *Educational Leadership*, April: 714–20.

Ruddock, J. (1983) *The Humanities Curriculum Project: An Introduction*, Norwich: University of East Anglia.

SCAA (1995) *GCSE Subject Criteria for Geography*, London: SCAA.

Schon, D. (1983) *The Reflective Practitioner*, London: Temple Smith.

Stenhouse, L. (1975) *An Introduction to Curriculum Research and Development*, London: Heinemann Educational Books.

Taba, H. (1962) *Curriculum Development: Theory and Practice*, New York: Harcourt Brace and World.

Tyler, R. (1949) *Basic Principles of Curriculum and Instruction*, Chicago: University of Chicago Press.

Chapter 6

The scope of school geography
A medium for education

Michael Naish

What is the scope of school geography as a means of enhancing pupils' education? To answer this question, we shall certainly have to consider what kinds of knowledge and understanding the study of geography can offer. Knowledge and understanding alone, however, do not necessarily constitute an education and we shall also need to discuss the range of skills which may be developed through the study of geography. Since geographical study will inevitably lead us into debate about the issues that arise from the way people use or misuse their environments and about the political nature of decision-making concerning the use of space, we shall also become involved in the important area of values education.

DEVELOPING VIEWS OF THE SCOPE OF SCHOOL GEOGRAPHY

This concept of geography as concerned with value-laden environmental situations is a relatively modern one and the subject has not always been viewed in this way. Let me briefly trace some key elements of the changing scope of school geography. (More detail is provided by Marsden in Chapter 2.)

During the early part of the nineteenth century, the little geography taught was of the 'capes and bays' variety, consisting largely of the rote learning of names of places and features, such as the rivers of Britain, and the location of these places and features. By 1880, geography was becoming more established in the elementary schools, with a clear division between physical and human geography. In the last years of the nineteenth century, there was a trend towards commercial geography and a greater focus on the links between physical and human phenomena. This was influenced by increasing interest in school geography on the part of the Royal Geographical Society, by the founding of the Geographical Association in 1893 and by the teaching and influence of Geikie, Mill, Mackinder and Herbertson (Graves 1975).

Geography experienced a growth period from about 1917 to 1933, as it increased in popularity as a subject both in schools and in the universities. By the mid-twentieth century it was well established as a popular subject and its main focus was on regional geography. The central interest was in recognizing, delimiting and analysing regions. Regions were normally delimited by physical features or by a combination of human and physical characteristics. Physical geography tended to receive separate attention as well as consideration in regional analysis and it was dominated by geomorphology, with meteorology and climate coming a poor second and consideration of biogeography and ecosystems a distant third.

In the late 1960s and through the 1970s, geography experienced what has been called a 'conceptual revolution'. The revolution had begun in North America in the early 1950s but it reached the UK much later, in the mid-1960s, and its impact on school examination syllabuses was not felt until the late 1970s. The main elements of the revolution were threefold. First, there was a move from regional geography to study of systematic specialisms, including, for example, geomorphology, economic geography, urban geography and agricultural geography. The second element of the revolution was the clarification of the key ideas, or central organizing concepts of the discipline: concepts such as spatial location, spatial distribution, spatial differentiation, spatial interaction and the region, for example. The third, dominating, element was the attempt to explain phenomena through a more scientific approach to the subject. This included the posing and testing of hypotheses and the construction of conceptual models such as those involved in central place theory, as opposed to hardware models, say of a volcano or an irrigation system. Use of the scientific method in this hypothetico-deductive approach necessarily entailed the collection of quantitative data as evidence and the statistical analysis of such data.

For some, the revolution, with its need for assumptions such as the featureless plain, and the reduction of human behaviour to quantified abstractions, represented a disastrous move away from the reality of human life on earth and counter-schools of thought rapidly developed. There was a strong challenge from behaviourists, who argued that the key factor in decisions about the use of space is the element of human choice, which is influenced, among other things, by the perceptions of the decision-maker. Behaviourism developed naturally, for some scholars, into a more humanistic approach to the subject. The other main prong of attack on the quantitative revolution came from those geographers who were more concerned with the inequalities which arise from the use of space and were involved in the investigation of issues such as social and spatial injustice in cities, or the impacts of multinational companies on conditions in the Third World. This socially and environmentally committed geography was characterized by a range of approaches, including a liberal, welfare approach, radical and Marxist approaches and structuralism. In the post-modern world, all approaches are subject to reconsideration and deconstruction, with an emphasis on the fragility and impermanence of social and spatial structures.

The 'conceptual revolution' (Davies 1972) had a significant impact on the scope of school geography in Britain. Early ideas were imported through the work of the American High School Geography Project, which was active in the 1960s (Graves 1968). The Project placed emphasis on the active investigation of situations on the part of pupils and students. Strategies involving role plays, simulations and games were quickly adapted by some school and university geographers in the UK, who recognized the teaching and learning potential of such approaches. The idea of employing the scientific approach, taken to be mainly concerned with the posing and testing of hypotheses, was also effectively taken up and applied with considerable drive to enquiry in fieldwork in particular (Chapallaz *et al.* 1970). Initially, Advanced level General Certificate of Education courses and then, more slowly, Ordinary level courses, were revised to take on board some elements of the conceptual changes. Most commonly, the new syllabuses focused on models in geography as the key area for attention and lists of conceptual models were included in syllabuses.

Unfortunately such syllabuses were not developed until the late 1970s, by which time geography at the research frontier had moved on. The conceptual revolution, typified by the adoption of logical positivism, had already been challenged, as described above, and new, stimulating ideas were characterizing research interests. Thus the syllabuses at school level for 14 to 19 year-olds, which inevitably influenced work for younger pupils, were fossilized in an out-of-date mode by the pace of change in geographical research. This is a problematic situation for the school curriculum and, in particular, for the examination syllabuses which at that time strongly influenced it. Research interests may advance and change quickly while examination boards, subject to inertia, are first slow to react and then, when they have reacted and invested time, money and commitment in the new development, reluctant to change yet again. This situation was influenced in those days by the fact that the boards are commercial concerns which need to take market forces and profit and loss into account.

SYLLABUS INERTIA

In the light of this analysis, the selection of content and the appropriate emphasis on skills development and values education is clearly no easy task. The danger is that curricula that are closely specified, as curricula represented by examination board syllabuses normally are, will become quickly out-of-date and will cease to reflect the nature of the subject either at research level or as it is manifested in higher education. The situation with regard to A Level geography in the mid-1970s illustrates this fossilization,

- mainly regional geography, focusing on explanatory description of areas
  – may tend to be repetitive;
- learning sets of facts about particular places
  – the main load on the mind is that of remembering a compendium of facts;
- lack of recognition of fundamental organizing concepts which provide a framework for study;
- strong dichotomy between the study of human geography (regional) and physical geography (systematic);
- examinations test mainly the skill of essay-writing, placing a premium on memory rather than critical thinking and other skills, particularly those used in geographical study and research;
- emphasis is towards the compilation of inventories rather than problem-solving or the understanding of general concepts and theories.

Figure 6.1 A caricature of Advanced level geography (1974)

or inertia, rather well. For a conference on geography for 16 to 19 year-olds at the Schools Council in 1974, I produced what I called a caricature of Advanced level geography, Figure 6.1 (see Naish *et al.* 1987).

The caricature suggested that geography at A level at that time was not fulfilling its potential role as a medium for education. Its content was limited in scope and out-of-date compared to what was happening in academic geography. It was encouraging the development of only a limited range of skills and had hardly begun to explore the attitudes and values inherent in environmental and spatial decision-making. The potential for transfer of learning from geography to other disciplines and interests was distinctly limited. While general aims of education were suggesting creative and developmental advances, geography remained largely trapped in old-fashioned content and constricting teaching and learning styles.

CURRICULUM CHANGE

Luckily, the 1970s was a decade of exciting curriculum change for geography. This was largely due to teachers making the most of the opportunity to become involved in curriculum development through the work of the Schools Council, which provided funding for curriculum development projects. By 1974, work had already been undertaken, or was in hand, for the development of geography for the age range 5 to 16 through the Environmental Studies 5–13 Project from 1967, History, Geography and Social Science in the Middle Years of Schooling, 8–13 from 1971 (Blyth *et al.* 1976), Geography for the Young School Leaver, 14–16 (Boardman 1988) and Geography 14–18 (Tolley and Reynolds 1977), both from 1970. From 1976 to 1985, the Geography 16–19 Project undertook curriculum development for the older age-group (Naish *et al.* 1987).

Through the work of these projects the idea of developing a curriculum framework for the selection of concepts and approaches became widely accepted. Building on the work of the Geography for the Young School Leaver and Geography 14–18 Projects, the Geography 16–19 Project set out to produce a curriculum framework for this age-group. In order to do this, a research phase was undertaken, during which the Project, working with a system of involved teachers and lecturers, investigated the needs of 16 to 19 year-old students and analysed the rapidly changing nature of the subject. On the basis of this research, it was possible to suggest broad aims. Such aims are not, however, necessarily operational and the next and key step was to produce the curriculum framework.

This document set out two main principles for 16–19 geography: a distinctive approach to the subject, the 'people–environment' approach, and the adoption of active enquiry as the main style of teaching and learning. Four overarching people–environment themes were proposed: The Challenge of Natural Environments, The Use and Misuse of Natural Resources, Issues of Global Concern and Managing Human Environments. The framework also offered advice on scales of study and on areal coverage. The Project then went on to exemplify the use of the framework in the construction of syllabuses, notably the Geography 16–19 A level syllabus with the University of London Examinations Board. A system of teacher support was set up, which included the production of a range of teaching materials.

PEOPLE–ENVIRONMENT AND THE SCOPE OF MODERN GEOGRAPHY

An examination of the key ideas of the Geography 16–19 framework will provide a helpful overview of the scope of modern geography in education, since the work of the Project, together with that of the other Schools Council projects, has been seminal in influencing recent developments.

The focus on the people–environment approach is seen as a way of helping teachers to cope with the rapid pace of conceptual and intellectual change in the subject. It offers a way of approaching key questions using the kind of geography which is most appropriate to the situation. It is based on the notion that people must interact with their environments in order to survive and in order to develop social groups, cultures and civilization. Through this interaction, people create spatial effects including locations, distributions and flows. The spatial effects change over time. Such matters have always been the central interest of geographical study, providing a focus for the kinds of questions asked by geographers, such as: Why is this location here? Why is it like this? How does this distribution or this flow come to exist? What influences it and why is it changing? How will it change in the future? How should it change? In using the word 'environments', the

Project wishes to include the full range of possible environments in which people interact, including physical, human and perceived environments.

More significantly, the interactions between people and their varied environments may cause problems, through misuse, overuse or ignorance. A very common form of problem envisaged here is the kind of interference in ecosystems that human activity causes and which often results in the input of too much positive feedback in the system. The dust-bowl effect of overfarming in the Midwest of the USA provides an example. Furthermore, the Project argues that issues arise from the interaction of people with environments and it defines 'issue' here as a situation where people are actually in conflict over decisions concerning the use of space. The recent events related to motorway developments in southern England, including the M11 in East London and the M3 near Winchester, provide striking examples of such conflict.

The people–environment approach, then, is to do with the questions, issues and problems that arise from the multifarious interactions of people and their varied environments, and geographers are concerned to study such questions, issues and problems. From the point of view of geography for 16 to 19 year-olds, the Project recommends that study should begin with the recognition of particular questions, issues and problems and then go on to investigate these using the most appropriate geographical approach. In this way it is possible to sample the main systematic branches of the subject in such a manner that the key concepts and methods of enquiry are satisfactorily covered. The significance of geographical enquiry in exploring and explicating important contemporary issues is amply demonstrated. Students come to see that what occupies prime viewing time on television and continuous coverage in the press – concern about the use of space and for environmental issues – is the very stuff of modern geography.

Students study people–environment questions, issues and problems through direct investigation of first-hand and secondary data. They carry through active, involving investigation, which they, and their teachers, find to be motivational. The enquiry is seen to be significant and interesting because it is about the world they are living in and their future in this world. Geographical study is about questions of genuine significance for the environment and for the quality of human life. Since virtually all questions about the use of space are political in some sense, students also become involved in the enhancement of their values education. They are encouraged to review the range of values and attitudes that impinge on a particular question, issue or problem, to investigate and evaluate the characteristics of such values and attitudes and to make a decision about their own stance. Such decision making may lead, in appropriate circumstances, to the taking of action with regard to the issue. In this way, the people–environment approach can help to develop the political literacy of the students.

In such study, students must necessarily be developing a range of skills and abilities. Some of these skills, such as map construction and interpretation, or the analysis of satellite images, may be thought of as specific to geography. Others, such as intellectual, social, communication, practical and study skills, are certainly susceptible to development through study in geography, but are not the exclusive domain of geography.

FRAMEWORKS ENCAPSULATE THE SCOPE OF GEOGRAPHY

In the late 1990s, some kind of framework approach is applied to the geography curriculum at all phases of education, primary, secondary and post-16. For the curriculum for 5 to 14 year-olds, the National Curriculum at Key Stages 1, 2 and 3 is in place (DFE 1995); for 14 to 16 year-olds, the GCSE National Criteria provide guidelines for Examination Boards (SCAA 1995); at post-16 level, the Subject Core and Principles for A and AS Examinations devised by SCAA form the structure of the framework (SCAA 1992, 1993). These frameworks in each case offer guidance on the selection of content and the development of skills and, to a varying degree, on the place of attitudes and values. They tell us what is the scope of modern school geography. Each of the frameworks shows the strong influence of the Schools Council projects.

Key Stages 1 to 3

In the case of the National Curriculum, teachers of 5 to 14 year-olds are given quite tightly specified guidance on content, which is designed to ensure that children are developing a range of 'geographical skills' through the activities of investigating places and themes and undertaking studies that focus on such geographical questions as: What/where is it?, What is it like?, How did it get like this?, How and why is it changing?, What are the implications? There is an emphasis on place, including knowing locations and finding out about the character of places and some issues concerning them. Care is taken to ensure that examples are selected from countries in different states of development and the themes, extending in number with older children, represent a number of geography's systematic interests.

The influence of the people–environment approach becomes clearer with increasing age. At Key Stage 1 (5 to 7 year-olds), the thematic study is concerned with the quality of an environment in a locality and pupils are to express views on the attractiveness of the environment, to investigate how the environment is changing and how the quality of the environment might be sustained and improved. At Key Stage 2 (7 to 11 year-olds), one of the thematic studies is about environmental change, which requires investigation of how people affect the environment and attempt to manage and sustain it. For Key Stage 3 pupils (11 to 14 year-olds), the people–

environment approach is more pervasive. There is the general statement that pupils should be given opportunities to 'consider the issues that arise from people's interaction with their environments' and one of the thematic studies is called Environmental Issues.

There are significant omissions from the English and Welsh Statutory Orders for Geography in the National Curriculum. There is no general overview of the nature of geography and its contribution to a child's education. No broad aims are expressed. There is also no specific reference to values education, but with the kinds of enquiry questions being encouraged and the focus on environmental quality and change, teachers have every opportunity to develop the potential of the subject in this direction. There is encouragement towards this in the level descriptions, which are intended as guidelines for teachers in assessing the performance of their pupils. At Level 8, for example, the highest of the levels, pupils may be beginning to 'account for disparities in development' and to 'recognize the causes and consequences of environmental issues'.

GCSE criteria

The GCSE criteria for geography provide the framework which all examinations consortia must use in the construction of syllabuses to be in place from September 1996. The criteria show a clear people–environment view of the subject in terms of content and approach. Syllabus content must include, for example, 'balanced coverage of physical, human and environmental aspects of the subject', 'study of the interrelationships between people and the environment' and 'study of the geographical aspects of social, economic, political and environmental issues'. Even more encouraging is the requirement that pupils must study the 'significance and effects of attitudes and values of those involved in geographical issues and in decision-making about the use and management of environments'.

The criteria place helpful stress on study of a range of places and environments, thus taking forward the concern with place begun in the earliest years of the National Curriculum. The need for study at a range of scales from local to global is also emphasized. There is encouragement, too, to give pupils the opportunity to appreciate the dynamic nature of geographical features, patterns and issues and the way new ideas and methods can 'lead to new interpretations'. Pupils are to be helped to develop a range of important 'geographical enquiry skills', which include research and communication skills.

Post-16

For the post-16 group, commonly known as the 16–19 age-range, the 'Subject Core for Geography' (SCAA 1993) provides the framework for course construction and, once again, the people–environment approach as developed by the Geography 16–19 Project is clearly recognizable. Examination Boards must ensure that the core comprises one-third of their A level syllabuses and two-thirds of their AS syllabuses. The core includes 'a theme which emphasizes the interaction between people and their environment at different spatial scales and focuses on the relevant systems and processes, their outcomes, changes through time and consequent issues, responses and strategies'. A selected physical environment and a selected human environment must also be studied, with a focus on characteristics, natural, physical and human processes, their interaction, consequent outcomes and change over time.

Emphasis is placed on personal investigative work using first-hand and secondary data and a range of skills listed includes not only the 'research' skills necessary for such work, but also 'the evaluative and interpretive skills involved in problem analysis, decision-making and a critical examination of geographical sources and evidence . . .'. Under 'knowledge and understanding', students are required to 'appreciate and analyse the role of values, perceptions and decision-making processes in geographical contexts', thus opening up the potential for a critical element of values education in the geography curriculum for 16 to 19 year-olds and older students. The picture of 16–19 geography offered by the subject core presents a strong contrast to the caricature of A level geography summarized in Figure 6.1.

THE QUESTION OF BALANCE

The scope of school geography refers to its content in terms of concepts and principles, but concepts and principles cannot alone comprise a geographical education. To them must also be added the factual and experimental learning that leads towards the acquisition of concepts and the understanding of principles. As part of the scope of modern school geography, it is argued that an active enquiry approach is the one most appropriate to the study of geography. Such an approach can be employed not only to help develop a range of significant skills and abilities, but also to open up the area of values education, where geography has a significant contribution to offer.

The key difficulty in managing the scope of geography to produce effective curricula is one of balance: balance between breadth and depth of study and balance between content and educational value. Courses should cover sufficient breadth, in terms of areal examples, to provide an overview of the global situation, but at the same time, study needs to be in depth, rather than superficial, if genuine conceptual learning is to be achieved. Curricula that are too heavy in content militate against skills development and the consideration of values and attitudes. The pressures exerted by content-loaded curricula force teachers towards didactic, expository styles of teaching. Achieving an appropriate balance between these forces remains the central problem of curriculum design.

REFERENCES

Boardman, D. (1988) 'The impact of a curriculum project: geography for the young school leaver', *Educational Review*, Birmingham: University of Birmingham, Occasional Publications.

Blyth, A., Cooper, K., Derricot, R., Elliott, G., Sumner, H. and Waplington, A. (1976) *Place, Time and Society 8–13: Curriculum Planning in History, Geography and Social Science*, Bristol: Collins–ESL for the Schools Council.

Chapallaz, D.P., Davis, P.F., Fitzgerald, B.P., Grenyer, N., Rolfe, J. and Walker, D.R.F. (1970) *Hypothesis Testing in Field Studies*, Teaching Geography Occasional Papers 11, Sheffield: The Geographical Association.

Davies, W.K. (1972) *The Conceptual Revolution in Geography*, London: University of London Press.

DFE (1995) *Geography in the National Curriculum*, London: HMSO.

Graves, N.J. (1968) 'The High School Geography Project of the Association of American Geographers', *Geography* 53, Part 1: 68–73.

Graves, N.J. (1975) *Geography in Education*, London: Heinemann Educational Books.

Naish, M., Rawling, E. and Hart, C. (1987) *Geography 16–19. The Contribution of a Curriculum Project to 16–19 Education*, Harlow: Longman.

SCAA (1992) *Principles for Advanced and Advanced Supplementary Examinations*, London: School Curriculum and Assessment Authority.

SCAA (1993) *Subject Core for Geography*, London: School Curriculum and Assessment Authority.

SCAA (1995) *GCSE Subject Criteria for Geography*, London: School Curriculum and Assessment Authority.

Tolley, H. and Reynolds, J.B. (1977) *Geography 14–18: A Handbook for School-based Curriculum Development*, Basingstoke: Macmillan.

Chapter 7

Progression and transition in a coherent geography curriculum

Michael Williams

In the persistent attempt to improve standards of attainment in school geography, it is essential that close attention is paid to establishing curriculum structures which facilitate geographical learning. In essence, the nature of geography as a school subject changes as pupils mature. Maturity brings intellectual accomplishment with gains in knowledge and understanding, changes in values and attitudes, and the acquisition of a broader range of skills. It also brings substantial changes in pupils' enthusiasms, experience and interests. The geography teacher's task is to achieve a match between the learner as he or she matures and appropriate subject-matter defined in terms of knowledge, attitudes and skills. Aspects of these three domains can be developed at particular stages of pupil development – some can be initiated in the early years while others are best left until later. In this chapter we shall discuss some of the principles which are currently being used within the framework of the National Curriculum to take account of progression and we shall highlight some of the difficulties inherent in the transition from stage to stage in the school system.

PRINCIPLES OF PROGRESSION

Any consideration of progression in geographical education can begin with the changing nature of the learner, or the nature of the subject, or the teaching–learning process. That these three are very closely related, however, is highlighted in a set of propositions suggested by Bennetts (1981):

1   Some ideas are inherently more difficult than others, some skills more demanding than others.
2   Many ideas can be approached at different levels of understanding.
3   An analysis of what is involved in particular learning tasks can help a teacher select appropriate methods.
4   Learning is facilitated by:
    a) building upon pupils' prior experience and knowledge
    b) avoiding any unnecessary difficulties or barriers.

5   Learning is facilitated when the experience provided and the tasks set by teachers are related to pupils' interests and capabilities and the overall course programme is designed to take account of the way in which pupils mature.
6   Assessment of pupils' progress is necessary in order to adjust the programme to meet the requirements of individuals.

The first two of these propositions were extended in a publication of Her Majesty's Inspectorate (1986: 40–2, 49–57) where it was stated that progression in geographical learning should involve the following:

• An increase in breadth of studies. There should be a gradual extension of content to include different places, new landscapes, a variety of geographical conditions and a range of human activities.
• An increasing depth of study associated with pupils' growing capacity to deal with complexities and abstractions. As pupils mature intellectually they are able to make sense of more complex situations, to cope with more demanding information, to take account of more intricate webs of inter-relationships and to undertake more complicated tasks.
• An increase in the spatial scale of what is studied. The growth in pupils' abilities to take account of greater complexities and to make use of general ideas enables them to undertake successful geographical studies of larger areas.
• A continuing development of skills to include the use of specific techniques and more general strategies of enquiry matched to pupils' developing cognitive abilities.
• Increasing opportunity for pupils to examine social, economic, political and environmental issues. Older pupils should not only be more skilled at evaluating evidence and the consequences of alternative courses of action, but should develop greater appreciation and understanding of the influence of people's beliefs, attitudes and values.

Figure 7.1 represents these principles as a staircase which the pupil climbs through the years of compulsory schooling. At each step attention must be paid to what has been learned earlier and what will be learned on the next step up. This will ensure that continuity is taken fully into account in aims, content, pedagogy and mode of assessment. Also, at each step consideration must be given to achieving an appropriate balance, acknowledging the need for differentiation between geographical knowledge, attitudes and skills on the one hand, and pedagogical strategies on the other. The reference to continuity is a reminder that the staircase metaphor ought not to divert one away from the spiral metaphor which emphasizes the persisting threads which render the curriculum coherent. These threads extend vertically through the years of schooling and laterally across the studies in any one year or stage.

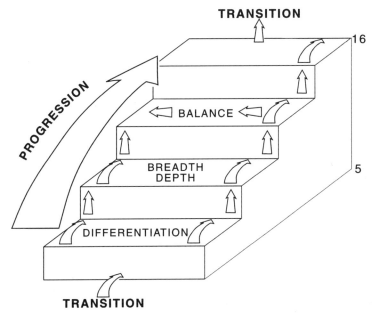

Figure 7.1 The curriculum staircase

PROGRESSION IN THE NATIONAL CURRICULUM

In the Draft Proposals for the revision of geography it is stated that:

> Progress has been secured across the key stages in terms of breadth of studies, depth of studies and complexity of concepts, an increase in the range of spatial scales of what is studied and a continuing development of a widening range of increasingly complex skills.
>
> (SCAA 1994: iv)

In the equivalent sentence for Wales there is one important change of phrasing where the sentence concludes with

> . . . the development and application of a widening range of increasingly complex skills.
>
> (CAAW 1994: iv)

What both proposals highlight is the need for attention to be paid both to progression from 5 to 16 years, i.e. from stage to stage, but also to progression within each Key Stage. It is difficult to disentangle both of these conceptions of progression from pupil assessment. To focus sharply on progression throughout the stages is to emphasize the importance of assessment at the end of the 5–16 period of schooling. To focus sharply on progression within a stage is to suggest that a summative assessment of pupils' attainment at the end of each stage is as important as the summative assessment at the end of Key Stage 4.

In the National Curriculum (SCAA 1994) proposals for geography the preference was for the latter, as is evident in the statement in the Orders. By the end of Key Stage 1, the performance of the great majority of pupils should be within the range of Levels 1 to 3, by the end of Key Stage 2 it should be within the range 2 to 5 and by the end of Key Stage 3 within the range 3 to 7.

What appeared under the heading of progression for each Key Stage is shown in Figure 7.2. A close reading of the statements for each Key Stage indicates that an attempt has been made to render each stage sufficiently discrete for meaningful assessment to take place at the end of the stage while, at the same time, seeking to provide some continuity between the stages. A more thorough analysis would have focused on a well-worked-out hierarchy of geographical learning, similar to the work of Bloom and his colleagues (Bloom 1956, Krathwohl et al. 1964) in their analysis of cognitive and affective domains. While there is evidence in the proposals of an awareness of the move in the cognitive domain from knowledge, at the lowest level, to evaluation at the highest level, via comprehension, application, analysis and synthesis, it is not presented systematically.

What teachers are required to do is put flesh on the framework by selecting themes and places and tracking these in a structured, orderly way through the Key Stages. Thus, for the study of the weather there is a clear shift from a concern with observing, recording and describing in Key Stage 1 to investigating and recognizing local and global patterns in Key Stage 2 to explaining spatial variation in Key Stage 3.

In practice, what is required is for each of the specified themes in the Geography Statutory Order (one theme in Key Stage 1, four in Key Stage 2 and ten in Key Stage 3) to be placed in a planning matrix which places alongside each theme the relevant knowledge, attitudes and skills plus mapwork, fieldwork and the use of information technology. A development of such a matrix would include a column for details of appropriate teaching and learning strategies.

Examples of the application of the principles of progression in the context of pre-National Curriculum and National Curriculum geography have been provided for several aspects of the subject, e.g. shopping patterns (Bennetts 1981), mapwork (Boardman 1986 and Sandford 1986), manufacturing industry (HMI 1986), economic activities (Bennetts 1995) and the incorporation of enquiry (CCW 1991).

Bennetts (1981: 174–5) has warned against being too logical in designing a scheme of work based on principles of progression. He argues that in geography there are many substantive viewpoints 'each of which presents its own criteria for the selection and organisation of important concepts and principles' and asserts:

Through the Key Stage, pupils will increasingly:

Key Stage 1	Key Stage 2	Key Stage 3
Broaden and deepen their knowledge and understanding of places and themes	Broaden and deepen their knowledge and understanding of places and themes	Broaden and deepen their knowledge and understanding of places and themes
	Recognize what places are like with accuracy and coherence	Make use of a wide and precise geographical vocabulary
Recognize and describe what places are like, using appropriate geographical vocabulary		
		Analyse, rather than describe, geographical patterns, processes and change
	Offer explanations for the characteristics of places	
		Appreciate the inter-actions within and between physical and human processes that operate in any environment
Offer their own explanations of what they observe	Identify physical and human processes and describe some of their effects	
		Appreciate the inter-dependence of places
Make comparisons between places and between geographical features	Apply geographical ideas learnt in one context to other studies at the same scale	
		Become proficient at conducting and comparing studies at a widening range of scales and in contrasting places and environments
Develop and use appropriate geographical skills	Acquire information, from secondary sources as well as first-hand observation, to investigate aspects of local and more distant physical and human environments	Apply their geographical knowledge and under-standing to unfamiliar contents
		Select and make effective use of skills and techniques to support their geographical investigations
	Develop and use appropriate geographical skills	Appreciate the limitations of geographical evidence and the tentative and incomplete nature of some explanations

Figure 7.2 Proposals for progression at each of Key Stages 1 to 3 of the National Curriculum

The fact that many ideas can be approached at different levels of understanding greatly complicates the notion of a logical route through a 'map of knowledge'. In practice there are usually alternative routes and sometimes no clear indication of what is best. Furthermore, . . . a number of return journeys may not be out of place, for the intellectual landscape can present a changing appearance to pupils who are growing in experience and maturity.

(Bennetts 1981: 175)

Not only are there difficulties inherent in the definition, structure and manner of reasoning (Gregg and Leinhardt 1994) of geography as a school subject, there are also difficulties derived from the differing curriculum cultures in which geography is embedded at each Key Stage. These are especially evident at the points of transition from one Key Stage to another and it is to this issue we now turn.

TRANSITION

Whereas the focus in the discussion of progression is principally upon the nature of the geography and the way pupils make progress in learning about it, the focus in transition is more upon curriculum culture and, within that, teaching and learning strategies. As HMI asserted:

> While programmes of learning activities extending over the 5 to 16 age range necessarily involve shifts in the nature of what is studied, the methods which are used and the environment in which learning takes place, sharp discontinuities can impede progression in learning . . . . Without effective coordination between teachers there can be unnecessary repetition of work and a failure to build on pupils' previous experience and learning.

(HMI 1986: 41)

In a study of a secondary school and its eight feeder primary schools, conducted before the passing of the Education Reform Act in 1988, we distinguished between planned discontinuity and unplanned discontinuity in geography curriculum provision. We wrote:

> One can also argue that continuity is not an unqualified blessing and that for some pupils it is a positive advantage to have discontinuity because they thrive on a total change of pattern. Planned discontinuity is a deliberate change in practice with the intention of stimulating pupils' growth and development. It stands in sharp contrast to unplanned discontinuity, the clarification of which is the starting point in any deliberate attempt to ease the transition from one sector of schooling to another.

(Williams and Howley 1989: 62)

Curriculum culture characteristics	Upper primary	Lower secondary
Ideology	Progressive, child-centred, strong welfare orientation	Classical, subject-centred and vocational
Curriculum design	Topic- or theme-centred, subject integration	Subject-centred
Classroom ecology	Open, generalist classrooms, mobile furniture	Specialist, subject-specific classrooms, immobile furniture
Preferred pedagogy	Projects and topics, active experiential learning with many opportunities for fieldwork, multiple learning resources, mixture of work and play	Subject-focused, much use of textbooks and teacher-prepared worksheets, fewer opportunities for fieldwork
Teacher	Generalist, trained through 4-year undergraduate (B.Ed.) or 1-year PGCE teacher-training course	Specialist, trained principally through 1-year PGCE teacher-training course

Figure 7.3 Contrasts in curriculum culture between upper primary and lower secondary schools

What we reported were unplanned discontinuities from teacher to teacher and year by year within individual primary schools and from primary school to primary school in terms of the aims, content and methods of assessment of geography. Further, not only were there unplanned discontinuities from geography teacher to geography teacher in the first two years of the secondary school, there were serious discontinuities in the aims, content, teaching methods and modes of assessment between the secondary school and its feeder primary schools.

One of the strengths of the National Curriculum Order for Geography is that it gives the opportunity for teachers in primary and secondary schools to confront directly a common definition of the subject, a set of aims for each Key Stage, and an attempt to provide a coherent set of attainment descriptions expressed through geographical skills, places and themes. In principle, these arrangements should reduce the scope for discontinuity.

However, the Order for Geography has to be adapted to the curriculum cultures of the schools. In Figure 7.3 we have identified some of the characteristics of Key Stage 2 in primary schools and Key Stage 3 in secondary schools which influence this adaptation. It is important for teachers on both sides of the curriculum boundary between Key Stages 1 and 2 to identify and recognize the strengths of each of their cultures with specific reference to geographical education. To achieve this requires the setting up of appropriate structures that will facilitate constructive and purposeful discussions. Experience suggests that, generally, there have been greater advances made in collaboration between primary school and secondary school teachers with regard, on the one hand, to the core subjects of science, mathematics and English and, on the other hand, to the special educational needs of particular pupils. It can be argued that as much attention should be paid to the foundation subjects as to the core subjects though it would be foolish to ignore the resource implications of any proposals for increasing inter-school collaboration. In many areas, and especially those in which primary school pupils and their parents are able to choose from a range of possible secondary schools in a locality, there are obvious difficulties in identifying precisely the feeder schools. Further problems are associated with personality difficulties across the boundaries.

Despite the difficulties, many schools have established close relationships which contribute simultaneously to assisting pupils to make an easy transfer between schools and to building curriculum bridges in geographical education. These relationships often go a long way further than the simple transfer of pupils' records demonstrating what they have achieved in geography by the end of year 6 and the details of topics taught to those pupils in the last year in the primary school. These examples serve to illustrate some of these practices.

A secondary school with six feeder primary schools, located in an urban area, arranged a week-long residential field studies course for all of the year 6 pupils. The programme for the week was arranged jointly by the year 6 teachers and two geography teachers in the secondary school, one of whom was also the year 7 tutor. The course was held in the summer term in a camp in a rural environment. Each day the pupils were divided into groups comprising pupils representative of each of the primary schools. They studied a river, a farm, a stretch of coastline and an area of woodland. The tasks were defined by the teachers who supervised the work co-operatively. They learned from each other and, in this way, developed an understanding of each other's methods of working. The secondary school teachers were able to provide specialist teaching equipment. The pupils were able to meet their future teachers in a relatively informal context as well as establishing friendship links with pupils from other schools whom they would meet again the following September.

In another secondary school, pupils from feeder primary schools were brought to the school in order to use specialist geography equipment, e.g. large-scale maps and globes and sets of aerial photographs, and to use computer software not easily accessible in the primary schools.

In yet another school, secondary school geography teachers participated as leaders in a one-day INSET course for teachers in which the focus was upon fieldwork planning and fieldwork study skills. Interestingly, there is much less evidence of primary school teachers contributing to secondary school INSET days. There can be little doubt that geography teachers in many secondary schools have much to learn from primary school teachers about such matters as the planning and arrangement of topic work, the organization of classroom displays, record-keeping of pupil progress, and ways of teaching pupils with special educational needs.

As a final example, senior secondary school pupils were taken to feeder primary schools to work with year 6 pupils on the acquisition of basic map and compass skills. They designed an orienteering route in the school grounds and taught the pupils how to use maps in order to follow the route.

While these examples are merely illustrative of interesting practice, it is important to emphasize the need for any arrangements to become more than one-off happenings and for structures to be built to consolidate such links and to provide the basis for future development. From such activities teachers should be able to learn more about the aims and objectives of geography teaching in the schools, teaching and learning strategies which are commonly employed in the feeder schools and the host secondary schools, and the modes of pupil assessment and record-keeping. Secondary school geography teachers are often unaware of such important aspects of their new pupils as their fieldwork experience and skills and their IT experience and skills.

CONCLUSION

Facilitating both progression and transition are important tasks for teachers of geography throughout the period of compulsory schooling and beyond. In this chapter the focus has been upon schooling in the 5–16 age-group but it is clear that the discussion can easily be extended to take account of progress in the years after secondary schooling. There are problems associated with progression and transition between the end of compulsory schooling at the age of 16 and between schools and post-secondary school courses and institutions. It has been emphasized that the importance of curriculum cultures must be recognized and their implications for pupil learning must be taken into account in the planning of geography programmes of study.

REFERENCES

Bennetts, T. (1981) 'Progression in the geography curriculum', in R. Walford (ed.) *Signposts for Geography Teaching*, Harlow: Longman.
Bennetts, T. (1986) 'Structure and progression in geography', in D. Boardman (ed.) *Handbook for Geography Teachers*, Sheffield: Geographical Association.
Bennetts, T. (1995) 'Geography at Key Stage 3: continuity and progression', *Teaching Geography* 20 (2): 75–9.

Bloom, B.S. (ed.) (1956) *Taxonomy of Educational Objectives, Handbook* I: *Cognitive Domain*, New York: David McKay Co.

Boardman, D. (1986) 'Relief interpretation', in D. Boardman (ed.) *Handbook for Geography Teachers*, Sheffield: Geographical Association.

Curriculum and Assessment Authority for Wales (1994) *Geography in the National Curriculum in Wales*, Cardiff: Curriculum and Assessment Authority for Wales.

Curriculum Council for Wales (1991) *Geography in the National Curriculum: Non-statutory Guidance for Teachers*. Cardiff: Curriculum Council for Wales.

Gregg, M. and Leinhardt, G. (1994) 'Mapping out geography: an example of epistemology and education', *Review of Educational Research* 64 (2): 311–61.

Her Majesty's Inspectorate (1986) *Geography from 5 to 16, Curriculum Matters* 7, London: HMSO.

Krathwohl, D.R., Bloom, B.S. and Masia, B.B. (1964) *Taxonomy of Educational Objectives, Handbook* II: *Affective Domain*, New York: David McKay Co.

Sandford, H.A. (1986) 'Objectives of school mapwork', *Teaching Geography* 12 (2): 22–3.

School Curriculum and Assessment Authority (1994) *Geography in the National Curriculum: Draft Proposals*, London: School Curriculum and Assessment Authority.

Weston, P., Barrett, E. and Jamison, J. (1992) *The Quest for Coherence*, Slough: National Foundation for Educational Research.

Williams, M. and Howley, R. (1989) 'Curriculum discontinuity: a study of a secondary school and its feeder primary schools', *British Educational Research Journal* 15 (1): 61–76.

Chapter 8

Differentiation in teaching and learning geography

Jeff Battersby

Within any class group there will be marked variations in the ways that pupils learn, the speed of their learning and the levels of attainment they achieve as well as the kind of learning difficulties and problems they experience. This would suggest that there is a need for differentiated teaching and learning strategies in all our classrooms, to match learning opportunities to learning needs of pupils.

Differentiation was identified as an equal opportunities issue by the Prime Minister, John Major, when he stated in 1992 that he wanted 'to ensure that we actively recognize pupils' abilities and aptitudes and create the means for this diversity to flourish. That is the way to genuine equality of opportunity' (Major 1992).

Differentiation in the National Curriculum is meant to be an enabling process focused on the development of the curriculum and concerned with creating optimum learning conditions for each child. Previously, differentiation was identified as a tool used to separate and rank the pupils, as a means of organizing them. Differentiation is now equated with good practice in teaching which allows for differences within a teaching group rather than leading to the distribution and allocation of pupils to a supposedly homogeneous group which could be taught as a separate unit.

Differentiation really came onto the curriculum agenda as a result of *Better Schools* (DES 1986a). The acceptable curriculum was identified as broad, balanced, relevant and differentiated. Differentiation has been a key issue in any discussion of curriculum change and planning and is seen as being essential to achieving a curriculum entitlement for all pupils. The Warnock Report (1978) stated that the purpose of education for all children is the same; the goals are the same but the help that individual children need in progressing towards them will be different.

In clearly identifying levels of attainment for each Attainment Target, the National Curriculum assumes that individuals do not progress at a uniform rate. It states that it will help alert teachers to problems experienced by individual children so that they can be given special attention. The National

Curriculum encourages teachers and pupils to operate on a more individual basis, to plan programmes of work which take account of pupils' achievements and which allow them to work at different levels to ensure that they each achieve their maximum potential.

Differentiation is based on an understanding of individual difference, and of the worth and value of each pupil's learning. Consequently, teachers need to differentiate in their curriculum planning according to Barthorpe and Visser (1991). However, Dowling (1990) and others feel that differentiation is a means of emphasizing and reinforcing inequalities in curriculum provision. The curriculum has to satisfy two apparently contrary requirements. On the one hand it needs to reflect the broad educational aims which apply to all children, of whatever ability and at whatever school, while on the other hand it needs to accommodate differences in the ability and other characteristics of children, even of the same age.

A number of important questions emerge in relation to pupil entitlement to the Key Stage Programme of Study. The Order for Geography states in its access statement that the Programme of Study for each Key Stage should be taught to all or the great majority of pupils in the Key Stage in ways appropriate to their abilities (DFE 1995). Can differences in pupils' abilities affect their access to the curriculum? Does differentiation imply teaching a different curriculum to pupils of different ability? Can we teach the same curriculum to all pupils by tailoring teaching strategies to the learning needs of the pupils?

Responses to these questions have implications for curriculum planning through schemes of work. Differentiation is not necessarily about creating individual programmes for individual pupils. In some cases this may be a good idea but not in others, as, for example, the pupil who learns more effectively in a group than in isolation. Differentiation is concerned with providing appropriate educational opportunities for all pupils and to match learning opportunities with individual learning needs.

As pupils' learning needs vary it will be necessary to employ a range of teaching styles and methods in the classroom. It calls for skilful teaching, detailed planning and preparation, and perceptive responses to the individual pupils. Detailed knowledge of each pupil's learning needs is essential if they are to be addressed successfully. This involves the careful selection of relevant learning resources, building suitable expectations into pupil's work programmes, and sharing learning objectives with the pupils. Individual pupils will then be enabled and encouraged to take increasing responsibility for their own learning, to measure their successes and achievements, to begin to identify their own learning needs and to help in meeting them.

The following essential elements must be included in course planning if successful teaching and learning for pupils are to occur:

- clear learning objectives and learning outcomes in terms of the pupil's knowledge, understanding and skills;
- a variety of teaching and learning strategies to differentiate the learning experiences of pupils;
- a variety of resources available to support pupils' learning;
- a variety of tasks and activities which provide different opportunities for pupil learning and for different outcomes;
- opportunities to vary in the pace and depth of learning;
- different strategies for assessment of pupil learning.
- effective feedback on the pupils' learning outcomes and target setting for their future learning.

(Battersby 1995: 26)

Furthermore, teachers need to consider the quality of the pupils' learning environment and to promote one which encourages and enables effective learning to take place. The curriculum needs to challenge the pupils, to have high expectations of involvement and attainment, to enable and encourage positive achievement as a realistic goal and engage pupils in active and enjoyable learning. Classrooms need to reflect this philosophy.

There are still important questions to address concerning how judgements are made about the appropriate teaching and learning environments for individual pupils and the expectations of an individual pupil's capabilities. The focus is now centred on differentiation in teaching and learning and how best this might be accomplished. Differentiation in learning can be achieved when pupils are presented with learning opportunities which enable them to learn effectively and to demonstrate what they know, understand and can do. In most learning situations the role of the teacher is as a facilitator of learning, providing structured situations which encourage investigation and enquiry using a variety of resources.

Differentiation is 'simply effective teaching' argues Waters (1995: 83). 'It is the planned process of opening out the curriculum to enable access to all pupils.' He summarizes a number of strategies for differentiation:

Planning

- clear learning objectives, shared with pupils
- the need to plan small achievable steps
- schemes of work that plan for revisiting
- schemes of work which have a full range of structured and open-ended tasks
- develop the model of core tasks with reinforcement and extension activities

Teaching

- using a wide range of activities and teaching styles
- clear instructions, explanations and expectations
- an awareness that each pupil has unique abilities
- the importance of the pace of a lesson
- the need for a balance of questioning techniques
- the use of open-ended questions and enquiries

- schemes of work with clear progression

- flexibility of approach and response to pupils
- encourage a supportive classroom atmosphere

Resources

- the importance of clearly designed, uncluttered materials matched to pupils' abilities
- using texts of appropriate readability
- using materials that are free of gender/ethnic bias
- the ease of access to learning resources
- classroom display that encourages learning and reflects high expectations

Pupil needs

- talking with teachers about their learning
- talking to each other about their learning
- sufficient repetition to consolidate learning
- varied activities to match pupils' attention span
- the use of pupil review to set realistic goals
- positive marking which points to improvement

ACHIEVING DIFFERENTIATION

Differentiation can be achieved by outcome, by the rate of progress, by task, by the resources available or by a combination of any of these. The following summary diagram (Fig. 8.1) serves to illustrate these strategies.

Differentiation by outcome

Differentiation by outcome results from pupils being presented with common or neutral tasks built around common resources with differentiated or different positive levels of achievement being identified to measure the pupils' responses to the tasks. The assessment criteria or mark scheme indicates the positive quality anticipated. Pupils might be shown a video extract of the shanty areas of Sao Paulo and be given the task of writing a newspaper report about life in the shanty slums. Some pupils may produce a limited summary of the video, others may outline the positive and negative aspects of living in the shanty, while other pupils may compare the shanties of Sao Paulo with other areas known to them. Thus there are different outcomes from the same resource input and identified task.

Differentiation by resources and by outcome

The same task could be presented to all pupils in a class but with varying resources, perhaps targeted to specific pupils. A range of textbooks and

1. Differentiation by outcome

Common stimulus   Common task   A range of outcomes

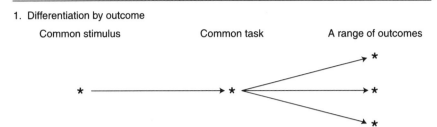

2. Differentiation by resources and by outcome

Varied resources   Common task   A range of outcomes

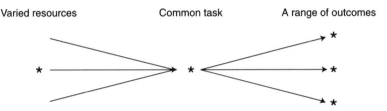

3. Differentiation by graded tasks and outcomes

Common stimulus   Series of tasks   A range of outcomes

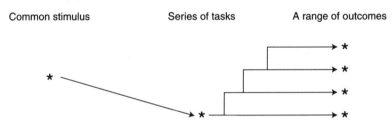

4. Differentiation by task and outcome

Common stimulus   Choice of tasks   A range of outcomes

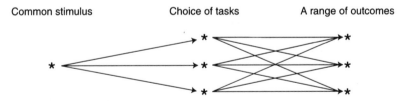

5. Differentiation by stimulus and by task

Stimulus targeted to ability   Task graded by ability   Outcomes appropriate to
                                                          predicted levels of ability

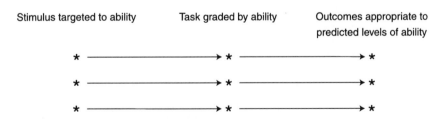

Figure 8.1 Differentiation strategies
Source: Davies 1990

newspaper extracts with different readability measures, different maps, diagrams and photographs may also be provided. The outcomes will be different and will reflect the suitability and accessibility of the resources in support of the task.

Differentiation by graded tasks and outcomes

The stimulus material and resources are common to all pupils, though these may vary in their difficulty and accessibility to different pupils. A series of tasks or questions can be set which become increasingly difficult, demanding and complex. Each of the tasks can be open to all pupils to attempt or some of the tasks may be too difficult or complex for certain pupils. Some pupils will be able to work through some of the tasks quickly while others will fail to go beyond the first one.

Stepped questions which also have an incline of difficulty enable the lower achiever to gain positive achievement in the early parts of each question while becoming less successful with the later parts; the able pupils will attempt successfully all parts of the question or task.

Consideration should be given to the overall diet presented to the pupils, especially if the same format is used in each lesson, assessment or teaching unit. Different tasks will present different challenges to different pupils. Data handling tasks will make different demands on pupils than a written report or a decision-making exercise. Those who find one more demanding may not find the other tasks equally difficult. The more appealing the task to the individual pupil the more it will enable that pupil to demonstrate knowledge, understanding and skills. Different learning and assessment styles will enable pupils to demonstrate a wider variety of their competences in geography.

Teaching and learning strategies should vary as should the tasks presented to the pupils. Initial tasks might involve a card sorting exercise where pupils are asked to categorize and match photographs, information, terminology and given examples to name, define and describe. A second task involving groupwork to research and summarise information from resources might require pupils to name, classify and describe a pattern from data resources which might also require pupils to extract information, interpret and explain it. An enquiry task which seeks to enable pupils to explain causes and effects, reviewing costs and benefits and analysing information, enables most pupils to engage with it. The examination of alternatives and an assessment of different strategies through a report or essay will make different demands on pupils. This variety of tasks will provide opportunities for all pupils to demonstrate some capability in their knowledge, understanding and skills in geography. The tasks themselves present an example of progression in demand and complexity, yet provide opportunities for a wide range of ability and opportunities to demonstrate subject competence.

Differentiation by task and outcome

Differentiation by task is achieved through the designing and setting of specific tasks for particular ability groups of pupils. All pupils are provided with the same stimulus resources and then either with a variety of tasks or with one main task, subdivided into a series of smaller ones. The example of the video input on a shanty slum may lead to pupils being presented with tasks which ask them to produce an annotated sketch map or diagram, to produce a cost-benefit analysis of the provision of new government housing and to write a report for the Brazilian government as to how effective this strategy might be in solving the housing crisis. Different outcomes will result from each of the tasks. Pupils may produce a simple, detailed or complex sketch map, diagram, analysis or report. Those whose ability is lower will be unlikely to manage the whole task, while those of higher ability will accomplish all elements.

Differentiation by stimulus and by task

Stimulus material is targeted to specific ability levels identified by the teacher. The materials might be a simple structured worksheet, one with some structured and some open-ended questions, or, for the most able, an assignment involving the testing of a hypothesis. Tasks which are graded to ability levels range from those which seek description and simple explanation to those which ask pupils to evaluate policies and strategies. Pupils produce outcomes appropriate to their predicted level of ability.

These strategies for differentiation suggest the idea of targeted work and specific strategies targeted to enable successful pupil learning. While these should enable the pupils to achieve positive outcomes to their learning, differentiation should not be so fine-tuned that it does not allow for the unplanned and unexpected outcomes. Pupils should do better than expected sometimes, but at others not quite reach their goal because it has been set just out of reach at that particular moment.

Differentiation in the assessment of a pupil's ability will be achieved through a combination of tasks set and the outcomes to them. Differentiation by task is achieved by targeting a task suitable to a pupil to ensure that the assessment is appropriate and the level of performance is as predicted. Differentiation by outcome is achieved through the nature of the pupil's response to a common task or series of tasks. The assessment criteria, or mark schemes, are critical to the success of this method of differentiation of pupils. Differentiation by a combination of task and outcome will be through the teacher deciding the most relevant strategy for a pupil to demonstrate their achievement. In reality this happens in most situations where a task may start off based on a common resource but develops into a series of differentiated sub-tasks, thereby producing different outcomes.

GCSE is firmly based on the principle of differentiation and the general assessment criteria state that all examinations must be designed to ensure proper discrimination so that candidates across the ability range are given opportunities to demonstrate their knowledge, abilities and achievements – that is to show what they know, understand and can do. Differentiated papers or differentiated questions within papers will be required accordingly in all subjects, while in the case of coursework differentiation will be achieved by presenting candidates with tasks appropriate to their individual levels of ability.

Differentiation guards against the dangers of under-achievement and unsatisfactory assessment experiences. If set tasks are too difficult for some of the candidates, the assessment will be a dispiriting experience for them and the marks that they gain are more likely to register random success with partially understood ideas than to give credit to a coherent set of concepts, skills or abilities. Conversely, if the set tasks are too easy, the assessment may be equally unsatisfying and discrimination among candidates may be the results of small slips rather than the evidence of higher abilities required for the award of the higher grades.

Differentiation, according to Stradling (1990), is a loaded word associated with long-standing debates about comprehensive schooling and more recent ones concerning the National Curriculum. The common curriculum is at odds with differentiation for it seeks to provide a common entitlement to all pupils irrespective of individual ability or need. Addressing and meeting individual needs legitimizes the differences we are trying to accommodate while providing a curriculum which is no longer common to all. The structure and content of the National Curriculum implies that mixed ability teaching is inappropriate and that such groupings do not meet the needs of individual pupils.

Differentiation in the National Curriculum is meant to be an enabling process which focuses on the development of optimum learning conditions for each pupil which can be achieved under a wide variety of organizational structures, including mixed ability teaching groups. This raises other important questions about how judgements are made concerning the optimum and appropriate learning conditions, expectations, strategies and outcomes which are identified for individual pupils. If differentiation results in inequalities the alternative is not a solution, but represents a failure to address the problem.

Pupils who are unable to develop their understanding of new ideas or become more proficient in their skills can be said to have learning difficulties. It is therefore necessary to identify strategies and opportunities which will enable such pupils to develop their competence and proficiency in these areas. It is necessary for teachers to reappraise their teaching methods in order to improve the learning opportunities for each pupil. Questions need to be asked which address the learning difficulties of the pupils as a consequence of the curriculum. Difficulties are all too often identified as relating to the pupil rather than as possibly arising from the curriculum. It is in this area that teachers can acknowledge their responsibility for teaching and learning in their subject and explore alternative strategies, structures and opportunities to enable all pupils to gain access to the curriculum and begin to achieve positively.

Differentiation in teaching and learning in the classroom and in schemes of work requires a fundamental rethinking of curriculum expectations and objectives. In the past, differentiated work for any pupil with learning difficulties has been through minor modification of questions and tasks on worksheets or reduced expectations of positive achievement in relation to the set tasks. The provision of alternative worksheets and resources has tended to marginalize those pupils who are experiencing difficulties in grasping new ideas, concepts or skills, and this in turn has created problems in the integration of these pupils with others in the class.

Hart (1992) argues that schools need to make a significant shift in pedagogy if pupils' learning needs are to be addressed. She feels that there is a need to create 'more opportunities for learning through talk and practical experiences, more emphasis upon co-operative work and self-directed activities'. This is illustrated in her summary diagram of 'curriculum imbalances':

written outcomes	◢ drama, oral presentation, drawing,
	◢ construction, collage
teacher-led discussion	◢ pupil-led discussion
learning through written word	◢ learning through talk
individual tasks	◢ co-operative tasks
teacher-initiated activities	◢ pupil-initiated activities
closed tasks (i.e. one right answer)	◢ open-ended tasks
whole-class teaching	◢ individual/small group teaching
teacher evaluation, marking,	◢ pupil self-assessment, peer
assessment	collaboration

Changes to these perceived imbalances would require changes in the organization and planning of teaching and learning strategies and associated learning opportunities to take into consideration ways of improving, extending and enhancing the curriculum in order to use and develop the basic literacy skills of reading and writing.

Other questions arise in relation to our responses to pupil achievements in the tasks presented to them. How far do we evaluate the relevance and the accuracy of the pupils' responses to their tasks if they apparently demonstrate a general understanding of the ideas and seem to gain positive achievement generally? Each pupil's response to each task needs to be evaluated to ensure that a correct range of learning opportunities is being offered to each pupil so that they reach their potential and are able to demonstrate what they know, understand and can do.

Hart makes the telling point that 'by encouraging a focus upon differences, differentiation diverts our attention away from making the crucial connection between individual responses and general questions about curriculum', and that we need to 'be alert to what individual children's responses may have to tell us about the appropriateness of curriculum experiences provided for all children'. We therefore need to shift the 'focus of attention from the abilities and characteristics of the children to the abilities and characteristics of the curriculum' (Hart 1992: 139–40).

We must discover how to create conditions which will enable all our pupils to learn successfully and must feed these into a virtuous circle of improvement in the quality of education for all. Differentiation has a significant part to play in this aim.

In practical terms there is a need to focus attention on classroom procedure, in relation to the learning objectives and any intended outcomes of pupils' knowledge, understanding and skills. These objectives should be shared with the pupils. Geography lends itself to a wide variety of teaching and learning strategies which should feature in all lessons so as to enable the pupils to develop their competence in the subject. Equally, a wide range of readily available resources suited to a range of pupils' preferred learning styles should be used in each lesson.

Differentiation can be achieved through the use of open-ended questions and tasks designed to enable pupils to demonstrate their knowledge, understanding and skills at a variety of levels. Structured or closed questions can also achieve this objective and provide for a more predictable outcome. Demonstration of achievement is dependent on the skill of the teacher asking appropriate questions while encouraging responses which allow a clear demonstration of a pupil's ability.

An awareness of the individual needs of pupils and the ability to make quick, yet accurate, judgements about them before diagnosing, introducing and implementing remedial action to meet such needs, represents the real art of the teacher. It is through such practices that the individual needs of pupils are addressed and met, highlighting differences in provision and response, differentiation in practice which is enabling equality of access to the entitlement curriculum.

REFERENCES

Barthorpe, T. and Visser, J. (1991) *Differentiation, Your Responsibility*, National Association of Remedial Education, Nasen Enterprises.

Battersby, J. (1995) *Teaching Geography at Key Stage 3*, Cambridge: Chris Kington Publishing.

Currie, S. and Whittle, R. (1984) *Reducing Under-achievement: Learning to Succeed Development Project*, Cardiff: Welsh Joint Education Committee.

Davies, P. (1990) *Differentiation in the Classroom and in the Examination Room: Achieving the Impossible?* Cardiff: Welsh Joint Education Committee.

Dearing, R. (1994) *The National Curriculum and its Assessment: Final Report*, London: SCAA.

DES (1986a) *Better Schools*, London: HMSO.

DES (1986b) *Geography from 5 to 16, Curriculum Matters 7*, London: HMSO.

DES (1988) *The Education Reform Act 1988*, London: HMSO.

DFE (1995) *Geography in the National Curriculum*, London: HMSO.

Dowling, P. (1990) 'The Shogun's and other curriculum voices', in Dowling, P. and Noss, R., *Mathematics versus the National Curriculum*, Basingstoke: Falmer.

Hart, S. (1992) 'Differentiation: part of the problem or part of the solution?', *Curriculum Journal* 3 (2): 131–42.

Major, J. (1992) in *Times Educational Supplement*, 28 February 1992.

National Curriculum Council (1989) *Curriculum Guidance 2: A Curriculum for all*, York: NCC.

National Curriculum Council (1990) *Curriculum Guidance 3: The Whole Curriculum*, York: NCC.

OFSTED (1993) *Handbook for the Inspection of Schools: Guidance on the Inspection Schedule*, London: HMSO.

Stradling, R., Saunders, L. and Weston, P. (1990) *Differentiation in Action*, London: HMSO.

Warnock, M. (1978) *Meeting Special Educational Needs*, London: HMSO.

Waters, A. (1995) Differentiation and classroom practice, *Teaching Geography* 20 (2): 81–3.

Chapter 9

Cross-curricular concerns in geography
Earth science and physical geography

Duncan Hawley

Geography is traditionally divided into two halves – physical geography and human geography – and it has been argued that one of the key justifications for the place of geography in the curriculum is its position as a bridge between the sciences and the arts (Rawling 1987). If geography is such a bridge, then one end of the geography bridge will rest on the ground of the sciences. In the past, the relationship between school geography and school science has tended to be separative, but the development of the National Curriculum has highlighted many of the similarities between the two subjects and provided a platform for reviewing the relationship between science and geography teaching and its implications for pupils in the classroom.

WHAT ARE THE EARTH SCIENCES AND HOW DO THEY RELATE TO GEOGRAPHY?

The term 'Earth sciences' gained wide usage in North America in the 1960s and became established a decade or so later in Britain. It has been applied to a collection of disciplines encompassing the study of aspects of the physical earth, varying from place to place and from time to time. However, a consensus of what constitutes earth sciences would include climatology, meteorology, economic geology, engineering geology, geochemistry, geomorphology, geophysics, hydrology, mineralogy, oceanography, palaeo-climatology, palaeoecology, palaeogeography, palaeontology, pedology, petrology, planetary geology, sedimentology, stratigraphy, structural geology, tectonics and volcanology (Allaby and Allaby 1990).

Most geography teachers will recognize and identify with some of the key aspects just listed and a glance at some of the recent geography A level syllabuses will see several of the Earth science disciplines (e.g. climatology, meteorology, geomorphology, hydrology) appearing as subheadings on the syllabus outline. They constitute, of course, what is known as physical geography, while the others could be grouped under a label of geology.

The origins of physical geography lie in environmental determinism and regional geography, which was the predominant approach to geography for the first half of the twentieth century. Thus no account of the geography of an area would be complete without an initial consideration of the nature and distribution of its rocks, landforms, soils, climate, rivers, minerals and vegetation. At a higher level of study a more detailed investigation was demanded and so developed the specialist subdisciplines of geomorphology, pedology, hydrology, climatology and biogeography, although at school level they remained grouped under the general heading of physical geography (Biddle 1985; Gregory 1985).

The 1960s saw the 'quantitative revolution' in geography sweep across higher education and by the 1970s this systematic process-oriented approach had permeated school geography. The change of approach had two effects, particularly on the teaching of geography in the 11 to 16 age-range. First, there was a shift towards teaching the predominantly social and human aspects of the subject, exemplified in the Geography for the Young School Leaver Project, which paid very little attention to physical geography. Second, there was a move towards a more systematic, quantified, process-orientated, data-testing approach, which owed much to adaptations from scientific methodology. Consequently a paradox emerged concerning the relationship between geography and Earth science – a strengthening of the nature of the disciplines with respect to methodologies, but a weakening in terms of content and concepts.

In the 1980s two curriculum innovation trends affected the way school geography was taught. Some secondary schools began to subsume geography into lower school humanities courses, combining variously with history, religious education and English. In other schools geography remained a discrete subject in the curriculum but the emphasis of the teaching shifted towards a 'people and environment' approach, highlighting the human response to natural phenomena as exemplified by the 'Natural Hazards' units that appeared in school geography departments' schemes of work and 'The Challenge of the Natural Environment' core module on the University of London Examination Board 16–19 A level course. It was retrospectively noted that physical geography was considerably weakened in school syllabuses with the introduction of GCSE in 1986. For many geographers the people–environment framework did not provide the rigour required to give proper attention to physical processes (Adamczyk *et al.* 1994).

PHYSICAL GEOGRAPHY AND EARTH SCIENCE IN THE NATIONAL CURRICULUM

Concurrent with these developments in geography teaching, there was a general move in science education toward the introduction of broad and balanced science courses, and these included aspects of Earth science. As

HMI commented, 'Astronomy and the Earth sciences can provide a suitable context for important concepts to be developed' (DES/Welsh Office 1985: 12). So it was no surprise when the Science National Curriculum emerged in 1989 that it included a whole Attainment Target – 'AT9 Earth and Atmosphere' – dedicated to Earth science. Science, being designated a core subject, was already in place and being taught in schools when the Geography National Curriculum Working Party was formed. Consequently, this led to a territorial clash over 'ownership' of Earth science and, in their Interim Report produced in late 1989, the Geography Working Party included comments on the 'problems at the interface between science and geography' (para. 3.41) and there were suggestions that content that was properly geographical should be removed from the Science Order (para. 3.44). Clearly, the Geography Working Party thought that the Earth sciences had been poached. Such a response indicated a fear that any attempt to include in the Geography National Curriculum those Earth science and environmental topics that were now established in the Science Order would fail, because it would be regarded as unnecessary duplication of teaching. No doubt it was perceived that the omission of Earth science material in the Geography Order would further weaken the place of physical geography in schools, and this stance was reiterated in the Geography Working Party's final proposals of June 1990.

A different view was put forward by the Earth Science Teachers' Association and the Association for Science Education, who supported the idea of physical geography being included in the Geography National Curriculum but opposed suggestions that any Earth science content should be removed from the Science Order. Their opinion was that the teaching of any similar content in geography and science would take fundamentally different approaches, drawing on different concepts and principles and so they proposed that physical geography would complement the material in the science curriculum and considered the interface between geography and science as a fertile area for the development of cross-curricular links (Wilson 1990).

In the event, very little material was removed from what was proposed in geography or from science, and the Geography Final Order contained a substantial physical geography Attainment Target. In spite of, or perhaps as a result of, all the 'political' posturing, it was decided (implicitly) that the issue of Earth science/physical geography overlap was not to be dealt with by statutory decree, but to be resolved at an individual school level.

The subsequent revision of the Science Order in 1991 resulted in the reduction of the number of Attainment Targets, from the original seventeen to five. Earth science lost its distinct status and became a strand within the Attainment Target termed 'Materials and their Properties'. The significance of this was that, for the most part, this Attainment Target was what many would recognize as chemistry, and in a good number of schools the responsibility for teaching Earth science came to rest with the chemistry specialists. The Dearing Review retained some of Earth sciences content under 'Materials and their Properties', but removed the requirement to teach about the atmosphere (weather and climate), which became the domain of the revised Geography Order.

The thrust of Earth science in the Science Order (Fig. 9.1) is on teaching about the characteristics of rocks (KS2) and the processes which determine their characteristics, including the concept of the rock cycle and an emphasis on weathering (KS3), culminating at KS4 in a consideration of how plate tectonic processes are involved in the formation, deformation and recycling of rocks. In addition, pupils at KS2 should be taught 'about the water cycle and the part played by evaporation and condensation' (DFE 1995a: 11).

APPROACHES TO LEARNING

Aside from content, another area of common ground between geography and science is to be found in the methodological approaches to the study of the subjects. The teaching of the Science Order is prefaced by two general requirements to incorporate into science teaching where appropriate. The first is a requirement for pupils to learn about the nature of science: systematic enquiry; science in everyday life; the nature of scientific ideas; communication and health and safety. The second requirement is to use the contexts derived from the subject-specific content to teach pupils about experimental and investigative methods: planning experimental work; obtaining evidence; analysing evidence and drawing conclusions; considering the strength of evidence. Geography teachers who have guided pupils through GCSE and A level courses will recognize the striking similarities between the latter and the structure of geography individual studies. The 'scientific' method is also clearly present in the Geography National Curriculum. Thus teachers are required to give pupils opportunities to 'identify geographical questions and issues and establish an appropriate sequence of investigation; to identify the evidence required and collect, record and present it; to analyse and evaluate the evidence, draw conclusions and communicate findings' (DFE 1995b: 10), through the approach generally referred to as geographical enquiry.

This similarity in methodology can confuse the issue of overlap and it may not be helpful to define subject distinctiveness only in terms of the process of investigation (Fisher 1993). However, it is generally acknowledged that a high proportion of learning in science is expected to occur through experimentation in the laboratory, which is the process whereby pupils investigate phenomena through the controlling and changing of variables. In contrast, controlling variables in geography is generally not an easy task (although it is possible to do so with some practical activities or through computer simulations), so that in geographical investigation we can

Key Stage One (5 to 7 Years)

Grouping Materials – *Pupils should be taught:*
- to sort materials into groups on the basis of simple properties, including texture, appearance, transparency and whether they are magnetic or non-magnetic;
- to recognize and name common types of material, e.g. metal, plastic, wood, paper, rock, and to know that some of these materials are found naturally.

Key Stage Two (8 to 11 Years)

Grouping and classifying materials – *Pupils should be taught:*
- to compare everyday materials e.g. wood, rock, iron, aluminium, paper, polythene, on the basis of their properties including hardness, strength, flexibility and magnetic behaviour, and to relate these to the everyday uses of materials;
- to describe and group rocks and soils on the basis of characteristics including appearance, texture and permeability.

Key Stage Three (11 to 13 Years)

Planning and experimental procedures – *Pupils should be taught:*
- to consider contexts, e.g. fieldwork, where variables cannot readily be controlled, and how evidence may be collected in these contexts.

Changing materials – geological changes – *Pupils should be taught:*
- how rocks are weathered by expansion and contraction and by the freezing of water;
- that the rock cycle involves sedimentary, metamorphic and igneous processes;
- that rocks are classified as sedimentary, metamorphic or igneous on the basis of their processes of formation and that these processes affect their texture and the minerals they contain.

Key Stage Four (14 to 16 Years) – Double Science

Planning and experimental procedures – *Pupils should be taught:*
- to consider contexts, e.g. fieldwork, where variables cannot readily be controlled, and to make judgements about the amount of evidence needed in these contexts.

Changing materials – useful products from metal ores and rocks – *Pupils should be taught:*
- that a variety of useful substances can be made from rocks and minerals.

Changing materials – geological changes –*Pupils should be taught:*
- how igneous rocks are formed by the cooling of magma, sedimentary rocks by the deposition and consolidation of sediments, and metamorphic rocks by the action of heat and pressure on existing rocks;
- how the sequence of, and evidence for these processes is obtained from the rock record;
- how plate tectonic processes are involved in the formation, deformation and recycling of rocks.

Figure 9.1 The Earth science component of the Science National Curriculum

only occasionally experiment in the laboratory (Harvey 1973). Consequently, learning through geographical enquiry tends to take an inductive route to explanation, bringing order to a variety of facts in order to reach a generalization, whereas learning in a science investigation more frequently adopts a deductive route which reaches explanation through repeated testing using different factors to narrow down the cause (Fig. 9.2). A perusal of any of the 'enquiry-led' or 'key question' textbooks for KS3 geography demonstrates that the inductive route to investigation is the approach most frequently adopted in geography.

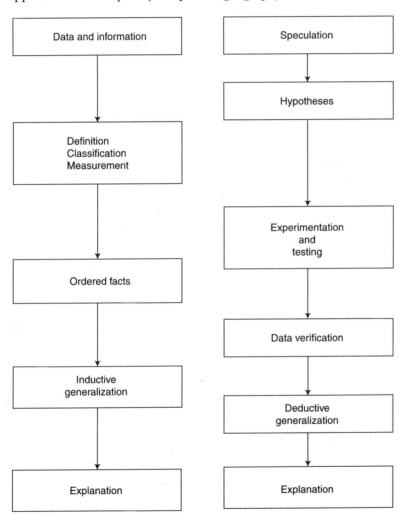

Figure 9.2 Inductive and deductive routes to explanation
Source: Harvey 1973

Thus the nature of the questions asked in each subject also differs, so that the point of arrival in a science investigation is often the point of departure for a geography investigation (Fisher 1993). Science questions to investigate volcanoes might include 'What is the effect of changes in the temperature, viscosity and composition of a lava on the shape of a volcano?' This can be tested by laboratory experiments in which the variables are altered (using a substitute material such as jelly to simulate the lava) and the results synthesized to isolate the key factors in determining volcano shape. A physical geography enquiry on the same topic might ask questions such as 'Do volcanoes with different shapes erupt in different ways?' In this instance the task of the pupil might be to examine data on the shape of volcanoes, frequency of eruptions, volume of material erupted, destructive properties of eruptions and so on. The data are classified and sorted to search for relationships and the outcome of the enquiry might lead to a discussion on the relative risks of living on different types of volcanoes.

Understanding the distinctions and their implications is important because it enables teachers of both science and geography to recognize how the approach and content of each subject can complement the other. Similarities can be exploited and/or reinforced in different contexts and any differences in approach can be used to provide different or alternative perspectives for pupils.

The main differences between aspects of Earth science taught in geography and science have been summarized as follows:

> In Science, the scientific principles underlying Earth processes are studied in an investigative way, involving laboratory experimentation through Sc.1. These Earth processes are related to their products in terms of weather conditions, Earth activity, different types of rocks, soils, etc.
>
> In Geography, evidence for activity of Earth processes is sought in the environment, and the theme of the impact of these processes on the landscape and human activities is developed.
>
> (Kennett and King 1993: 3)

Some examples of this complementary approach are shown in Figure 9.3.

CROSS-CURRICULAR CO-ORDINATION AND COLLABORATION

Having established that science and geography may approach Earth science in different manners but may still be complementary for pupils' learning, the importance of cross-curricular liaison and links becomes evident. Co-ordination and collaboration between different subjects need to be recognized as key aspects of a teacher's professional responsibility because

Topic	Science	Geography
Erosion	Investigate processes of erosion, e.g. abrasion, attrition	Visit a stream bed and look for evidence of erosion of the bed and rounding of pebbles
Volcanic activity	Investigate the properties of molten material and relate these to the characteristics of volcanic activity and the products which result	Consider the relationship between different types of volcanic eruption and the resultant landforms, e.g. Mt Etna, Mauna Loa – Hawaii
Weathering	Investigate the action of freezing and thawing, heat and cold, acid attack on rocks	Examine the effects of weathering on local buildings and on a range of different landscapes
Earthquakes	Investigate fracturing in materials and transmission of waves through various media, link to faulting in rocks	Use secondary sources to locate earthquake zones and describe the effects of earthquakes on people and the landscape
Deposition of sediment	Investigate the rate of settling and angle of rest of sediment, study the formation of 'deltas' in a stream table or in the field	Video, photograph, map and fieldwork. Compare the theoretical processes with the development of specific examples, e.g. the Mississippi Delta and local flood-plains

Figure 9.3 A complementary approach to cross-curricular co-ordination of the Earth sciences in science and geography

Source: National Curriculum Council 1993

thoughtful cross-curricular co-ordination can lead to more effective teaching. It can enhance the curriculum in a number of ways.

From the teacher's perspective collaboration can lead to:

- a saving of time and energy, if teachers share responsibility for those aspects that are common to both subjects;
- teachers learning from each other and gaining different perspectives and approaches to teaching;
- a recognition and sharing of appropriate knowledge and expertise in terms of subject content and teaching approaches;
- more reliable assessment of pupils.

From the pupil's perspective collaboration can lead to:

- increased motivation since similar topics in different subjects are more likely to be complementary rather than just more of the same;
- a greater knowledge and understanding of a topic because the topic has been studied from different perspectives;
- more successful learning since what has been learned in one subject is developed in another;
- enhanced progress because of the transfer of learning across subjects.

There is little evidence indicating the current state of co-ordination and collaboration between geography and science teachers in secondary schools, or on what effect the National Curriculum might have had on such inter-subject co-operation. A survey of forty-three geography and science teachers in Devon schools undertaken in 1986/7, just before the introduction of the National Curriculum, revealed that with one exception the teachers possessed no significant knowledge of reciprocal teaching in other courses. When questioned on what they knew about the related teaching in the other subject, the most frequent response from the teachers related how they had discovered the overlap by accident, either from pupils or from informal chance discussion or, as in one case, from notes left on the blackboard. In one extreme case, a class had experienced a science lesson on anticyclones immediately followed by a geography lesson on the same topic (Trend 1996). It seems probable that this situation is being replicated in the National Curriculum era. As one Sussex school reported, 'A class politely endured the geographical "rendering" of "The Water Cycle" but then protested when asked to complete a homework on exactly the same material as they had already done in Science!' (Adamczyk et al. 1994: 12). If such states of affair are to be avoided the issue becomes how best to collaborate between the subjects to ensure that pupils receive high-quality learning experiences which enable them effectively to use their learning across the two subjects. Assuming that teachers in the science and geography departments are enthusiastic about adopting the professional responsibility for curricular co-ordination, foci for collaboration between the departments can be developed through a number of different aspects (Trend 1993).

COMMON CONTENT

The most obvious area for collaboration is identifying common content, and further co-operation might be developed by the 'sharing' of teaching to avoid repetition or duplication. For example, in the teaching of tectonic processes at KS3, teachers in a geography department might agree to include teaching about how the idea of continental drift and plate tectonics came about and was developed into a theory, which would contribute to the

Key Stage 2

- Adaptation of plants and animals (different plants and animals found in different habitats)
- Rock and soil types based on textures and permeability
- Evaporation
- Condensation
- Dissolving
- Water cycle

Key Stage 3

- Competition for resources
- Rock types based on processes of formation
- Rock cycle
- Weathering
- Acids and bases (and their applications)
- Atmospheric acid and chemical weathering
- Quantitative relationship between speed, distance and time
- Frictional forces affecting motion
- Renewable and non-renewable energy resources

Key Stage 4

- The impact of human activity on the environment
- Carbon cycle
- Seismic waves
- Earth's internal structure
- Plate tectonics
- Radiation

Figure 9.4 Some concepts taught through the science curriculum that are useful in the teaching of geography

requirement in the science curriculum to teach about the nature of scientific ideas. Content does not have to be interpreted only in terms of knowledge but can also include concepts and skills. A list of concepts taught in science that might be useful to draw on in the teaching of geography is given in Figure 9.4.

SEQUENCE AND PROGRESSION

An associated but more developed collaborative stage is the planning of sequence and progression, where schemes of work for both subjects are adapted or planned in such a way as to allow coherence in building on and taking forward the knowledge, skills and concepts learned. For example, a science unit of work on acids and bases might be followed by a geography unit of work on energy sources and the effects and management of environmental pollution, or science teaching about rock-forming processes and the rock cycle might precede the teaching about landform development in geography. The key point here is that collaboration is not just about content but is also dealing with prerequisite learning.

PROCESS OF INVESTIGATION

Another aspect for collaboration is the similarity between the geographical enquiry process and scientific investigation. It is possible here to co-ordinate deliberately the development of particular aspects of the processes, so that pupils are given, for instance, opportunities to develop simultaneously their skills in collecting evidence or to extend their abilities to analyse evidence using a variety of graphical techniques in both geography and science. Clearly, it would be possible to save considerable teaching time in both subjects and to develop pupils' competence to a greater level if teachers had confidence in being able to make use of and develop skills and ideas they knew were being taught concurrently in the other subject.

EQUIPMENT AND RESOURCES

This aspect of collaboration may be well established in some schools, but in as many others it is likely to be an *ad hoc*, chance arrangement. There may well be respectable geological collections to be found in cupboards in geography classrooms that could be put to good use in the science laboratory. Similarly, science departments often hold a range of equipment that could prove useful for geography fieldwork or may possess some relevant computer software that could be borrowed. A good working relationship developed here could be very profitable for both subjects.

EXPERTISE

It may be possible to capitalize on using teachers' professional or educational backgrounds. In many science departments, much of the responsibility for teaching the Earth sciences component rests with chemistry specialists who may welcome the Earth science knowledge of a geographer. In some schools the geography department has taken on the responsibility for the Earth science teaching in both geography and science, although there will be some geography teachers who would not feel comfortable teaching and managing a practical session in a laboratory. However, the effective use of expertise does not necessarily have to involve shifts in timetabling. The particular knowledge and interests of a teacher could be made available through helping to develop a unit of work and might operate at a number of different levels, from writing a unit of work to checking content and resource materials for accuracy. Helpful advice given in this way could help to reduce teaching errors which sometimes occur when subjects are being taught by people without subject-specific expertise. (For examples of Earth science 'howlers', see Fielding 1990 and Bates 1995.)

CONCLUSION

Earth science and physical geography are inextricably linked through themes which deal with similar subject-matter, by some common skills and by broadly common approaches in methods of study. There is a contribution to these common themes that can be made through the teaching of both the science curriculum and the geography curriculum. This teaching is likely to be most effective and to have most impact on pupils' learning if it is co-ordinated, so that the curriculum is enriched through the distinct perspectives that each subject brings to the common aspects of learning.

REFERENCES

Adamczyk, P., Binns, T., Brown, A., Cross, S. and Magson, Y. (1994) 'The geography-science interface: a focus for collaboration', *Teaching Geography* 19(1):11–14.

Allaby, A. and Allaby, M. (1990) *The Concise Oxford Dictionary of Earth Sciences*, Oxford: Oxford University Press.

Bates, D. (1995) 'Editorial', *Teaching Earth Sciences* 20(3):86.

Biddle, D.S. (1985) 'Paradigms and geography curricula in England and Wales 1882–1972', in Boardman, D. (ed.) *New Directions in Geographical Education*, London: The Falmer Press.

Department for Education (1995a) *Science in the National Curriculum*, London: HMSO.

Department for Education (1995b) *Geography in the National Curriculum*, London: HMSO.

Department of Education and Science/Welsh Office (1985) *Science 5–16: A Statement of Policy*, London: HMSO.

Fielding, D. (1990), letter in *Teaching Earth Sciences* 15(4):91–2.

Fisher, J. (1993) 'The empirical inductive tradition and some of its implications for Earth science teaching', *Teaching Earth Sciences* 18(1):12–15.

Gregory, K.J. (1985) *The Nature of Physical Geography*, London: Edward Arnold.

Harvey, D. (1973) *Explanation in Geography*, London: Edward Arnold.

Kennett, P. and King, C. (1993) *National Curriculum Earth Science at Key Stage 3: A Teacher's Guide to the 'Science of the Earth' Approach*, Sheffield: Earth Science Teachers' Association.

National Curriculum Council (1993) *Earth Science For Secondary Teachers, An INSET Handbook*, York: National Curriculum Council.

Rawling, E. (1987) 'Geography 11–16: criteria for geographical content in the secondary school curriculum', in Bailey, P. and Binns, T. (eds) *A Case for Geography*, Sheffield: The Geographical Association.

Trend, R. (1993) *Science/Geography Links at Key Stage 3*, Exeter: Devon Learning Resources/Devon County Council.

Trend, R. (1996) 'Fostering collaboration as a means of enhancing geoscience teaching in Devon, England', in Stow, D.A.V. and McCall, J.G. *Geoscience Education and Training: In Schools and Universities, for Industry and Public Awareness*, Joint special publication of the Commission of Geoscience Education and Training of the International Union of Geological Sciences and the Association of Geoscientists for International Development, AGID Special Publication Series 19, Rotterdam: Balkena.

Wilson, C. (1990) 'National Curriculum Geography Working Group (the ESTA response), National Curriculum Geography Working Group (the ASE response)' *Teaching Earth Sciences* 15(1):18–23.

Chapter 10

Cross-curricular concerns in geography
Citizenship and economic and industrial understanding

Daniella Tilbury

CROSS-CURRICULAR THEMES – WHOSE CONCERN?

I don't have time to even think about the themes. There is a lot to cover in geography.

(A geography secondary school teacher, May 1993)

Since the first appearance of cross-curricular themes (CCTHs) in 1990, it has become increasingly apparent that incorporating them into the curriculum has been a difficult task for teachers. The statement above, recorded before the Dearing Report of 1994, sums up many teachers' reactions to these cross-curricular components. The 1995 Orders have since given schools more discretion to decide their response to CCTHs and other elements of the whole curriculum. The slimming down of the National Curriculum has not only brought greater freedom, but also more curriculum space and time for teachers to consider the CCTHs within their work.

This chapter argues that, despite their low status within the National Curriculum, the CCTHs constitute one of the most exciting and potentially most transformative curriculum innovations yet to be experienced in England and Wales. It identifies a number of reasons why teachers should grasp the opportunities that the slimmer 1995 Orders bring and make the CCTHs their concern as geography educators. Arguments are developed with specific reference to economic and industrial understanding and education for citizenship.

THE INDIVIDUAL IN A CHANGING WORLD

The CCTHs of health education, economic and industrial understanding, education for citizenship, careers and guidance, and environmental education are inextricably and unavoidably linked to contemporary social, economic and political issues. They attempt to prepare pupils for the world outside and beyond school. These cross-curricular themes share six characteristics:

1   They are relevant to the pupils' current and future experiences.
2   They contribute to the pupils' knowledge and understanding.
3   They involve pupils in discussion over questions of values and belief.
4   They rely on decision-making and practical activities.
5   They explore the inter-relationship of the individual in the community.
6   They prepare pupils for life in a changing world.

Recognizing the changing nature of society, the CCTHs not only promote the development of skills, knowledge and attitudes which pupils need to deal with change but also encourage them to be active agents shaping change. This educational approach, which supports a reconstructivist view of the curriculum, provides potentially an exciting development for schools. It complements the more passive, academic and knowledge-centred view of education contained in the subject Orders and reintroduces breadth and balance into the slimmer programmes of study.

Regrettably, the attempts to reduce the Attainment Targets have led to a narrower view of the curriculum and pupils' experiences. As a result, the themes now have a vital contribution to make to curriculum learning. In Morrison's words, 'it is not enough that students should possess a body of knowledge. They also need to know what to do with it and how it enables them to be active participants in society' (Morrison 1994: 21).

TEACHING AND LEARNING FOR CHANGE

The Curriculum Guidance booklets and Advisory Papers which detail the nature of the CCTHs also identify pedagogic characteristics which are common to all the themes. These documents promote democratic learning methods which recognize the individual within the group, promote citizenship and social co-operation. They value active, participatory, collaborative, problem-solving and experiential learning methods. Such approaches encourage critical thinking, independence, assertiveness, co-operation, self-determination, freedom and the development of more imaginative forms of expression. They serve to empower individuals to ask critical questions, and to make and enact choices about their futures. The development of these qualities and skills form part of an education for life in a changing world.

Unlike the subject Orders, with their detailed content specification and contrasting *laissez-faire* approach towards pedagogical practices, the National Curriculum booklets on the CCTHs have recognized that content and pedagogy need to be mutually reinforcing. These documents acknowledge the role of active learning approaches in encouraging individual and collective participation in social, economic and political issues.

ECONOMIC AND INDUSTRIAL UNDERSTANDING

Economic and Industrial Understanding (EIU) is a theme which explores the links between the pupil and economic aspects of everyday life. Through EIU students study certain basic economic concepts, investigate a number of economic issues, make judgements and decisions about their own lives, and develop attitudes needed to participate 'responsibly' in economic activity (NCC 1990a).

EIU plays an important part in preparing learners for the responsibilities and opportunities of life in an industrialized society. Through its approach to learning, EIU provides pupils with the knowledge and skills necessary not only to understand but also to question the workings of the economic system. Ultimately, EIU can give pupils the confidence to play a more active and enquiring role in the economic issues of everyday life and empower pupils (and their societies) to shape personal and collective economic futures.

Relevance

EIU adds relevance to the curriculum in that it increases pupils' understanding of themselves and the world in which they are growing up. Through considering questions such as 'Should the local council build a sports complex or a new school?' 'Where should a local firm locate itself and what might be the impact on jobs and the environment?' and 'Should the government increase spending on health?' EIU encourages pupils to be better informed about the economy in general and the world of work in particular (CCW 1994). Through its learning approach EIU can promote a critically reflective and analytical perspective of the way in which contemporary society uses its resources (CCW 1994). At another level, EIU encourages pupils to explore links between their personal lives and these wider social concerns, especially in areas such as consumerism and the world of work.

EIU is relevant to schoolchildren of all ages. Young children experience and make economic decisions when they go shopping with parents or even when they spend their pocket money at the school tuck-shop. They are also aware of different types of shops and services and the variety of jobs and careers. There is a body of research and literature (PSIC 1989; Smith 1988) which supports the assertion that Key Stage 1 pupils are conscious of economic activity and decision-making.

Contribution to pupils' knowledge and understanding

EIU aims to develop economic literacy and awareness through studying (i) the world of industry, business and employment (ii) consumerism and personal economic decision-making and (iii) the economy and public affairs at the local, national and international level.

Different focuses of study can be developed from the knowledge areas identified above. There has been much criticism of the interpretation adopted by the National Curriculum Council (1990a) and Curriculum Council for Wales (1990) documents, which provide the official guidance on developing EIU through the National Curriculum (Carter 1991; Morrison 1994). The EIU exemplars used place emphasis on particular concepts, especially those which endorse a free market view of the economy. They also ignore questions which might challenge capitalist development.

As part of EIU, pupils are expected to learn that 'Companies compete in business through innovation, price and advertising, aiming to increase their share of the market and sell more goods and services' (NCC 1990a: 31). Carter (1991) is critical of this partial view and argues that to gain a full understanding students would need not only to understand how this works in practice but also to look critically at the impact of an increase in market share for one company and how this may result in a decrease in the share of another, as well as critically examine the place of this market-centred principle in areas like education and health.

Through EIU pupils develop knowledge and understanding of influences on consumers such as prices and advertising of consumer rights and responsibilities. The particular example included in the document refers to 'How design of goods and services including packaging and advertising affects consumer choice' (NCC 1990a: 31). There is no mention of the social and environmental consequences of packaging (Carter 1991). The result is that it is left to teachers to stand outside the contents of the documents and raise questions about the underlying assumptions of the specified knowledge. Morrison (1994) suggests that teachers should work *on* as well as *with* the guidance documents.

Questioning of values and beliefs

EIU provides pupils with the opportunity to review their own daily economic experiences, beliefs and values. Through clarifying their beliefs and considering alternative viewpoints, EIU attempts to extend the pupils' understanding of how values and beliefs determine economic decisions and actions. This CCTH also encourages pupils to reflect upon, question and examine critically economic and industrial decisions taken at a social level.

Individual in the community

EIU was a response to the dominant enterprise culture of the 1980s and was initially part of a wider movement which aimed to establish closer links between school and industry. It is, therefore, not surprising to find that EIU requires schools to build close partnerships with local industries and community organizations which provide valuable contacts and resources for the development of pupils' understanding of industry, business and the world of work (NCC 1990a: CCW 1991b).

The Welsh guidance document on EIU argued that by the time they have completed their compulsory education all pupils should have:

- had first-hand experience of industry and the world of work through contacts with a range of industries . . . [and that visits] should be structured so that pupils have an opportunity to talk to and question adults within their community;
- participated in activities which promote the qualities of enterprise and the ability to work together with others as part of a team;
- had the opportunity to work collaboratively with adults in and from the community.

(CCW 1990: 3)

The CCW (1991b) details, with the use of examples, how the links between the individual and the community can be developed.

Decision-making and practical activities

Placing pupils in the role of decision-maker, investigating the problem, gathering information, considering the alternatives and views of others, weighing up the impact of the decision and finally coming to and justifying a decision is an important focus of EIU activities. Through EIU pupils interpret their own daily economic experiences and question the basis on which they make decisions and the consequences of these decisions at a personal and social level. Similarly, pupils study how economic decisions are made in society and analyse the values and beliefs which inform these judgements.

The CCW (1990) illustrates how a study which looked into the suitability of a site for a leisure centre and the likely demand within the community for the facilities it would offer (years 6 and 7), or a study into local tourism and leisure industry and its impact on the local economy (years 7 and 9) invite pupils to become involved with EIU at a practical level.

Dealing with and shaping change

EIU attempts not only to interest but also to involve pupils in economic change. Through EIU pupils learn how 'economic activity has changed and is changing and the effects of such changes' (DFE 1995: 13). Most importantly, through values analysis, decision-making, problem-solving, practical and action-orientated activities, pupils learn to cope with as well as shape change.

EIU THROUGH GEOGRAPHY: WORKING WITH AND ON THE ORDERS

The objectives and content of EIU greatly overlap with those of geographical education. Geography teachers' past involvement with GSIP (Geography Schools and Industry Project) and recently with GNVQs (General National Vocational Qualifications) have highlighted the subject's contribution to economic understanding.

Economic literacy is arguably crucial for geographers interpreting a changing world. Economic factors linked to issues of standards of living and quality of life are often primary determinants of the human and physical characteristics of places. Geography develops understanding of the reasons behind the location of such different economic activities as a small food shop, a large chemical plant or a hospital (CCW 1994).

Economic issues are central in any debate about environmental quality. Technological and economic development are inextricably bound up with questions about the protection and preservation of the physical and social environment. EIU can promote understanding about the causes, effects and ways of tackling environmental problems, whether they be on a local or global scale. Furthermore, there is a growing recognition that the misuse of the environment has economic costs.

The Geography Orders provide several opportunities for economic and industrial considerations and the development of EIU as a CCTH. For example, at KS1 children 'identify some of the jobs done by adults who provide goods and services for the community'. KS2 pupils study 'how people affect the environment e.g. by quarrying' (DFE 1995: 5). At KS3 students:

> become aware of the global context within which places are set, how they are interdependent and how they may be affected by processes operating at different scales e.g. how a locality is affected by a regional economic policy or a world trade agreement.
>
> (DFE 1995: 10)

However, there are few references in the geography document to the need for reviewing or questioning values and beliefs relating to economic activity. The Orders require pupils to engage predominantly in acquiring knowledge. In fact, there has been much concern over the lack of opportunities for the study of values and attitudes in the Geography National Curriculum Orders. Rawling (1991) believes that the Orders provide

> us with a view of geography as a subject mainly concerned with putting across specific items of knowledge and information, with developing

basic understanding and with learning a narrow range of 'geographical skills'. Pupils are not to be encouraged to handle evidence, to consider alternative views, to evaluate material from different sources critically, to ask awkward questions.

(Rawling 1991: 18)

This problem has been accentuated by reductions in the Attainment Targets which have further restricted the possibilities for values education. This is a reason why EIU is of importance to geography teachers. Through its approach, EIU fosters discussion of values and beliefs and provides a more holistic approach to learning.

Teachers can enrich their geography curriculum, reintroduce breadth into the slimmer programmes of study and balance the more knowledge-centred view of education contained in the subject Orders by integrating with CCTH into their teaching. This can be accomplished by developing the references to economic understanding in the Orders so that learning incorporates the six characteristics outlined in the previous section.

EDUCATION FOR CITIZENSHIP (EFC)

It [EFC] is of paramount importance in a democratic society and in a world undergoing rapid change. Schools must lay the foundations for positive, participatory citizenship.

(NCC 1990b: 1)

Education for Citizenship in the National Curriculum (or Community Understanding in Wales) is concerned with preparing pupils for the world in which they live (NCC 1990b). It aims to encourage participatory democracy through increasing awareness and understanding of responsibilities and rights and by 'providing opportunities and incentives' for pupils to become active citizens (NCC 1990b: 1).

Although the National Curriculum documents outline a clearly defined rationale for this CCTH, the term 'citizenship' has been the subject of much energetic debate. Its contestable nature has led to a variety of interpretations. As acknowledged by the NCC (1990b), education for citizenship (EFC) in schools was, in the past, primarily concerned with knowledge about the machinery and processes of government. Now, the advisory documents offer a different interpretation which involves pupils in discussions about fairness, equality, community and shared values. However, pupils are expected to take on board this concept of citizenship unquestioningly. The booklet makes no reference to the need for pupils to appreciate that 'citizenship' is a controversial concept.

Much contention surrounds the Welsh document, which adopts the term 'Community Understanding' and places great emphasis on the need to explore notions of Welsh cultural heritage and a sense of place. Commentators object to pupils not being offered the opportunity to examine critically alternative notions of citizenship. In fact, Morrison (1994) argues that the key verbs used in the documents focus mainly on understanding and exploration rather than critique. He believes that the contents of these documents need to be interrogated rather than just accepted.

Despite the shortcomings of these official booklets, their contents reveal that EFC does share some common ground with the other CCTHs. Its essence and underlying characteristics contribute to an education for life outside and beyond the school.

Relevance

Both EFC and Community Understanding (CU) serve to add relevance to the curriculum through preparing pupils to deal with the moral and cultural dilemmas which face them and through encouraging them to play an active and meaningful role in the communities where they live.

Through role-play pupils involve themselves in issues such as bullying and racism and explore links between their personal lives and wider social concerns. They also investigate the consequences of individual and collective actions for themselves and others.

Contribution to pupils' knowledge and understanding

CG8 (NCC 1990b: 3) argues that through EFC pupils should develop knowledge and understanding of:

1 *The nature of the community* – which includes recognizing that individuals belong to a range of communities and studying how communities combine change with stability, how communities are organized and the importance of rules and law, how communities reconcile the needs of individuals with those of society.
2 *Roles and responsibilities in a democratic society* – which involves exploring the nature of co-operation and competition between individuals, groups and communities, and considering the similarities and differences between individuals, groups and communities.
3 *The nature and basis of duties, responsibilities and rights* – which includes the role of custom and law in prescribing duties, responsibilities and rights, and the nature of fairness, justice and moral responsibility.

These three areas also underpin the framework offered by the CCW (1990). However, the Welsh document gives greater prominence to knowledge about the distinctive features of culture in communities.

Both documents add to the curriculum an important dimension of knowledge and understanding which can serve to fuel questions about social and political alternatives in our society.

Questioning of values and beliefs

EFC encourages pupils to analyse critically the values and beliefs of individuals and groups in the community. Through an EFC study, pupils explore how their moral codes may be influenced by personal experience.

Community Understanding places greater emphasis on discrimination and the moral questions which surround it. It encourages pupils to explore their own standpoints regarding issues such as vandalism and sexism. Through CU pupils are expected to question and examine critically the values and beliefs that influence communities and democracy.

Individual in community

Both documents require pupils to explore relationships between themselves and the community. As part of an EFC study primary pupils may establish links with local hospitals or those living in sheltered accommodation (NCC 1990b). Secondary students may become involved in the wider community through fund-raising or may campaign for (or against) change in the community (e.g. a new motorway or the pedestrianization of the city centre). Student placements within the community, for example, decorating for the elderly, are also encouraged (NCC 1990b).

Decision-making and practical activities

CG8 (NCC 1990b) suggests that as from Key Stage 1, pupils should be given opportunities to participate in decision-making (e.g. through identifying jobs that need to be done, deciding who should do what and devising rotas). Practical activities at the secondary level may include assuming responsibility for an aspect of school or community life (e.g. keeping the school free from litter or running a community fair).

The CCW (1990) identifies the need for individuals to recognize that decision-making operates at a number of levels ranging from the family and school level, to national government and international agencies. Pupils, it argues, need to examine how decision-making at different levels works and to be aware of the role they can play in these processes.

Dealing with and shaping change

> Pupils should be aware of the ways in which their own communities have changed and are changing and of the relationships between conflict and change. . . . They should understand how people can work for and achieve change, either as individuals or as members of a group.
>
> (CCW 1991b: 8)

The NCC booklet recognizes the need for pupils to anticipate and participate in change. It suggests that even at KS1, children could participate through becoming involved in 'making the dining hall a more pleasant place to eat' or 'making the school more welcoming' (NCC 1990b: 11). Both documents provide examples of tasks ranging from individual, group to whole-school activities which involve the pupil in change at every Key Stage.

The CCW document also identifies an active participatory role for pupils. It argues that CU must:

> assist them in taking responsibility for and control of their own lives. At the same time they will be encouraged to contribute, as active participating critically reflective members of the communities in Wales or wherever they may subsequently live.
>
> (CCW 1991b: 2)

GEOGRAPHY AND CITIZENSHIP: WORKING WITH AND ON THE ORDERS

The CCW (1990) proposed a framework for teaching about the community through this CCTH. A close look at the framework reveals that its components, which include becoming a member of a community, patterns of social life and active citizenship, all make reference to a number of geographical concerns (CCW 1991a: 9):

Becoming a member of a community

'They should recognise the specifically Welsh characteristics of the communities in which they live and in the process develop a sense of place.'

Patterns of social life

'Pupils should be aware that in Wales some communities are rural, whereas others are more urban and cosmopolitan.'

Active citizenship

'They should explore what citizenship means at various levels e.g. what it might mean to be a citizen of Wales as well as a world citizen.'

People, work and the distribution of resources

'Pupils should know how and why wealth and resources are distributed unevenly between individuals, groups, nations and continents. . . . They should consider the relationship between economic, social and environmental factors in community development on both local and global levels.'

All these components highlight the citizenship dimension of school geography, which is almost absent from the Geography Orders.

Geography teaching can be enriched by the inclusion of the citizenship dimension. The slimming down of the National Curriculum has not only meant that references to the CCTHs within the Orders have been deleted but also that the process of geographical learning has been limited and weakened by the attempt to make the curriculum more manageable. Now, geography in the National Curriculum provides the context for pupils to understand the societies to which they belong but they are given few opportunities to question (never mind change!) the world in which they live.

Geography education, as defined in the Orders, enables pupils to study how industrial societies cause environmental damage. There is little scope within the slimmer Orders for pupils to develop the knowledge, values and skills needed to tackle this problem. Education for Citizenship (or CU) can address this gap in geographical learning.

At the root of geographical understanding lies an appreciation of how political, economic and social factors shape the local to global environment and influence social decisions. However, the study of these factors has been underplayed throughout the drafting process of National Curriculum Orders. Although there has been much objection to the low profile of such dimensions (see Huckle 1993), the 1995 Geography Orders appear to make (limited) references to political, economic and social influences (especially at the lower Key Stages). The inclusion of EFC in geographical work could compensate for this weakness and prepare pupils for life and change in a complex world.

CONCLUSION: GEOGRAPHY EDUCATION FOR A CHANGING WORLD

> The Dearing Review has said very little about such themes but one of its guiding principles has been to give schools more scope to teach how they want to. The conclusion which geographers should draw from this is that if cross-curricular themes have helped to enrich a piece of work, then they should not be abandoned.
>
> (Grimwade 1995: 62)

In the aftermath of the Dearing Review, what of the CCTHs? The CCTHs' role and place in the curriculum is now a matter for schools and teachers to decide.

CCTHs enrich the school curriculum through making learning experiences more relevant to the pupils' everyday life and through involving the individual in community issues. Furthermore, the themes can compensate for the weaknesses and gaps in the Geography Orders. Through integrating the themes into schemes of work teachers can advance the quality of geographical learning in the school curriculum. The Final Orders alone do not provide pupils with an education for life in a changing world. For these reasons, this chapter has argued, geography teachers must grasp the greater curriculum space and time that the slimmer Orders bring and make the CCTHs their concern.

REFERENCES

Baglin Jones, E. and Jones, N. (1992) *Education for Citizenship*, London: Kogan Page.

Carter, R. (1991) 'A matter of values', *Teaching Geography* 16(1):30.

Curriculum Council for Wales (1990) *Economic and Industrial Understanding: A Framework for the Development of a Cross-Curricular Theme in Wales*, Advisory Paper 7, Cardiff: CCW.

Curriculum Council for Wales (1991a) *Community Understanding: A Framework for the Development of a Cross-Curricular Theme in Wales*, Advisory Paper 11, Cardiff: CCW.

Curriculum Council for Wales (1991b) *Industry and Enterprise in Cross-Curricular Work*, Cardiff: CCW.

Curriculum Council for Wales (1994) *Developing EIU Through Geography and History*, Cardiff: CCW.

Dearing, R. (1994) *The National Curriculum and its Assessment: Final Report*, London: SCAA.

Department for Education (1995) *Geography in the National Curriculum*, London: HMSO.

Edwards, J. (1993) *Developing Citizenship in the Curriculum*, London: David Fulton Publishers.

Grimwade, K. (1995) 'Revising courses', *Teaching Geography* 20(2):62–4.

Huckle, J. (1993) 'Environmental education and sustainability: a view from critical theory', in Fien, J. (ed.) (1993) *Environmental Education: A Pathway to Sustainability*, Geelong: Deakin University Press.

Morrison, K. (1994) *Implementing Cross-Curricular Themes*, London: David Fulton Publishers.

National Curriculum Council (1990a) *Education for Economic and Industrial Understanding*, Curriculum Guidance 4, York: NCC.

National Curriculum Council (1990b) *Education for Citizenship*, Curriculum Guidance 8, York: NCC.

Primary Schools and Industry Centre (PSIC) (1989) *Primary Schools and Industry Kit*, London: Polytechnic of North London.

Rawling, E. (1991) 'Spirit of inquiry falls off the map', *Times Educational Supplement*, 25 January, pp. 15–18.

Smith, D. (1988) *Industry in the Primary School Curriculum*, East Sussex: The Falmer Press.

Chapter 11

Environmental education and development education
Teaching geography for a sustainable world

Daniella Tilbury

For the survival of the World and its people teachers must do far more than just teach about global issues. We must find ways to change hearts and minds. This can be a response to reasoned argument and evidence or to experience where empathy will lead to commitment to action. Teachers hold the responsibility for educating their participants to work for future change that will help create a better world for all. Together we must work towards a more ecologically sustainable and socially just society locally, nationally and globally.

(Calder and Smith 1993: 2.1)

INTRODUCTION: EDUCATING FOR SUSTAINABILITY

Over the last decade there has been growing concern over global inequalities, the stability of ecosystems and sustainability of existing lifestyles. Issues about quality of life of current and future populations are now at the forefront of public concern (Dunlap *et al.* 1992). As a result the 1990s have seen strong support for the idea of schools playing a critical role in educating for sustainability (BGPSD 1995; EDET Group 1992; IUCN, UNEP, WWF (1991); UNESCO 1992; UNESCO 1995).

Education for sustainability addresses quality of life issues through combining environmental education and development education. Environmental education, until recently, has focused on the quality of the physical environment, while development education has been traditionally concerned with economic growth and development of the social environment. Evidence that many people around the world exploit their local environment for daily survival coupled with the realization that social and economic factors are a contributory (and often major) cause of environmental problems has altered the course of environmental education in the 1990s. Similarly, recognition that real improvements in quality of life are dependent on the reconciliation between economic development and environmental conservation has changed the agenda for development education.

Now problems such as climatic change, deforestation, land degradation and desertification, depletion of natural resources, loss of biodiversity, overpopulation, food security, drought, poverty, and urban decay are primary concerns for both environmental and development education. Such matters as environmental deterioration and human development are also central to geography.

This chapter argues that geography education is uniquely placed to develop links between environmental and development education in the context of education for sustainability. It begins with a discussion about the nature of these complementary disciplines and how they have been redefined in the 1990s to meet the challenge of educating for sustainability. The role and place of this new approach in geography education is explored. The chapter presents a framework for planning and assessing education for sustainability through geography.

THE PURPOSE AND NATURE OF ENVIRONMENTAL EDUCATION

Environmental education is an area of learning which seeks to interest and involve students in local to global environmental problems. From the beginning when the term 'environmental education' was first used (at a meeting of the International Union for Conservation of Nature and Natural Resources, Paris, 1948), this area of learning has sought to address real issues and directly promote environmental improvement. However, its introduction into the curriculum in the 1970s was problematic, as environmental education was never accepted as a concept in its own right, being confused with a diversity of disciplines which use the environment as a vehicle for teaching.

A historical review reveals how the term 'environmental education' has at times been synonymous with environmental studies, urban studies, outdoor education and conservation education and has been taken to mean a variety of activities which consider the environment for educational aims. The effect of this has been to distract from the real purpose of environmental education, which evolved in response to concern over the quality of the environment and the need for education to improve the existing environmental predicament (Tilbury 1993).

As a result a mismatch between the purpose and practice of environmental education occurred. Instead of involving students in the real complexity of environmental issues, lessons focused on the local and geophysical topics. Environmental education was thus limited to the study, rather than the improvement, of pupils' environment.

These curriculum identity problems continued during the 1980s until environmental education became a cross-curricular theme of the National Curriculum. Curriculum Guidance 7 (NCC 1990) and Advisory Paper 17

(CCW 1990) gave environmental education a new curriculum status, acknowledging it 'an essential part of every pupil's curriculum' (NCC 1990: 1). These documents re-established the original goals of environmental education, promoting *active involvement* of pupils in environmental issues. The aims of environmental education were clarified as being to:

> arouse pupils' awareness and curiosity about the environment and encourage active participation in resolving environmental problems.
>
> (NCC 1990: 3)

Although the role of environmental education as a cross-curricular theme in the National Curriculum was underplayed by the Dearing Review, a number of recent influential reports have continued to raise its profile within education. Among these is the British Government Panel on Sustainable Development, which stressed that:

> Education on environmental issues and on environmental values should be available throughout life to enable citizens to see for themselves the need for sustainability and to help convey the necessary sense of individual responsibility for a healthy environment.
>
> (BGPSD 1995: 12–13)

Such support for environmental education can be found in many other national and international documents. These documents not only revitalize environmental education's primary goal of immediate *environmental improvement*, but also call for the promotion of *sustainable lifestyles* in the long term. They advocate a new approach, environmental education for sustainability (EFS), which differs significantly from the apolitical, naturalist and scientific work which was carried out under the environmental education banner of the 1970s and 1980s.

EFS seeks to nurture a sense of *personal responsibility* towards the environment and attempts to equip pupils with skills and knowledge to give effect to this responsibility. This is achieved through environmental education's *action-oriented, participatory goals* and by involving pupils in real *local to global issues*.

These documents, recognizing that poverty is often at the root of environmental exploitation, highlight the social and economic factors which contribute to environmental problems. They call for the reconciliation between environmental conservation and economic development and promote a form of environmental education which integrates the complementary disciplines of *environmental* and *development* education. This new approach promotes a *critical* understanding of global issues and requires that pupils explore the *socio-economic* as well as the *political* dimensions of environmental problems.

ENVIRONMENTAL EDUCATION: ITS PLACE AND ROLE IN GEOGRAPHY

Geographical content and methodology have a great deal to contribute to environmental education. Geography, which studies the interactions between humans and the physical environment, contributes to an understanding of the processes affecting the environment and encourages an interest in its management and protection. Most significantly, environmental problems have a spatial dimension which makes a geographical understanding crucial to environmental education.

Geographical concepts such as sustainable development, exploitation, stewardship and responsibility, respect, protection, dependence and interdependence, co-operation, urbanization and industrialization, globality, complexity, citizenship, and equity are integral to environmental education. Similarly, teaching and learning styles usually associated with geographical education can make a methodological contribution to environmental education. Geography education places emphasis on problem-solving and enquiry-based learning, role-play, simulations and fieldwork which encourage pupils to carry out practical investigations and become actively involved in environmental management. Such approaches can have a significant impact on pupils' environmental education experiences.

These overlaps between geography and environmental education have been acknowledged by the National Curriculum – initially geography was regarded as 'the principal vehicle' for the delivery of environmental education (NCC 1989).

Although the contributions of school geography to environmental education have been progressively weakened through the revisions of the National Curriculum, geography still plays a leading role in developing the objectives of environmental education. The final Geography Orders (DFE 1995; WOED 1995) require consideration of sustainable development at all Key Stages (Huckle 1995). At KS1 pupils are expected to be taught how the quality of the environment can be improved (WOED 1995) and sustained (DFE 1995). Pupils at KS2 are required to know how and why people seek to manage (WOED 1995) and sustain (DFE 1995) their environment through a thematic study of environmental change. Environmental issues figure prominently in the DFE Geography Orders at KS3, which include consideration of how sustainable development, stewardship and conservation affect environmental management. Students who are at Level 8 are expected to be able to understand and apply the concept of sustainable development. The Welsh Orders encourage students at this level to explore the nature, causes and potential effects of global environmental change. The environmental dimension permeates geography in the National Curriculum, with opportunities throughout the place and thematic studies to develop environmental education.

DEVELOPMENT EDUCATION: AN EVOLVING GEOGRAPHICAL CONCERN

Development education grew from the concerns of aid and charitable organizations, the churches and the United Nations over socio-economic conditions in the poorer nations. Seeking greater political support and financial aid from economically developed countries, they agreed to promote this new form of public education. At the time, development education aimed to increase awareness of Third World famine and poverty and gain support for socio-economic change in 'less developed countries'.

Although the term 'development education' was first used in the 1960s it did not find its way into higher education until the 1970s. Initially development education took the form of optional course units on population growth and standards of living in Third World countries. These concerns were later integrated into undergraduate geography degree courses and geography A level examinations in schools, establishing it as an integral part of geographical study. Since then, the nature and characteristics of development education have evolved in response to the changing needs and concerns of the last decades.

Although the term 'development education' is still used and although its ultimate aim of *improving socio-economic* conditions remains unchanged, much of its initial principles and assumptions have been revised. Development education has now broadened its scope and seeks to *improve the quality of life* of people across the globe. It has turned its attention to the development concerns of both developed and economically developing countries and placed a new emphasis on their *interdependence.*

Evidence that the gap between rich and poor has continued to widen (despite progress made in areas like trade, communication, science and technology, health education and civil rights) (Dunlap *et al.* 1992) has prompted development education to take a more *critical and political* stance. This area of learning now challenges conceptions of power, fairness, justice and human rights across the globe. It explores the impact of economically developed countries on the poorer nations through colonization, racism, unfair trade, multinational corporations and arms sales. Many have extended their use of the term 'Third World' to encompass not only 'less developed countries' but also marginalized groups, like the homeless, unemployed, ethnic minorities, indigenous people and women across the world. Development education is no longer teaching about the Third World but about human rights, self-reliance and social justice in both developed and developing countries.

The environmental dimensions now figure more prominently in development education as a result of a growing realization that, although the survival of many depends on the *preservation of the natural environment,* much of the world's population still use their environments unsustainably to meet their basic daily needs.

The link between development and environment can be traced back to the influential Brandt Report (ICIDI 1980). This document questioned a world economic order which encouraged the poorest agricultural countries to over-use their soils and forests to produce commodities for the West. Soon after, the Brundtland Report (WCED 1987) argued for the need for more sustainable forms of development. It promoted a longer-term view which depended upon conserving natural resources and called for an attitude to development of anticipation and prevention rather than of reaction and cure.

It was the United Nations Conference on Environment and Development which secured a place for the concept of sustainability in development education. Its Agenda 21 (UNESCO 1992) promoted forms of *appropriate development*, and recognized that progress in quality of life depended upon protecting the physical environment.

So far the 1990s have been landmark years for development education, with conferences like the World Conference on Education for All (Juptien, Thailand 1990), the International Conference on Population and Development (Cairo, Egypt 1995) and the World Summit for Social Development (Copenhagen, Denmark 1995) which have increased the profile of development across the world. All have placed significant emphasis on the need for a *holistic* conception of development which incorporates educating for environmental as well as social sustainability. More significantly they highlight the role of development education in promoting knowledge, values and skills which will enable pupils to influence their environment and bring about a more just and fair world order.

LOCATING DEVELOPMENT EDUCATION WITHIN THE GEOGRAPHY CURRICULUM

Key issues for development education include population growth, food security, urbanization, energy, industry, ecosystems, the international economy, conflict, and environmental degradation. These are inherently geographical concerns. It is therefore not surprising to find several references to development within the Geography Orders of the National Curriculum.

However, although there is scope for introducing this area of learning in the early Key Stages (particularly through the study of a locality), the term 'development' does not appear until later on at KS3. Students at this level are expected 'to account for disparities in development and show some understanding of the range and complexity of factors that contribute to the quality of life in different places' (DFE 1995: 19; WOED 1995: 24).

There are various opportunities for integrating development education within the place and thematic studies component of KS3. In England, pupils are to be taught through place studies 'about the ways in which the country may be judged to be more or less developed . . . how the country is set within a global context and how it is interdependent with other countries' (DFE 1995: 11). Through thematic studies students investigate the concept of development in greater depth and consider the ways of identifying differences in development, their effect on the quality of life of different groups of people as well as how the interdependence of countries influences development.

The English curriculum also expects KS3 students to 'understand and apply the concept of sustainable development' (DFE 1995: 19) and to link it with stewardship, conservation and environmental planning and management.

Although students in Wales are required to study an economically developing country, the concept of development is more implicit within the Orders. There is no specific reference to the need for considering the concept of development, but students are expected to consider related concerns – population distribution and change, resources and the environment, and global environmental change.

EDUCATION FOR SUSTAINABILITY: A PLANNING FRAMEWORK

The Geography Orders offer great potential for integrating education for sustainability into Programmes of Study. However, in order to exploit this opportunity, teachers need to be clear about the aims and characteristics of this area of learning.

By drawing from the contents of the major reports cited previously in this chapter, it is possible to develop a framework for planning EFS through geography. This framework, presented below, provides a basis for teachers who wish to integrate this area of learning into their programmes of study.

Planning education for sustainability

The aim of EFS is to develop and bring about immediate improvements in quality of physical and social environments and to promote sustainable living. The objective of EFS is to develop knowledge, values and attitudes, skills necessary for understanding and addressing environmental and development problems.

These goals can be developed through integrating the following key components into geography programmes of study:

Knowledge of environment and development problems

Through geography lessons pupils must learn about the major *environment and development problems* (e.g. climatic change, deforestation, land degradation and desertification, depletion of natural resources, loss of biodiversity, overpopulation, food security, drought, poverty, and urban decay) through *issue-based learning*.

They must be given opportunities to explore how these issues relate to their everyday lives and how their *lifestyle decisions, choices and actions* have an impact on the quality of the physical and social environment. The dependence and *interdependence* of people and places should be a central theme of these studies.

Teachers must promote a holistic outlook, through promoting a *multi-dimensional* (e.g. social, economic, political, historical, cultural, aesthetic) study of environment and development problems at a *variety of scales*.

Investigations into environment and development issues should be closely integrated so that lessons focus on developing closer links between *environmental quality, ecology and socio-economics*. More specifically, pupils need to explore the term *sustainable development* and question what forms of development are desirable and acceptable.

Critical thinking skills

Critical thinking skills are needed to interpret the root causes of environmental problems and to examine personal and political contributions to change. Critical thinking is also required to challenge bias and support rational decision-making.

A number of geographical questions form the basis of critical thinking. *Who makes decisions affecting the quality of the social and physical environment? Why are they made? According to what criteria? Whose interests do they serve? Are long-term consequences considered? Which decisions and choices promote sustainable living? How can these be promoted? What opposition are these likely to encounter?*

In order to answer these questions pupils must embark on the task of critical appraisal. This requires consideration of the different value positions and their perceptions of environment and development issues. Pupils also need to engage in a critical review of their own environmental and political values.

Values education

Geography lessons need to *teach values for sustainable living*, including those of social responsibility, concern for all life forms, harmony with nature, understanding and tolerance of different values, and commitment to work with and for others.

Geography should also *teach about values*, so that pupils develop an awareness of the existence of different value positions and how they influence environmental quality.

Involvement and action

Geography education must involve pupils in real or simulated processes of *environmental decision-making and action*. This involvement is seen as the most effective way of developing the action skills needed to investigate, evaluate and implement solutions to problems.

Geography teaching must challenge pupils on a personal level and engage them in changes towards sustainable lifestyles. At a public level pupils should be encouraged to take responsibility for the care and management of the environment either directly, through participation in practical conservation projects, or indirectly, as informed and concerned adults through the democratic process.

In order to achieve this orientation, teaching and learning strategies which invite participation of the learner are needed. Only participatory learning creates a climate within the classroom which explicitly values and affirms each individual and empowers pupils to exercise responsibility for their own lives and for the environment. It promotes the dynamic qualities of initiative, assertiveness, independence, commitment, readiness to accept responsibility and creativity, all of which are required for constructing a sustainable world. Games, simulations and role-plays as well as class and group discussions are a few of the active learning strategies which can be developed through geography.

Assessing education for sustainability

Assessing progress is critical to ensuring that the aims of sustainability are achieved. However, the issues-based, values-focused characteristics and goals of education for sustainability pose a number of problems for existing models of assessment.

The traditional methods, currently implemented within the National Curriculum, are inappropriate for the task of assessing personal development in this area of learning. The more significant outcomes of EFS, such as the appreciation of the surroundings, understanding and tolerance of different values, are likely to be neglected within a central examination system. Although there is a place for written examinations, alternative approaches to assessment are also necessary for the successful monitoring of its goals. These approaches may include 'process' assessment through dialogue with children and observations of behaviour as well as self-assessment. Achievements in EFS need to be monitored under four of the components previously listed.

Assessment of knowledge of environmental and development problems

Assessing pupils' environmental knowledge and understanding may be simply achieved by testing students on the acquired knowledge through recall as well as through requesting written/oral explanations. Teachers should also assess the pupils capacity to analyse environmental problems and reveal underlying causes and effects, to synthesize factors which influence the physical and social environment, and to evaluate the impact of their own lifestyles on environmental quality.

Assessment of critical thinking skills

The high-order skills of critical thinking are very abstract and difficult to assess. Pupils' ability to answer critical questions and justify their responses can be assessed through discussion or written work. A process-orientated form of assessment is required for monitoring pupils' examination and development of their own environmental and political positions. Self-evaluation can also serve as an important assessment tool.

Assessment of environmental values and attitudes

Alternative assessment procedures must be used to measure attitudes and values since these are difficult to assess via traditional written examinations. Observation is often the best method of assessing achievement in this area. This can be done by keeping records of pupils who participate in conservation projects or belong to environmental groups. Student diaries can be useful for evaluation purposes and may provide information about affective changes students might be experiencing.

Assessment of environmental action

Involvement in real issues is seen as the most effective way of assessing action skills. Environmental action is easier to evaluate through direct observation. The thinking behind the chosen action (or non-action) must also be assessed. This can be done orally or via a written form.

In evaluating action skills, the efficiency (performing with least amount of energy and time) and effectiveness (accomplishment of what was intended) of environmental action must form the basis of the evaluation. Evaluations could monitor development in all six categories of environmental action—negotiation, persuasion, consumerism, political action, legal action, and ecomanagement (Tilbury 1995).

CONCLUSION: TEACHING GEOGRAPHY FOR A SUSTAINABLE WORLD

Why teach geography for a sustainable world? There are sound educational as well as social and environmental reasons for why geography teaching should address issues of sustainability.

Education for sustainability is of intrinsic value to education. It not only contributes to the improvement of the physical and social environment but also to the quality of the educational experience. One of the aims of education as defined by the Education Reform Act is to prepare pupils 'for the opportunities, responsibilities and experiences of adult life' (DES 1988: 2). Today's pupils need opportunities to reflect and act upon the world around them. These pupils will be tomorrow's consumers, voters and decision-makers, ultimately responsible for the development and implementation of environmental policies and practices. EFS is therefore relevant to their current experiences and future responsibilities.

Furthermore, social anxiety over environmental matters makes it vitally important that geographical education addresses this major issue of the time and that through it the potential for future change is established. Otherwise, Orr contends (1992: 145), to 'stand aloof from the decisions about how and whether life will be lived in the twenty-first century . . . would be to miss the Mount Everest issue on the historical topography of our age and condemn ourselves to irrelevance.'

REFERENCES

British Government Panel on Sustainable Development (1995) *First Report*, London: Department of the Environment.

Calder, M. and Smith, R. (1993) 'Introduction to development education', in Fien, J. (1993) *Teaching for a Sustainable World*, Brisbane: Australian Association for Environmental Education.

Curriculum Council for Wales (1990) *Environmental Education*, Advisory Paper 17, Cardiff: CCW.

Department for Education (1995) *Geography in the National Curriculum*, London: HMSO.

Department of Education and Science (1988) *Education Reform Act*, London: HMSO.

Dunlap, R., Gallup, G. and Gallup, A. (1992) *The Health of the Planet Survey*, Princeton: G.H. Gallup International Institute.

Environment Development Education and Training Group (1992) *Good Earth-Keeping Education, Training and Awareness for a Sustainable Future*, London: UNEP-UK.

Huckle, J. (1995) 'The greening of geographical education: a challenge still to be realised', paper presented at the University Department of Education Tutors Conference, Exmouth.

Independent Commission on International Development Issues (ICIDI, 1980) *North–South: A Programme for Survival*, The Brandt Report, London: Pan Books.

IUCN, UNEP, WWF (1991) *Caring for the Earth: A Strategy for Sustainable Living*, Gland: IUCN.

National Curriculum Council (1989) *National Curriculum: Geography Working Group Interim Report*, London: HMSO.

National Curriculum Council (1990) *Environmental Education*, Curriculum Guidance 7, London: NCC.

Orr, D. (1992) *Ecological Literacy: Education and the Transition to a Post-modern World*, Albany: State University of New York Press.

Tilbury, D. (1993) *Environmental Education: Developing a Model for Initial Teacher Education*, Unpublished PhD thesis, University of Cambridge.

Tilbury, D. (1995) 'Environmental education for sustainability: defining the new focus of environmental education in the 1990s', *Environmental Education Research* 1(2):195–212.

UNESCO (1992) *UN Conference on Environment and Development: Agenda 21*, Switzerland: UN.

UNESCO (1995) *Re-orienting Environmental Education for Sustainable Development, Final Report*, Inter-regional Workshop, Athens.

Welsh Office Education Department (WOED) (1995) *Geography in the National Curriculum*, Cardiff: HMSO.

World Commission on Environment and Development (WCED) (1987) *Our Common Future*, The Brundtland Report, Oxford: Oxford University Press.

Chapter 12

Equal opportunity and the teaching of geography

Brian Gonzalez and Elizabeth Gonzalez

> Equal opportunity is about helping all children to fulfil their potential. Teachers are highly concerned when their pupils underachieve and are aware that educational outcomes may be influenced by factors outside the school's control such as pupils' sex or social, cultural or linguistic background.

> Teachers have a major role in preparing young people for adult life; this means life in a multicultural, multilingual Europe which, in its turn, is interdependent with the rest of the world. It is a world in which the roles of men and women are changing and both sexes are likely to have dual responsibilities for home and work.

These two quotations taken from the National Curriculum Council's document *The Whole Curriculum* (NCC 1990: 2–3) encompass the concept of equality of opportunity and define, albeit in general terms, the role that we as geography teachers can assume within the whole curriculum. Equality of opportunity is not only about access to the curriculum for all our students. It is also about content, methodology and relevance to citizenship. Geography, like most subjects in the school curriculum, has had to justify its role and relevance in education. It is only when we closely analyse the forces which are currently affecting our schools and society in general that the question of gender and race in the teaching of the subject assumes an all-encompassing importance.

A geography that 'ignores gender issues is impoverished and incomplete' (Bowley 1992: 349). Similarly, a geography that is racist and not multicultural in its outlook will not 'emphasize the development of tolerance as well as the celebration of differences between cultural groups' (Hacking 1992: 41). Concern over equality of life between the sexes, cultural groups and different parts of the world is fast becoming an important determining factor in the teaching of geography. This is clearly leading to a more critical geography in which controversial issues are investigated and pupils asked for their opinions and strategies for solving them (Hacking 1992).

The aim of this chapter is to highlight some of the basic issues which we, as teachers of geography, need to be aware of and adopt and adapt purposefully in our teaching strategies.

CURRICULUM DEVELOPMENT AND EQUAL OPPORTUNITIES

Education, like politics, is influenced by slogans (Nisbet 1974). In the 1970s words like 'autonomy' and 'accountability' became fashionable. Certain phrases and words influenced policy-making and then faded away. The introduction of the GCSE and the National Curriculum forged a new language. 'Criterion referencing' became fashionable. Pupils have to meet 'targets' as defined by the Education Reform Act of 1988. The National Curriculum defined Attainment Targets as the knowledge, skills and understanding which pupils of different abilities and maturities were expected to achieve by the end of each Key Stage.

A major innovation of the GCSE when it was introduced in the mid-1980s was the adoption of 'national criteria' to determine all syllabuses. Two types of criteria were formulated. The General, which set up the framework for syllabuses and examinations, and the Specific which highlighted in more detail the aims, objectives, content and assessment of all GCSE subjects. The system required that every possible effort should be made to ensure that both syllabuses and examinations were free of 'political, ethnic, gender and other forms of bias' (paragraph 19 of the *General Criteria*). Also, linguistic and cultural diversity had to be taken very much into account.

In *GCSE, A Guide for Teachers* (Secondary Examination Council 1986) the following areas were seen as presenting novel issues for the teaching of geography:

1   The influence on geographical situations of values and attitudes.
2   The relevance of geography to students in a society faced by major issues such as development, use of resources and environmental quality.
3   The contribution of geography to education in a multicultural society.

The question of values and attitudes has become one of the most significant changes. Bias, in gender and race, has become less tolerable and teachers are being asked to consider very closely such concepts as 'values inculcation', 'values analysis' and 'values reasoning'. We have to encourage our students to see themselves, regardless of gender or race, as part of a system in which they can act according to their values and attitudes within a geographical context.

The National Curriculum, that other major educational upheaval of the last decade, also highlighted the importance of values and attitudes. This time, however, it was not to be within the domains of the examination system. Pupils as young as 5 have to be made aware. In 1990, the National

Curriculum Council highlighted a commitment to providing equal oppor-tunities for all pupils and recognized that preparation for life in a multi-cultural society is relevant to all pupils and should permeate every aspect of the education system.

That the National Curriculum got out of hand has been well documented and we as teachers need no reminding of it. It became (some may argue it still is) an over-burdened and over-prescriptive subject-based curriculum. A need to integrate the different components became apparent and the National Curriculum Council proceeded to identify the 'links' essential to the whole curriculum. Five themes were developed: Economic and Indus-trial Understanding, Careers Education and Guidance, Health Education, Education for Citizenship, and Environmental Education. Overlapping of these themes was deemed possible and different subjects were encouraged to encompass them in a purposeful manner. The themes identified the skills required for living in present-day society and the subjects were asked to adapt their traditional content into a relevant framework of education. Within the context of sexism and racism geography has been identified as an important means to achieving the goal of 'tolerance'.

More recently, a revised National Curriculum for geography has been introduced as a result of the Secretary of State for Education's invitation to Sir Ron Dearing to slim down the National Curriculum. Dearing recom-mended a substantial reduction of the volume of material required by law to be taught so as to give greater flexibility to the teachers. The major reduction in content was achieved through the reduction in the number of specified studies of places (Battersby 1995: 58). The Geography Order has become a 'minimal entitlement' from which one can start planning geo-graphy courses (Rawling 1995). Place knowledge and understanding are best developed together with values and attitudes of people, places and environments. Ranger (1995: 67) recommends asking the following ques-tions when choosing places as a strategy for identifying and developing values and attitudes:

- How can the pupils' local area be linked to the chosen place of study?
- How can the pupils' own experiences contribute to the study of the chosen place?
- How will the cultures, religions and history of the chosen place of study be analysed?
- Will the emphasis be on people or places?

Questions such as these initiate the process of developing a broad and balanced geographical curriculum in which, consciously and purposefully, bias in gender and race has no relevance.

PSYCHOLOGICAL BASIS OF GENDER DIFFERENCES IN GEOGRAPHY

Statistics issued by examination boards consistently show that geography as a school discipline is more popular with boys than girls. A commonly held view is that there is a relationship between spatial ability and gender. Roder (1977) concluded that there are fewer females in geography because of an inherent weaker spatial skill when compared to males. The basis for this difference is twofold. First, there are the physiological differences between the sexes and, second, there are the socialization processes experienced by children from a very early age.

Numerous studies into gender-related variations in spatial skills have shown that:

- Cognitive maps of female adolescents are less accurate than those of males.
- Males are better spatial visualizers than females (Brown and Broadway 1981).
- There are differences between individuals in terms of their cognition of urban environments (Moore 1979).
- Gender-based differences in spatial skills follow a developmental pattern.
- Boys outperform girls in the reading of graphs and maps (Bettis 1974).
- There is a relationship between the accuracy of sketch map representation and gender.

Psychological research has shown that, on average, males are more proficient than females in spatial visualization and spatial orientation (Gilmartin and Patton 1984). 'Spatial visualization' refers to the ability to manipulate spatial stimuli mentally whereas 'spatial orientation' is the capacity to understand the arrangements of elements in a pattern. Gilmartin and Patton have suggested two possible explanations for these diferences. First, there are hormonal differences between genders. Male hormones, in particular androgens, can be positively correlated with spatial skills. Tests quoted by the authors show that in 13 to 18 year-old girls spatial scores were lower in more 'feminine' girls and higher in more androgenized or more 'masculine' girls. Second, the effects of brain lateralization should be taken into account. Female behaviour seems to be dominated by the left and males by the right hemispheres. The left is associated with verbal ability and the right with visuo-spatial skills. In a study of functional maturation of cerebral hemispheres, Witelson (1976) concluded that right-hemisphere functional maturity was achieved in males earlier than in females. The tests consisted of 6 to 13 year-old pupils of both sexes being asked to feel pairs of different nonsense shapes and then having to identify the pair felt from a visual display containing the pair along with other shapes. The left hand proved to be more successful in even the youngest boys but not in girls until age 13.

Maccoby and Jackson (1977) identified four basic psychological differences which are important in understanding the variations in geographical ability between gender:

- Women have a superior verbal ability.
- Men have a more aggressive behaviour.
- Men have on the whole higher skills in mathematics.
- Men have higher skills in visuo-spatial tasks.

Another school of thought on the relationship between gender and spatial ability argues that males and females are in essence 'programmed' by society, i.e. that processes of socialization resulting from cultural factors instil in children at a very young age basic skills which either inhibit or enhance specific cognitive styles such as spatial skills and awareness.

Rheinfold and Cook (1975) carried out a study into the contents of the bedrooms of 1 to 6 year-old boys and girls. Not surprisingly, they found that males had significantly and substantially more 'masculine' toys encouraging spatial games and awareness. Boys had vehicles, sports equipment, machines and toys of a military nature. Girls had more 'feminine' toys like dolls, doll's houses and domestic toys. Harper and Sanders (1975) also concluded that boys are more likely than girls to wander from home, to use more space, to seek large areas for exploration and play, and to spend more time playing outdoors. Thus, in many instances, boys will receive more chances, encouragement and training with respect to the acquisition and development of visuo-spatial skills (Harris and Liben 1981). Boys, in general, are more active in their play than girls.

Other researchers have studied the cognitive mapping abilities of childen. Mathews (1984) commented on the difference between the sexes in terms of environmental knowledge. It was established that boys of different ages showed an awareness of places further away from home than girls. Also, the influence of gender expectation by parents and general socialization processes lead to girls having a different perspective of space, and this is clearly demonstrated by exercises relating to mental mapping.

Clearly, then, psychological studies have shown that there are inherent differences in geographical ability between the sexes. Unfortunately, there are few geographical studies into psychology-related processes and many uncertainties can be highlighted. For example, what kinds of spatial abilities are useful for what kinds of geographical tasks? Can the skills identified by the psychologists be learned through instruction and practice? Are there developmental patterns in spatial aptitude which influence geographical abilities? Again, as teachers of geography we need to be made aware of the cognitive factors and processes operating in or missing from our teaching/learning environment. In order to treat our audience equally we need to know where their differences lie.

EQUAL OPPORTUNITY AND ATTITUDES TOWARDS GEOGRAPHY

Studies into the attitudes of pupils towards geography have shown that differences exist between the preferences of boys and girls. A clear indication of this is the number of students from both sexes who opt for GCSE geography. Geography is more popular with boys than girls. Bramwell (1987), in a study of 199 boys and 218 girls in the fourth year of single-sex and mixed-sex comprehensive schools, found that there were significant gender differences in the frequency with which learning difficulties were experienced and in the preferences for different learning activities and topics. The table below shows the learning activities and topics used as the basis of Bramwell's study.

Learning activities used in geography	Topics studied in geography
Writing dictated notes	Physical geography
Copying from blackboard	Weather
Filling in maps and diagrams	Natural environments
Looking at slides	Farming
Watching a video	Transport
Listening to a tape	Industry
Ordnance Survey mapwork	Rural settlements
Drawing maps	Urban settlements
Working from worksheet	Development
Working from textbook	Developed areas
Drawing graphs	
Creative writing and drawing	
Project work	
Group work	
Geographical games	
Role-playing	
Fieldwork	

Significant differences of experience by gender of the following learning activities were identified in the study:

Gender experiencing activity most frequently

Girls	Boys
Writing dictated notes	Creative writing/drawing
Filling in maps and diagrams	Working in a group
Drawing maps	Geographical games
Working from a worksheet	
Working from a textbook	
Drawing graphs	

With regards to preferences, significant differences by gender were experienced in the following activities:

Gender preferring activity

Girls	Boys
Writing dictated notes	Filling in maps/diagrams
Copying from blackboard	Watching a video
Working from a worksheet	Ordnance Survey mapwork
Working from a textbook	Drawing maps
Drawing graphs	
Working in a group	
Geographical games	

Differences in topic preferences also exist. Girls seem to prefer studies of natural environments, farming, rural settlements and the Third World. Boys showed a greater preference for physical geography, transport, industry and the developed areas of the world.

Bramwell's study and some research currently being undertaken by Brian Gonzalez highlight the variety of factors which may have an influence on subject choice. These factors can be divided into four:

- **Personal interactions**
  How well does the pupil get on with the teacher?
  Have the pupil's friends chosen the subject?
  What do their parents think about geography?
- **Perceived relevance**
  How useful is geography for the pupil's chosen career?
- **Subject characteristics**
  What does the pupil think of the work covered by the geography syllabus?
  What is the success rate of geography as an examination subject?
- **School characteristics**
  What are the timetabling constraints?
  What facilities are available?
  How much fieldwork is done?
  With what other subjects is geography included in the options block?

Bramwell found that there were more similarities than differences between the sexes. However, heads of department must make it their role to find out the reasons why students do not opt for the subject.

DEVELOPMENT GEOGRAPHY

The 'geography of welfare' has increasingly gained prominence in the geography curriculum. The introduction of GCSE and the National Curriculum has made students aware of a world of contrasts. Topics such as population dynamics, poverty, unemployment and the existence of rich and poor are highlighted in our schools. Such contrasts led to development education. Binns (1995) points out that development as a thematic study is specifically mentioned only in the Key Stage 3 statutory requirements and that there are many opportunities for introducing development-related issues elsewhere in the curriculum, for example in primary schools with locality studies about places. Pupils, it seems, are experiencing and are being made consciously aware of a multicultural society at all levels.

Development education is not new. In 1975 the United Nations defined it as the concern for issues of human rights, dignity, self-reliance and social justice in both developed and developing countries. The Development Education Association was established in 1993 with the aim of providing understanding of the patterns and processes affecting human living standards. It identified the importance of developing skills in a variety of situations and stressed the following:

- Skills of recognizing personal values and the influences that these may have
- Skills of empathy with people in different situations and within different cultures
- Skills of acquiring information and of critical analysis of the information
- Skills of recognizing the validity of different points of view
- Skills of forming one's own conclusions
- Skills of recognizing the way we relate with the world
- Skills of recognizing possibilities for future action.

Development education, in which geography has a very important role to play, depends very closely upon values and attitudes. It could be argued that it is impossible to teach about other people and their cultures without an active awareness of values and attitudes. Indeed, there is perhaps no such practice as value-free human geography. As teachers of the subject we must acknowledge this and realize that one of our roles as educators is to make our pupils understand the nature of their values and attitudes and their significance to everyday experiences. The fact that they are the result of experiences, such as the culture into which they and their families and friends are born, and that they are fundamental in decision-making, has to play an important role in curriculum planning. The DES, in one of their earlier documents on the geography curriculum for the 11–16 age-group, had stated that pupils could be helped to think about their attitudes and develop values through the content of geography by acquiring information about important issues, diagnosing problems and identifying the values and attitudes of others. Daniels and Sinclair (1985) identified the values and attitudes we should aim to promote in our teaching of geography:

- that all people are of equal value and deserve equality of opportunity;
- that empathy is an essential human quality which needs to be encouraged and fostered;
- that anti-discriminatory policies should be supported and substantiated;
- that exploitation and oppression of persons for any reason should be exposed and openly criticized.

In 1985 the Swann Committee (DES 1985) stressed that teachers and schools had a responsibility to prepare their students for life in a multi-ethnic society. It was of the opinion that initial teacher training courses should assimilate the principle of equal opportunities. Unfortunately, as Tomlinson points out, teacher training is subject to 'hesitancy, indecision, and slowness to respond' (Tomlinson 1989: 135). There is a clear need for recognition of the key role played by geography teachers in preparing pupils for life.

EQUAL OPPORTUNITIES AND RESOURCES

There has been a shift in geographical education from knowledge to understanding of places as well as the increasing role of interdisciplinary consideration of themes such as education for citizenship. Therefore, just as in history where students develop the skills of empathy and critical questioning of sources of information, geography too should foster a more empathetic way of studying equal opportunities and should work towards a genderless and multicultural stance. Geography uses a wide range of resources ranging from textbooks, newspaper and magazine articles, travel brochures, and advertisements to photographs, slides, videos and sound recordings. These bring with them a set of assumptions, values and attitudes based on cultural characteristics (Hicks 1993). One way of identifying bias is to follow a strategy similar to the one outlined by Connolly (1992) and illustrated in Figure 12.1.

Connolly sees the use of such a matrix as a prelude to identifying values and attitudes in resources and as an exercise for both pupils and teachers. A similar exercise was carried out by GEON (Geography and Equal Opportunities Network) and the results, analysed by Connolly, are shown in Table 12.1 (after Connolly 1993). The gender bias of some textbooks published in 1991/2 is very clear.

Evaluation exercises clearly show that selecting resources requires thought and that there are no simple solutions. The information gathered, however, should serve to illustrate their deficiencies and make pupils as well as teachers critically aware of bias. Daniels and Sinclair (1985: 85) found that 'working directly with the materials helped to clarify' their ideas and suggested some key questions that geography teachers should ask about their lesson materials:

Title _____ Publisher: _____ ISBN: _____

(1) AUTHOR(S):		SEX:		EDITION DATE:	

(2) ILLUSTRATIONS	Male only	Female only	Black only	White only	Mixed	Illustrations without any people
Photographs						
Sketches						

(3) ROLE OF PEOPLE IN ILLUSTRATIONS	Male roles	Female roles		White people's roles		Black people's roles
Photographs						
Sketches						

(4) Are the sketches lifelike or stereotyped?

(5) Language use of sex specific terms in general situations (add to list)	He	She	His	Her	Man

(6) ROLE PLAY AND EXERCISES	Male roles	Female roles	White roles	Black roles
	Total	Total	Total	Total

(7) OMISSIONS

(8) WOMEN AS AN IDENTIFIABLE GROUP

(9) How are black people generally depicted as an identifiable group?

(10) Are there any people with physical disabilities shown? In what situations?

Figure 12.1 Book evaluation matrix

Source: Geography, Genderwatch! © Cambridge University Press 1992

Table 12.1 Gender bias of KS3 textbooks published 1991/1992

Textbooks and Publishers	Authors M	F	Photographs Male only	Female only	No people	Visual Images Drawings Male only	Female only	No People
Access to Geography 1 (Oxford University Press)	2	1	16	13	35	5	1	11
Enquiry Geography (Hodder & Stoughton)	2	2	6	3	67	18	10	17
Exploring Geography Local Environment/UK (Hodder & Stoughton)	2	0	14	3	42	12	1	22
Exploring Geography UK within Europe (Hodden & Stoughton)	0	2	3	0	85	4	1	28
Environments (Folens)	1	0	20	4	25	4	3	9
People and Places (Folens)	1	0	3	0	39	34	31	16
Geography Today 1 (Collins)	6	1	30	0	66	7	0	23
People in the EEC (Heinemann)	2	0	8	1	56	4	0	2
People, Water and Weather (Heinemann)	1	1	6	4	36	9	1	20
People and the Land (Heinemann)	2	0	6	11	60	0	2	25
Key Geography – Foundations (Stanley Thornes)								
Jigsaw Pieces (Cambridge University Press)	1	0	19	15	69	10	2	20
World View 1 (Heinemann)	2	0	29	6	149	12	2	1

Source: GEON

- Does it contain bias? If so, of what nature?
- Does it contain stereotyping without qualification?
- Does it present information from different points of view?
- Does it present alternative possibilities and answers with equal emphasis and seriousness?
- Does it describe geographical patterns with reference to the influence of attitudes/values?
- Does it make clear the importance of attitudes to race, religion, colour, sex and status to development in the study area?
- Does it make clear the links between the place and/or issue now and in the past?
- Does it provide enough information for pupils to be able to achieve an informal evaluation of their own and others' understanding, feelings, attitudes and decisions?

For a more comprehensive list of curriculum evaluation questions the section on Equal Opportunities and the National Curriculum by Jane Connolly in Kate Myers' *Genderwatch* is strongly recommended.

CONCLUSION

Equality of opportunity in education is equality of a person's potential. In this brief chapter we have seen, from our experience, that in the context of gender and race the role of the geography teacher is to be critical of bias in resources and methodology. One very important role which we are rapidly developing is to help our students identify and critically evaluate their values and attitudes within a geographical context. The quantitative revolution and emergence of 'economic man' gave geography a status, but it also took from it the human dimension. Human geography and environmental education need not be devoid of feelings.

> In particular, geographical education promotes understanding, tolerance and friendship amongst all nations, racial and religious groups and furthers the activities of the United Nations for the maintenance of peace.
>
> (IGU 1992)

Geography should encourage on the part of the individual 'a readiness to participate in solving problems of their communities, their countries and the world at large' (IGU 1992).

REFERENCES

Battersby, J. (1995) 'Rationale for the revised curriculum', *Teaching Geography* 20(2).
Bettis (1974) in Harris, Liben *et al.*
Binns, A. (1995) 'Geography in Development', *Geography* 80(4).

Bowley, S.R. (1992) 'Feminist geography and the changing curriculum', *Geography* 77(4).

Bramwell, J. (1987) 'Pupils' attitudes towards geography in the lower school: an investigation into gender differences', *Geography* 72(1).

Brown and Broadway (1981) in Harris, Liben *et al.*

Connolly, J. (1992) 'Geography: equal opportunities and the National Curriculum', in Myers, K. *Genderwatch – After the Education Reform Act*, Cambridge University Press.

Connolly, J. (1993) 'Gender-balanced geography: have we got it right yet?', *Teaching Geography* 18(2).

Daniels, A. and Sinclair, S. (1985) *People Before Places*, Development Education Centre.

DES (1985) *Education for All*, The Swann Report, HMSO.

DES (1985) *General Criteria*, HMSO.

DFE (1995) *Geography in the National Curriculum*, HMSO.

Gilmartin, P. and Patton, J. (1984) 'Comparing the sexes on spatial abilities; map-use skills', *Annals of the Association of American Geographers* 74(4).

Hacking, E. (1992) *Geography into Practice*, Longman.

Harper and Sanders (1975) in Harris, Liben *et al.*

Harris, I., Liben, L. *et al.* (1981) *Spatial Representation and Behaviour Across the Life Span*, Academic Press.

Hicks, D. (1993) *Development Education in Geographical Education: Reflection and Action*, Oxford University Press.

IGU (1992) 'International Charter on Geographical Education', *Teaching Geography* 20(2):95–9.

Maccoby and Jackson (1977) in Harris, Liben *et al.*

Mathews, H. (1984) 'Cognitive mapping abilities of young boys and girls', *Geography* 69(4).

Molyneux, F. and Tolley, H. (1988) *Teaching Geography; A Teaching Skills Workbook*, Macmillan.

Moore, P. (1979) in Harris, Liben *et al.*

Myers, K. (1992) *Genderwatch: After the Education Reform Act*, Cambridge University Press.

NCC (1990) *The Whole Curriculum*, National Curriculum Council.

Nisbet, J. (1974) *Curriculum Innovation*, Croom Helm.

Ranger, G. (1995) 'Choosing places', *Teaching Geography* 20(2).

Rawling, E. (1995) 'What's new?', *Teaching Geography* 20(2).

Rheinfold and Cook (1975) in Harris, Liben *et al.*

Roder, J. (1977) in Harris, Liben *et al.*

SEC (1986) *GCSE, A Guide for Teachers*, Open University Press.

Geographical Association (1995) 'International Charter on Geographical Education', *Teaching Geography* 20(2).

Tomlinson, S. (1989) 'Training for Multiculturalism', in V.A. McClelland and V.P. Varma *Advances in Teacher Education*, Routledge Education.

Witelson, G. (1976) in Harris, Liben *et al.*

Part III

Chapter 13

Instructional design

Michael Williams

INTRODUCTION

The focus in the previous section was on curriculum planning and course design, including such issues as scope, sequence, continuity, balance and differentiation. In this section, it moves nearer to the classroom, to aspects of geography teaching and learning in the context of topics and units of work. Just as curriculum design encompasses the totality of the pupil's experience of geography in school, so in instructional design the emphasis is on the translation of a Programme of Study into a series of teaching units made up of classroom lessons and other organized learning experiences. Instructional design is the purposeful and systematic organization of teaching and learning strategies for specific groups of learners.

Underpinning this chapter is a concern with the efficiency of geographical instruction, i.e. with the maximization of learning outcomes for particular groups of pupils. One of the key questions to be addressed has been framed in the general context of effective schooling:

> How is it that two teachers with the same educational background and professional aspirations who are teaching in the same objective school context – in schools with similar levels of resources and community characteristics, for example – can develop substantively different instructional goals, practices and student learning outcomes?
>
> (McLaughlin and Talbert 1990: 1)

Implicit in this quotation is the assumption that geography teachers, as individuals or as members of geography departments, are not autonomous in their curricular and instructional decision-making. They are circumscribed by circumstances within and outside their schools. Clearly, at national level, there are the statutory requirements of the National Curiculum and school inspection in England and Wales. At the local community level, there are distinctive and unique pressures emanating from the socio-cultural and economic characteristics of governing bodies, families and active community groups. Within the schools, there are those characteristics which constitute a school's ethos or climate, including the quality of senior management, the pattern of pupil groupings, the availability of financial and material resources, the morale of the staff as a whole, and the status ascribed to geography. While acknowledging the significance of those contextual factors, we shall discuss the principles of instructional design in a general way on the premise that they can be applied to all school contexts.

In Figure 13.1, the principal features of instructional design are presented as a system. Entering the system are pupils individualized by their personality characteristics. When they enter into the study of a particular geographical unit of work or topic their aptitudes, experience, enthusiasm and interest with regard to that unit of work or topic are of prime importance. The teacher takes account of these in designing the unit of work or topic and he or she will also have distinctive aptitudes, experience, enthusiasm and interest. At the conclusion of the study of a unit of work or topic, the pupils should have achieved a number of learning outcomes and this achievement should be capable of assessment.

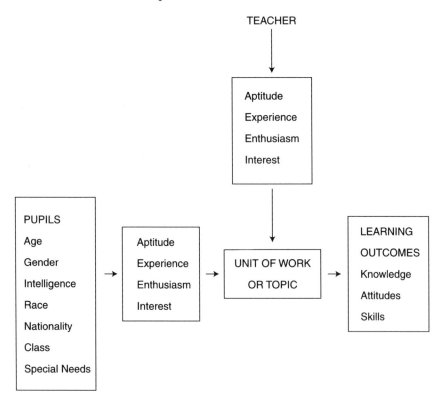

Figure 13.1 Instructional design as a system

INSTRUCTIONAL DESIGN AS A SERIES OF STEPS

Irrespective of particular pupils, teachers or geographical topics, instructional design can be described as a series of steps:

1 Identification of pupil needs.
2 Analysis of the identified needs.
3 Prioritization of pupil needs.
4 Statement of topic aims.
5 Statement of instructional objectives.
6 Specification of geographical content.
7 Arrangement of geographical content.
8 Auditing resources.
9 Planning of teaching and learning strategies.
10 Planning of pupil assessment.
11 Implementation of teaching and learning strategies and pupil assessment.
12 Monitoring the whole instructional design.
13 Formative evaluation.
14 Summative evaluation.

This is a detailed and analytical approach to what is more commonly referred to as preparation, teaching and follow-up. It may also be referred to as a three-stage sequence of pre-instructional, instructional and post-instructional processes. Central principles underpinning the series of steps are the following:

- instructional design is a rational process which follows a logical sequence of steps;
- instructional design is learner-centred: it commences with the needs of the learners;
- instructional design is comprehensive in that it takes into account all those factors which contribute to the achievement of learning outcomes;
- teaching of lessons is only part of the whole instructional process;
- aims are distinguishable from objectives;
- pupil assessment is distinguishable from evaluation.

It is not surprising when one reads both of these lists to find in an expert text on instructional design the comments:

> The job of the teacher in carrying out instruction is highly demanding in terms of time, effort and intellectual challenge. . . . Trying to accomplish both immediate and long-range instructional design, while teaching 20 or 30 students, is simply too big a job for one person, and it can readily lead to the neglect of essential teaching functions.
>
> (Gagne, Briggs and Wager 1992: 5)

Instructional design should, therefore, be perceived as a collaborative exercise. This is important in the context of a particular topic but it is also important in achieving continuity and sequence between topics and in locating a topic alongside others in other subjects. In a primary school context, where geography is commonly located as one component in an integrated, inter-subject topic, the notion of collaboration takes on a different meaning than in the secondary school context where geography is usually taught by specialist teachers.

With these principles in mind we can turn to the list of steps and group these in order to simplify the discussion.

PUPIL NEEDS

It would be easy to suggest that the existence of statutory requirements for geography reduces the amount of attention that should be paid to the needs of particular groups of pupils. However, it is obvious that unless careful attention is paid to the needs of pupils then there is little hope of teachers designing and implementing the appropriate strategies to enable the pupils to achieve the levels defined by the government.

It is commonplace to think of pupils as belonging to three broad groups: gifted, average and those with special needs. This classification is obviously crude and for realistic classroom purposes must be refined. One approach to this is to classify pupils on the basis of the teacher's conceptions of their psychological characteristics. Getzels (1991: 107) proposes four such conceptions: the empty organism, the active organism, the social organism, and the stimulus-seeking organism. The empty organism implies that the pupil receives information from a teacher, responding to stimuli from a teacher who operates a system of rewards and punishments. The active organism is the pupil as an active learner at the centre of the learning process, transforming information communicated by the teacher to his or her own forms of understanding. In the case of the social organism, the emphasis is on the learning of the individual as a member of a group and the learning of the group as a whole. The stimulus-seeking organism is defined by the learner's curiosity and exploratory activity.

This approach has to be placed alongside the changing nature of pupils as they mature. The needs of the developing learner must be taken into account, and in this regard the work of Piaget and his colleagues is usually quoted. Using empirical data, Piaget was able to identify four developmental stages in the formation and handling of concepts from early childhood to adolescence: the sensori-motor stage, pre-operative thought stage, concrete operations stage, and the formal operations stage. While these are not age-specific, they offer helpful guidance when we consider such aspects of geographical learning as spatial ability or graphicacy.

A further approach to needs comes from the nature of the statutory requirements for geography. Because of the division of the Orders into four Key Stages, with each stage having statements of aims and content, there is an assumption that these are appropriate to the needs of pupils in the stages. While the Statutory Orders indicate that attention must be paid to pupils with special educational needs, and, in the Welsh Orders, there is a specific requirement that the contributions of geography to a *curriculum Cymreig* should be addressed, there is no specific reference in the Orders as to how either of these should be accomplished. These considerations are important in the analysis of the geographical needs of a particular group of children.

With regard to the prioritization of needs, this has three parts. First, there is the weighting of the needs in terms of their importance, e.g. that needs directly linked to National Curriculum requirements should have the highest importance. Second, that the needs should be met in an orderly way, e.g. in sequence or through a spiral where meeting particular needs is a recurring issue over time. Third, that the needs of particular groups within a class – gifted, average, special needs in a geographical context – are systematically addressed.

AIMS AND OBJECTIVES

In the opening paragraph to this chapter, it is stated that instructional design is purposeful. This is to affirm the importance of aims for geographical instruction. It would be difficult to argue that the design of units of work or topics was purposeless.

The Statutory Orders make clear what the aims are for geography at each Key Stage. Translating these aims into instructional objectives is not easy. The general principle is that each aim should be associated with specific learning outcomes. The learning outcomes define precisely what are the instructional objectives for a unit or topic. The word 'precisely' is used to highlight the need to think of learning outcomes as 'observable behaviours the learner should possess at the conclusion of instruction' (Popham and Baker 1970: 11). While, superficially, this appears logical and straightforward, it becomes complicated when you consider such learning activities as geographical enquiry, role-play and problem-solving that are arranged precisely because of their open-ended nature. While the learning procedures may be specified in advance, determining the learning outcomes before the activity takes place is altogether more difficult because of the unpredictable ways in which pupils will engage in the tasks. While the teacher will be able to answer the question 'What will they be doing?', the answer to the question 'What will they have learned?' is much more difficult to articulate. For formal pupil assessment purposes, it is essential to define instructional objectives but it is also essential to recognize that not all that is taught should be assessed.

In specifying instructional objectives, the distinction between knowledge and understanding, attitudes and skills is essential. At its simplest, we can quickly recognize the distinction between knowing the precise location of a particular place and understanding where it fits into a spatial pattern, and how we are disposed towards that place, e.g. in terms of its attractiveness, and how we set about locating places on maps or globes. While this example illustrates responses to the 'What?' 'What's it like?' and 'How?' questions, it conceals the complexities beneath.

Bloom and his colleagues (Bloom 1956; Krathwohl *et al.* 1964) provided a taxonomy of objectives for the cognitive (knowledge and understanding) and affective (values and attitudes) domains. Just to illustrate how precise such a taxonomy is, and to highlight the fact that within each taxonomy there is a hierarchy of increasing intellectual accomplishment, we can quote six levels from the cognitive domain: knowledge, comprehension, application, analysis, synthesis, and evaluation. It should be noticed that each of these levels was further subdivided by Bloom and his colleagues into several categories.

In theory a neat line can be drawn from the identification of pupil needs to the specification of aims and objectives for geographical instruction. In reality, there is often confusion between aims and objectives and difficulty in defining and prioritizing instructional objectives. Yet, without some clarity in these processes, the next steps of selecting content and appropriate teaching and learning strategies become problematic.

CONTENT

In England and Wales the specification of the geography content for pupils aged 5–14 is in the Statutory Orders. For older pupils, the content is defined within the syllabuses provided by examinations boards. Here the content is defined in terms of themes, places and skills. The information is presented in a skeletal form with brief statements – often headings and subheadings – for each theme or skill, with examples quoted in order to provide some non-statutory guidance. A teacher in a school will need to decide how best to arrange for the content to be covered, with attention being paid to the following:

- scale: local, regional, national, international, global;
- similar and contrasting environments;
- pupil experience and interests e.g. the background of second generation immigrant pupils;
- newsworthiness of topics;
- school exchanges and overseas visits;
- international links with the local community, e.g. the presence of foreign businesses.

Some of these considerations may be overridden by the content of the textbooks, the availability and accessibility of video and IT resources, and the programmes presented for schools by radio and television companies.

What is essential for geography teachers is to decide, given the specification of content in the Orders, the sequence in which themes, places and skills will be addressed within a Key Stage. In which year, term and weeks will particular themes be covered? To what extent will skills learned in one theme be built upon in the study of other themes? How can a field study experience be designed both to facilitate learning in one or more themes and to form the basis for comparative studies with other locations? How do the knowledge and skills learned in one theme, topic or unit of work contribute to one or more cross-curricular themes or dimensions?

Answers to these questions are provided partly in the findings of a resources audit. What teaching resources – textbooks, maps, atlases, video recording equipment, IT equipment, fieldwork experience, etc. – are available at specific times? If such resources are shared between subject departments or are located in particular places or are available only at certain times of the year, then the planning of content is narrowly constrained.

TEACHING AND LEARNING STRATEGIES

The structure of a unit of work or a topic in geographical instruction can be conceptualized as a journey on which a pupil sets out having attained some learning relevant to the topic and seeks in a determined way to acquire more learning. Gagne, Briggs and Wager (1992: 190) have listed, from a teacher's perspective, the steps in the journey:

1 Gaining attention.
2 Informing the learner of the objectives.
3 Stimulating recall of prerequisite learning.
4 Presenting the stimulus material.
5 Providing learner guidance.
6 Eliciting the performance.
7 Providing feedback about performance correctness.
8 Assessing the performance.
9 Enhancing retention and transfer.

These steps are a response to the geography teacher's question, 'What shall I be doing in a lesson or series of lessons?'. There is a different response to the question also set by the teacher, 'What will the pupils be doing?'. They could be listening, reading, writing, engaged in mapwork or fieldwork, problem-solving or enquiry, individualized deskwork or group work, testing hypotheses or gathering data. Our analysis indicates that whatever the teacher or the pupils are doing is related directly to the anticipated learning outcomes, defined as aims and/or instructional objectives.

What is clear is that different geography teachers employ different methods to achieve the same learning outcomes. To some extent, this is a reflection of teacher characteristics. McLaughlin and Talbert (1990: 3) assert that effective teaching depends on how teachers think and feel about what they do and they identify four central dispositions: motivation, conception of task, enthusiasm over subject-matter, and sense of efficacy. Motivation refers to 'teachers' willingness to expend consistently high effort in their work'. Conception of task 'involves teachers' belief that they are responsible for encouraging individual accomplishment and for responding to a wide range of student needs'. Enthusiasm over subject-matter 'describes teachers' excitement about sharing their subject-area knowledge and discipline with students'. Sense of efficacy 'reveals teachers' belief that they are making a positive difference in their students' growth and capacity'. To these can be added teachers' receptivity to proposals for change in the nature of their subject and the way it is taught, learned, examined and evaluated.

Geography teachers have available a great variety of teaching and learning strategies on which they can draw. They vary from traditional chalk-and-talk lecture presentations through the use of audio-visual resources and the employment of new technologies, to simulations, enquiries and fieldwork.

To highlight the variations within classrooms we can quote the three models described by Tolley and Reynolds (1977) and link these with the psychological perceptions of the learner defined by Getzels, to which we referred earlier.

In the first of these models – the transmission–reception model – the pupil is perceived as an empty organism. The classroom is designed in a formal way to facilitate the transmission of information from the teacher directly to the pupil. Desks are arranged in neat rows, the teacher occupies a dominant position at the front of the class. Information is presented through lectures and chalk-and-talk recitations with the pupil recording the information in a way determined by the teacher. The second model is the behaviour-shaping model in which the teacher is perceived as a provider of sequential, structured learning experiences to pupils as a social group. The emphasis is on pupils recognizing and applying geographical concepts. Third, there is the interactionist model in which the emphasis is on individual pupils and the teacher engaging in enquiry and problem-solving in a collaborative way. The pupil is seen as a social organism and the classroom design and the extended clasroom takes this into account. Classroom furniture is arranged to promote pupil–pupil and teacher–pupil interaction.

MONITORING AND EVALUATION

As we have already emphasized, designing and implementing a topic or unit of work is a purposeful, staged activity. At the outset, it is always difficult to predict precisely how each step will develop and it is thus essential that teachers adapt and modify their carefully prepared plans in the light of prevailing circumstances. In this process of adaptation and modification we can distinguish between monitoring and evaluation.

Monitoring refers to the recording of what takes place as a topic or unit of work is being developed. It is a descriptive activity which takes into account what the pupils did, what the teacher did and how resources were used. Evaluation extends the process of monitoring to emphasize the value that ought to be placed on the various steps in planning and implementing. It is an ongoing process which has both formative aspects, i.e. evaluation at particular points which influences action in the succeeding steps, and summative aspects, i.e. the overall evaluation at the conclusion of a topic or unit of work.

While pupil assessment figures prominently in evaluation, it is only one component of it. Pupil assessment includes only those aspects of learning that can be formally measured. It demonstrates the extent to which instructional objectives have been met. While knowledge, understanding and skills can be measured using various tests, attainment in the affective domain, including values and attitudes, is much more difficult to measure. Evaluation, however, has to take account of such matters as the appropriateness of selected teaching and learning strategies for individuals and groups within a class; the effectiveness of particular social groupings; the quality of learning resources; the timing of learning activities; the motivation guaranteed by content and teaching and learning strategies; and the demands placed upon the teacher's energy and enthusiasm.

Assessment, monitoring and evaluation are important processes in the self-improvement of the teacher. Careful assessment, monitoring and evaluation should lead to changes in the way new topics or units of work are planned and implemented. It should be possible to identify areas where greater efficiency can be achieved, i.e. where learning outcomes can be attained in a shorter period of time with a minimum of distraction for pupils and teachers.

CONCLUSION

In this chapter we have advocated the need for a systematic and purposeful approach to instructional design. The emphasis has been upon the technical aspects of this approach. This is not to suggest that applying the analysis to any teaching context will ensure that a course will be effectively presented. Clearly, there is a great variety of teachers' behaviour and teachers' personality characteristics which will modify any technical design. However, by following the principal steps in instructional design at the pre-instructional, planning stage, teachers should be able to anticipate likely areas of difficulty and prepare possible alternative strategies should difficulties arise. Similarly, at the end of a topic, a unit of work or a course an analytical approach to the evaluation is likely to lead to an improved design for any future instruction.

REFERENCES

Bloom, B.S. (ed.) (1956) *Taxonomy of Educational Objectives, Handbook* I: *Cognitive Domain*, New York: David McKay Co.

Gagne, R.M., Briggs, L.J. and Wager, W.W. (1992) *Principles of Instructional Design*, Fort Worth: Harcourt Brace Jovanovich College Publishers.

Getzels, J.W. (1991) 'Paradigm and practice: on the impact of basic research in education', in D.S. Anderson and B.J. Biddle (eds) *Knowledge for Policy: Improving Education Through Research*, Lewes: Falmer Press.

Krathwohl, D.R., Bloom, B.S. and Masia, B.B. (1964) *Taxonomy of Educational Objectives, Handbook* II: *Affective Domain*, New York: David McKay Co.

McLaughlin, M.W. and Talbert, J.E. (1990) 'The contexts in question: the secondary school workplace', in M.W. McLaughlin, J.E. Talbert and N. Bascia (eds) *The Contexts of Teaching in Secondary Schools: Teachers' Realities*, New York: Teachers College Press.

Piaget, J. and Inhelder, B. (1969) *The Psychology of the Child*. London: Routledge and Kegan Paul.

Popham, W.J. and Baker, E.I. (1970) *Systematic Instruction*, Englewood Cliffs, NJ: Prentice-Hall.

Tolley, H. and Reynolds, J.B. (1977) *Geography 14–18: A Handbook of School-based Curriculum Development*, Basingstoke: Macmillan Education.

Chapter 14

Cognitive acceleration in geographical education

David Leat

INTRODUCTION

In the schools of England and Wales there are many really hard-working and exciting secondary school geography teachers, producing high-quality teaching materials and stimulating their pupils. They use innovative teaching methods, going well beyond normal expectations. Nevertheless, I would argue that there is a particularly serious problem in some geography teaching. Essentially, there is too much concern with teaching and not enough with learning, too much emphasis on substantive aspects of geography and not enough on the intellectual development of pupils.

On the surface, the continuing improvement in General Certificate of Secondary Education (GCSE) results would tend to indicate that my argument is wrong. If there is a problem, what are the symptoms? First, although I may harbour some doubts about the OFSTED (Office for Standards in Education) school inspection process, a report from the Chief Inspector of Schools on the teaching of geography (OFSTED 1995), based on a large sample of English schools, paints a worrying picture. It is reported that the quality of teaching was good or better in only 42 per cent of lessons. Video evidence of geography teaching that inspectors judge as satisfactory leads one to question the figure of 17 per cent that inspectors regarded as less than satisfactory. Nearly all lessons ought to be good with only an occasional lapse into the satisfactory. Some of the weaknesses detected are fundamental: challenge, pace and motivation in lessons were often unsatisfactory, weak subject knowledge, over-reliance on textbooks, undemanding activities and insufficient attention to real places and particular circumstances were common.

Second, one can raise doubts about the quality of textbooks that are currently popular. The uncertainty surrounding the introduction of the National Curriculum and its associated assessment procedures had a natural consequence in a desire among teachers to find a safety net: a series of textbooks that would support them through a period of substantial change. Geography is often taught in secondary schools by non-specialists, frequently over-burdened senior managers, especially in Key Stage 3 (KS3), and they often want a book that can be picked off the shelf. Books written to be virtually 'teacher-proof ', requiring minimal skilled intervention by the teacher, do not increase teacher professionalism and actually serve to encourage the creation of an unspoken pact in which teachers demand little, for which, in return, the pupils do not misbehave.

Finally, many pupils get low grades at GCSE and some who are entered for the examination fail to get any grade at all. While it is unfair to blame the individual teacher, or indeed the community of teachers, it does represent a collective failure by the prevailing educational system: eleven years of compulsory education should not leave pupils with GCSE grades D, E, F and G unless they have serious learning difficulties. An analysis by the Avery Hill Project team of pupils' examination papers in the Avery Hill GCSE (Midland Examinations Group/Welsh Joint Education Committee) showed that approximately 40 per cent of candidates gained no marks on the case-study element of questions in the 1990 structured questions paper (Battersby, Webster and Younger 1995). While lamenting this evidence, one must applaud the boards for undertaking the analysis.

ANOTHER APPROACH

To generalize, perhaps grossly, curriculum planning and development have tended to proceed on the assumption that differences in ability are irremediable and that therefore a specific curriculum for the less able has to be devised. Thus, we have setting and streaming, selective schools, tensions between academic and vocational education and a concern for summative assessment that concentrates on sorting the sheep from the goats. This is a conservative (small 'c') approach that assumes that intelligence, whatever that may be, is fixed. In my twelve years as a schoolteacher I worked largely on that assumption! One adapted the curriculum to fit the pupils so that they could cope easily with it.

However, there is another perspective that can make pupils, teaching and schools look very different indeed. This view is underpinned by substantially different assumptions – that intelligence is not fixed and can be developed, and that the curriculum for lower-achieving pupils should be aimed at changing the characteristics of the learners, so that they can enter into the mainstream curriculum experienced by the rest of the school population. This is a very value-laden view, but there is a growing body of evidence that provides some substantiation for it. It is also clear, though, that there are substantial barriers at teacher, school and government policy levels to implementing this alternative view.

By way of a brief summary, the strongest evidence for the success of the 'changing the pupil' approach comes from the Cognitive Acceleration in Science Education project (CASE). There is evidence that CASE materials, when used appropriately in years 7 and 8, or 8 and 9, improve GCSE results in science, mathematics and English two or three years later. The other thinking skills programmes that are used in British schools are Somerset Thinking Skills, Instrumental Enrichment, Philosophy for Children, and CoRT (Cognitive Research Trust) Thinking Skills. For both Instrumental Enrichment and Philosophy for Children there is good evidence to demonstrate gains in achievement and motivation where the programmes are implemented well. A useful summary of the programmes, their theoretical underpinnings and the research evidence is provided by Adey and Shayer (1994).

COGNITIVE ACCELERATION IN SCHOOL GEOGRAPHY

Since 1992 I have been working with the assistance of some outstanding former University of Newcastle PGCE students and local geography teachers to develop a geography curriculum that teaches thinking. This work and the group involved in it have come to be called Thinking Through Geography (TTG). We have drawn heavily on the CASE model, but have made some adaptations. Using various definitions of thinking (Nickerson, Perkins and Smith 1985) TTG has set three broad aims:

- to devise adaptable strategies and curriculum materials that make geography lessons more stimulating and challenging;
- to help pupils understand some fundamental concepts in geography in an explicit way so that these can be transferred to new contexts;
- to aid the intellectual development of pupils so that they can handle more complex information and achieve greater academic success.

We have developed more than twenty strategies and six units for KS3 and, in the process, identified and clarified a number of principles for curriculum design and teaching. These principles are briefly described below and further elaborated in the teaching example.

Constructivism

Constructivists argue that we all learn largely through the framework of what we already know (Driver 1983). New information will be understood only if it can be interpreted through existing knowledge structures. An important principle, therefore, is getting pupils to access their existing knowledge or to provide concrete experiences that will serve as the framework for their understanding of a topic or issue. It is well understood that pupils are assisted in their understanding of, for example, condensation by reference to breathing on cold window-panes, but it is less well appreciated that their understanding of conflict in National Parks can be assisted by reference to conflict and its resolution within families.

Challenge

The failure of most geography textbooks and much geography teaching is that they fail to challenge pupils. The pupils are given work that they can easily do (busywork); there is an unwritten contract between some classes and teachers: easy work in return for no trouble. Challenge, or work that makes you really think, is essential to intellectual development. The challenge may sometimes take the form of cognitive conflict, whereby pupils' existing understanding is established and then challenged by new experience or evidence. In many instances the challenge is provided by one of the strategies invented, gathered, developed and widely tested by the TTG. Examples include concept mapping, who/what/where/why/when, classifying, speaking graphs, relational diagrams, and reading photographs. Many of the activities deliberately include some ambiguity and an important part of many tasks is the process through which pupils clarify the task.

Talk between pupils and between teachers and pupils

Talk is a prerequisite of much learning and many of the activities are designed to be undertaken by groups. This emphasis on language and group work provides one of the pillars of differentiation in the materials. This will be familiar ground to teachers who have used materials from Development Education Centres and Action Aid. Attention has to be given by teachers to creating an environment in which pupils are encouraged to give their views and ideas and to be taken seriously as conversational partners. (For a fuller discussion, see Wells 1987.)

Concept elaboration

School geography revolves around a relatively small number of key concepts. The materials and teaching style make these concepts very visible and potentially transferable, facilitating their elaboration over time. Examples include planning, systems and causation.

Debriefing

The materials provide learning experiences. Within this context the role of the teacher changes. Teachers encourage pupils to explain their work, help them to understand the significance of what they have done, and put names to the reasoning patterns that they develop. This can be likened to providing pupils with a filing system to help them to retrieve knowledge, concepts and ideas.

Metacognition

This is becoming an over-used term that can be taken simply to mean an awareness of one's own thinking. The aim, through teachers' debriefing, is for pupils to be able to recognize types of problems or situations and select and apply appropriate strategies or reasoning patterns. More broadly, however, it may be conceptualized as making thinking, or 'how you tackled a problem', a legitimate and valued focus for discussion within the class. In this way pupils move towards being autonomous learners (Brown 1987).

Transfer

Once a strategy, concept or reasoning pattern has been established it is necessary to compare it against other contexts in geography, other subjects or everyday life so as to encourage transfer. To give a very simple example, after an activity in which pupils have been making decisions, there is an opportunity for the teacher to introduce the word 'factor' as something that influences decisions, as part of the debriefing process, and they can use the example of the factors that influence where people go for holidays as a context from everyday life. (For a fuller discussion see Perkins and Salomon 1988.)

Appealing to all the senses

We are becoming increasingly aware of the need to develop pictorial, symbolic, photographic, concrete and even aural resources to appeal to those for whom text is a barrier. At present, olfactory resources have defeated us, but they remain a challenge.

A WORKED EXAMPLE

Flooding is a familiar topic in KS3. The Programmes of Study (Department for Education 1995) specify that pupils should be taught 'the causes and effects of river floods and how people respond to and seek to control the flood hazard'.

Phase 1

Imagine that your home gets flooded to a depth of two feet or 60 cm.

1 Make a list of all the damage that might be done by the water, both inside and outside the house.
2 If the flooding lasts on and off for a week, what further problems might be created for you and the rest of your family, especially if your neighbourhood is flooded?

3 If you have an hours warning, what could your family do to reduce the damage and problems caused by the flood? Who might you need to contact for help?

4 What would you expect the emergency services, council, government and public utilities to be doing to help?

Commentary

This homework is employing a constructivist approach because it is drawing upon pupils' knowledge of their own homes as a starting-point. They would be encouraged to crawl around on their hands and knees to see what is below the 60 cm mark. They could be encouraged to talk to their parent(s)/guardian(s) about the difficulties that might ensue and what help could be expected. Disbelief has to be suspended by those who live in blocks of flats or on hills!

Phase 2

At the start of the next lesson the pupils would be asked to form groups of between two and four members to pool their data. A time-limit of five to ten minutes needs to be set. Pupils are then asked to generate some categories of action for 'How people respond to and seek to control the flood hazard'. This could be framed as 'Look at all the information that you have got. Try to put it into groups of things that people do to reduce, escape from, repair and prevent damage from floods'. Depending on the pupil group, the teacher may have to do some preparatory work on the notion of categorizing, but most KS3 groups will find this accessible.

Commentary

The talk between pupils is crucial at this stage as pupils, sometimes clumsily, extend their understanding of the possible effects of floods and the human response. Pupils are talking themselves into meaning. Furthermore, the classifying activity is challenging, there is no obvious answer and it is not something that they are routinely asked to do. Importantly, however, they are still working from their own knowledge base: no new content has been introduced by the teacher yet.

Phase 3

The teacher now asks one group, perhaps not the most able, to outline their categories. He or she then calls on another group who may have a somewhat different grouping and gradually encourages the class to consider whether any improvements can be made, but without giving what they consider to be the best or right answer. The types of category generated are diverse, but one can expect some of the following: moving goods and people, emergency rescue, repair services, community (friends, family and neighbours) action, financial assistance, local council services, and flood prevention. Following this, the pupils are then presented with an extended piece of text on the floods which affected the village of Singleton in southern England in January 1994. The piece focuses on the experiences over one week of a couple whose home was flooded. The pupils are asked whether their categories fit the evidence of the human response in this case.

Commentary

Here is a further opportunity for challenge. Do the categories fit or do they need amending? It is important that the teacher creates an atmosphere in which it is acceptable and even desirable to change one's ideas by positively reinforcing those who make some amendment. Debriefing is another principle that surfaces here as the teacher tries to draw out extended answers without trying to impose a teacher version.

Phase 4

The scale and context are now shifted radically to Bangladesh, a developing economy sorely troubled by floods. A traditional view might suggest that several weeks need to be spent giving a background geography to Bangladesh. In this case, it is considered more appropriate to be concise. Atlases can be used to locate Bangladesh and identify the main rivers and their source in the Himalayas, whose snow-melt and rainfall plays such a large part in the regime of the rivers. It may be sufficient to tell pupils that Bangladesh is a very poor country, where the majority of the people live at very high density in rural areas, in a largely subsistence economy. Whatever decision is reached, the next task for the pupils is: 'For a flood of a similar size to the Singleton flood, will Bangladesh or Britain be worse affected?' Pupils are encouraged to use their categories as a basis for this difficult comparison.

Commentary

Here is a further opportunity for challenge as the pupils measure the rigour of their categories in the new context and struggle with the evaluation of the differential impact of flooding on different societies. There is a strong values dimension present as assumptions about Britain and Bangladesh are exposed. The stark difficulty facing them is that there is no clear answer. The Bangladeshis perhaps have less to lose in physical terms, but does their smaller capital base make them more vulnerable and is the relative value greater? Are they used to such disasters and take them as a matter of course? Are the British more vulnerable because our technological society is thrown out of synchrony by the loss of power supplies and piped water? Which society recovers more easily? Furthermore, pupils are asked to consider whether they wish to adapt or change their categories. It is very encouraging when pupils do change their categories as it is a positive marker that cognitive conflict has taken place as a result of some serious thinking. Obviously, talk between pupils has been important again.

Phase 5

Finally, the teacher has the task of encouraging the pupils to see that their categories have a wider relevance. Do the categories fit the human response to other natural hazards such as earthquakes, tropical storms, droughts and fires? Do they need any further amendment? Do they perhaps fit domestic disasters such as car crashes and burglaries?

Commentary

The teacher is bridging the outcomes of this activity to other contexts in debriefing the pupils at the end of the activity, drawing from their categories a framework that helps them understand planning in the context of hazards, i.e. that planning can be undertaken by individuals, organizations and governments and that some of this planning relates to prevention and some to dealing with the aftermath (pupils' versions may vary from this). They may also start to address prediction. They are beginning to put flesh on some of the characteristics of planning and therefore to understand the concept better. If the shape of their thinking seems valuable in other circumstances, then, in the view of the pupils themselves, thinking about thinking may begin to look like a rewarding activity. When one begins to think consciously about thinking then one is entering the state of meta-cognitive awareness. In this state, transfer of learning from one context to another without external assistance becomes more probable, especially as the teacher has introduced other contexts – earthquakes, droughts and even car crashes – to which the new learning can be applied.

It is important to realize that these materials and tasks ask for substantial changes in thinking and classroom behaviour from teachers. We, TTG members, do not find this change easy and, for example, we are at an early stage in developing our debriefing skills. The kernel of the change is in the pattern of interaction (discourse) in the classroom as open questions become more common, pupils are allowed to take the initiative, and the teacher is no longer the sole arbiter of correctness. Moreover, subject-matter shifts in importance: it is still crucial but it becomes more the means to the end rather than the end itself. Pupils' intellectual and social development have become the prime focus.

INTELLECTUAL DEVELOPMENT AND PERFORMANCE IN GEOGRAPHY

Some pupils are better at geography than others. Some of this variation is accounted for by interest, motivation and quality of teaching, but much of it must be attributed to intellectual development. Piaget's description of stages of development (Piaget and Inhelder 1969) identified concrete operations and formal operations. Formal operational thinkers have substantial and important advantages in dealing with school-work: they can deal with (operate on) the relationships between more than two variables, they can formulate hypotheses, and they can synthesize apparently unconnected information. One needs to think about the implications of this for GCSE geography teaching. Some tasks that pupils are set are impossible for them because of their level of intellectual development.

It is helpful to be more specific about performance in geography. To clarify this, I have analysed the difference in quality in the work of pupils, across the ability range from a number of schools, in a common task. This task involved giving pupils thirty pieces of information on separate cards about the Kobe earthquake that occurred in Japan in 1994, which not only provide a background to the causes of the disaster but also give a strong narrative thread concerning the members of a particular family, the Endos. The pupils were asked why one of them dies and the other survives. It is a very open task, initially tackled as a group activity and later as an individual written task.

Three clear levels emerged with some exceptional performance beyond the range at both ends.

Level A

The written response consists largely of statements from the cards, with little apparent sequencing. There may be some rudimentary linkage and some inference – going beyond the given data – especially in the case of the named characters. The meaning or implication of many data items is not clear from their use for they are frequently just copies. There may be some misinterpretation of the data items.

Level B

The significant difference at this level is that the linkage between the information is generally good; there is some sequencing and direction to the narrative. Words and phrases, such as 'because', 'so', 'then', 'which meant', and 'this caused', become more frequent, indicating that one piece of data is linked to another and relationships are being understood. Quantification and qualification begin to appear, making the explanation more specific and detailed. However, the narrative is largely at the level of the trigger or more superficial causes of the death and destruction: the earthquake struck; the construction of the house was inadequate; the emergency services had problems; and there were many fires. Some misinterpretation of the data is to be expected.

Level C

At this level pupils' answers are more specific, more detail drawn from their pupils' geographical knowledge is given, and misinterpretations are less common. Second, there are more frequent generalizations as pupils begin to go beyond sequencing of information to group data together to isolate contributory background factors such as the lack of preparaton induced by a perception of low risk, rather than giving a narrative. There is more inference, going beyond the given data, and speculation, indicating that they are making more connections with their existing knowledge. They thus demonstrate understanding.

These differences not only provide a framework of assessment, they also signal the need for a certain approach to curriculum development. The level C pupils are those likely to get grades A and B at GCSE, so more pupils ought to be operating at this level. It is fairly certain that there would be a strong correlation between the levels obtained in this task and the Piagetian levels and between both of these and eventual GCSE results. (For more on intellectual levels and levels of outcome in pupils' work, see Biggs and Collis 1982.)

CONCLUSION

The argument in this chapter is that a geography curriculum developed on the principles outlined above and using procedures like those in the worked example has a far greater chance of bringing pupils to perform at level C than the sterility that characterizes many textbook series and classrooms observed in OFSTED inspections. The alternative model presented here is more likely to equip pupils to handle complex information and relationships, tackle challenging tasks and transfer learning to new contexts. It is also more likely to keep them interested. Some things are excusable in education, but boring pupils is not one of them.

REFERENCES

Adey, P. and Shayer, M. (1994) *Really Raising Standards*, London: Routledge.

Battersby, J., Webster, A. and Younger, M. (1995) *The Case Study in GCSE Geography: Experiences from the Avery Hill Project*, Cardiff: Welsh Joint Education Committee.

Biggs, J. and Collis, K. (1982) *Evaluating the Quality of Learning: the SOLO Taxonomy*, New York: Academic Press.

Brown, A.L. (1987) 'Metacognition, executive control, self regulation and other more mysterious mechanisms', in Weinhart, Franz, Kluwe, and Rainer (eds) *Metacognition, Motivation and Understanding*, London: Lawrence Erlbaum Associates.

Department for Education (1995) *Geography in the National Curriculum*, London: HMSO.

Driver, R. (1983) *The Pupil as Scientist?*, Milton Keynes: Open University Press.

Nickerson, R.S., Perkins, D.N. and Smith, E.E. (1985) *The Teaching of Thinking*, Hillsdale, NJ: Lawrence Erlbaum Associates.

Office for Standards in Education (1995) *Geography: a Review of Inspection Findings 1993/94*, London: HMSO.

Perkins, D.N. and Salomon, G. (1988) 'Teaching for transfer', *Educational Leadership* 46:22–32.

Piaget, J. and Inhelder, B. (1969) *The Psychology of the Child*, London: Routledge and Kegan Paul.

Wells, G. (1987) *The Meaning Makers: Children Learning Language and Using Language to Learn*, Cambridge: Cambridge University Press.

Chapter 15

Language and learning in geography

Graham Butt

INTRODUCTION

The importance of geography teachers gaining an understanding of how the use of language can affect the learning of their subject is undeniable. Language provides the medium for learning geography in every classroom and should therefore be a major consideration in the planning and preparation of lessons.

The term 'language' is perhaps deceptively straightforward at first glance. However, it encompasses a huge variety of talk, reading and writing that children undertake; the relationship between these activities and the process of learning; and the nature of communication between the teacher and the learner. The action of learning is closely associated with that of comprehending and using different forms of language. All teaching methods and materials used by the geography teacher therefore have important implications for language and understanding.

Research into the use of language specifically within the geography classroom is somewhat piecemeal, although valuable contributions have been made by Williams (1981), Hull (1985), Slater (1989) and Carter (1991). Nonetheless there is a considerable amount of literature exploring the relationship between language and learning (Piaget 1959; Vygotsky 1962; Chomsky 1968, etc.) as well as a major report – the Bullock Report (DES 1975) – which for a time stimulated a variety of subject specialists to explore the ways in which both teachers and children used language in the classroom. The inter-relatedness of language and learning, and the effects of the use of language on both conceptual development and the learning process, were major considerations of much of the work carried out. Unfortunately the impetus for these 'Language Across the Curriculum' studies did not continue after the late 1970s, leaving many of the issues surrounding talking, writing, reading and learning in geography largely unexplored. The role of language in the process of learning in geography is therefore widely acknowledged, but not fully investigated.

Recently the Language in the National Curriculum (LINC) report produced materials based on existing good practice in the use of language, but was suppressed by the government for not fully emphasizing the importance of grammar in pupils' work.

Geography teachers must be aware of the importance of their role in guiding the form and function of language used within the classroom and the impact this has on children's learning. Slater (1989: 109) carefully outlines the two distinct functions of language use in geography lessons as being 'to communicate what has been learned and is known', as well as being 'part of the *activity* of learning'. The distinction between the two functions is important, although often confused or conflated. Recently there has been a greater focus on the latter, i.e. 'talking and writing to learn'.

TALK WITHIN THE GEOGRAPHY CLASSROOM

Casual observation soon confirms the way in which teacher talk dominates the geography classroom. Teachers tend to talk much more than pupils during each lesson and closely control the amount of talking in which pupils are allowed to engage. Most children become quickly aware of the times which the teacher considers to be appropriate for talking, the acceptable content for discussions and the length of time they are permitted to talk. Very rarely are pupils able to negotiate what is talked about: the teacher controls the process and creates the rules by which communication takes place.

The teacher is in a very powerful position to direct how talking is used to help children learn. This 'gatekeeping' role can either be performed to the benefit of children's learning – if the teacher encourages a wide range of different types of talk – or to its detriment – if the teacher totally dominates what is said in the classroom. It is important that children are enthused and encouraged by what the teacher says, but this is only one part of the language and learning process. Evidence suggests that children must themselves engage in talking about geography, as well as listening, if they are to understand fully the subject's concepts and terminology.

Additionally, pupils often associate language forms used by the teacher with 'assessment', rather than as a part of the process of facilitating learning. Many geography classrooms exist where closed oral 'question and answer' sessions directed by the teacher are merely:

> guessing game(s) whereby the teacher has the knowledge, and tries through questioning to extract the right answers from the pupil. They in turn reach towards the preferred response, the correct answer. Alternatively they adopt a variety of strategies to keep their heads below the parapet.
>
> (Carter 1991: 1)

Here, talk, in the form of question and answer, can actually restrict much of the learning process. Such activities probably do not involve the majority of

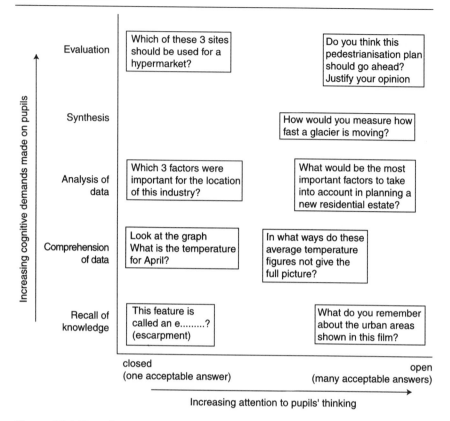

Figure 15.1 Two dimensions of questioning
Source: Roberts 1986: 69

children in the class and those that do participate are often not learning in the most profitable ways. Guessing the right answer represents only a very limited representation of how talking can enhance learning!

Roberts (1986) refers to these two dimensions of questioning by highlighting the type of thinking that different questions entail, and considering whether the questions posed are either open or closed. This is clarified by the above diagram (Fig. 15.1).

A number of important points are raised by this diagram. The 'y' axis shows the increasing cognitive demands made upon pupils – most questions that teachers ask actually fall into the lowest categories on this axis, consisting of recalling knowledge or comprehending data. Few of the questions that teachers ask tend to 'stretch' pupils into higher orders of thinking involving synthesis and evaluation. The implicit message this may give to children is that being able to remember facts in geography lessons is more important than working things out.

	Question type	Explanation
1	a data recall question	Requires the pupil to remember facts, information without putting the information to use. 'What are the main crops in this country?'
2	a naming question	Asks the pupil simply to name an event, process, phenomenon without showing insight into how it is linked to other factors. 'What do we call this process of coastal deposition?'
3	an observation question	Asks pupils to describe what they see without attempting to explain it. 'What happened when the soil dried?'
4	a control question	Involves the use of questions to modify pupils' behaviour rather than their learning. 'Will you sit down, John?'
5	a pseudo-question	Is constructed to appear that the teacher will accept more than one response, but in fact s/he has clearly made up his/her mind that this is not so. 'Is this an integrated railway network, then?'
6	a speculative question	Asks pupils to speculate about the outcome of an hypothetical situation. 'Imagine a world without trees, how would this affect our lives?'
7	a reasoning question	Asks pupils to give reasons why certain things do or do not happen. 'What motivates these people to live so near a volcano?'
8	an evaluation question	Is one which makes a pupil weigh up the pros and cons of a situation or argument. 'How strong is the case for a bypass round this village?'
9	a problem-solving question	Asks pupils to construct ways of finding out answers to questions. 'How can we measure the speed of the river here and compare it with lower down?'

Figure 15.2 Analyses of questions
Source: Carter 1991: 4

The 'x' axis represents the extent to which pupils consider a range of possible answers in their attempts to respond 'successfully' to the teacher's question. If the question is closed there is probably only one right answer, but if it is open a greater degree of thinking about a range of possible answers should occur. Most questions asked by teachers are of the closed recall type, essentially asking children to tell the teacher what is already known, rather than attempting to work towards new understandings.

This idea is taken further by Carter (1991) who lists a variety of question types starting with closed recall questions and ending with more open evaluative and problem solving ones (Fig. 15.2).

The more open the questions become, the more likely it is that the answers given by pupils will be tentative and exploratory, in itself evidence that new learning is occurring. Some teachers may feel threatened by this as these responses often deviate from the 'known' and 'expected' and possibly create a potential loss of academic control.

An important element of all oral question and answer within the classroom is the teacher's intention. Is it to explore concepts, ideas and thoughts and engage in supported, but often tentative, thinking to create new learning (often by using open questions)? Or is it to repeat what the teacher already knows along a rigidly determined pathway? The former approach may liberate pupils' thinking, the latter restricts it to the teacher's predetermined route. I would suggest that a balance of both is required within the geography classroom.

Marsden (1995: 94) helpfully lists a variety of factors which he considers illustrate good questioning:

- asking questions fluently and precisely;
- gearing questions to the student's state of readiness;
- involving a wide range of students in the question and answer process;
- focusing questions on a wide range of intellectual skills, and not just on recall;
- asking probing questions;
- not accepting each answer as of equal validity, though sensitively;
- redirecting questioning to allow accurate and relevant answers to emerge;
- using open-ended as well as closed questions so that creative thought and value judgements are invited.

Even when the teacher receives the 'right' answer to a recall question, this should not simply be taken as evidence that a pupil (or indeed the whole class) fully understands the concepts surrounding the response. For example, many pupils may know that the central area of large cities in the developed world is referred to as the 'CBD', but fewer may appreciate that this actually stands for 'central business district', and fewer still may be capable of providing an acceptable definition of its land uses, activities and *raison d'être*.

GROUP WORK AND LANGUAGE

Giving children the opportunities to discuss their own ideas in geography lessons is therefore important if effective learning is to take place. Whole-class teaching rarely gives each child the chance to talk. In many schools there is now a realization that active and pupil-centred styles of teaching and learning are often the best ways of promoting such talk, either as a part of group work, or in role-plays, simulations or decision-making exercises.

Many geography teachers are understandably nervous about allowing pupils too many opportunities to talk. They may fear a potential loss of control, or may simply be unsure about whether pupils will actually discuss what they have been asked to. These are natural concerns, for handing over learning activities to children is not always easy. However, unless such a transference occurs children will not learn for themselves. Establishing effective discussion in groups takes time. Some children find it difficult to take responsibility for their own learning and initially their work may be hesitant and uncertain. Time pressure is a constant concern for teachers and there may be a temptation not to pursue group work, especially if the initial results appear to be both messy and complex.

Research evidence suggests that pupils actually engage in higher-order thinking when discussing questions or problems in groups. As Slater confirms, 'Through talk, children clarify their ideas, come to realise what they do not understand and yet work through what they do know to make new connections' (1989: 111). If the discussion tasks are clearly set, the duration of the group work firmly established, reporting back procedures clarified, and teacher interventions timed correctly, the results can be impressive.

Group work has the added advantage of giving all children the chance of saying something in class. It also helps them to develop their social skills and to take greater control of their own learning. Handling group work requires a deft, supportive and sensitive touch from the teacher, who must appreciate when to intervene and when to stand back. Over-enthusiastic interventions often take the initiative away from the pupils, who should be developing an understanding of their roles and responsibilities in maintaining discussions and completing set tasks.

What has become clear is that teachers who have a restrictive and dominant teaching style, often involving a lot of traditional 'chalk and talk', impair their pupils' learning and concept development through restricting pupil talk. The importance of teacher control is not denied, but there must be opportunities for pupils to advance their learning through discussion.

WRITING

In examining the learning associated with writing it is first necessary to understand the different forms that both talking and writing can take – namely transactional, expressive and poetic. The transactional form is the one most commonly evident in geography lessons, being used to convey factual information, express ideas and concepts, and record facts in an ordered and logical sequence. Expressive forms of writing (or talking) are more personal and exploratory, what Slater refers to as 'thinking aloud on paper' (1989: 112). They reveal what the writer feels or believes, and are not inhibited by the more formal and structured patterns regularly seen in the transactional mode. Importantly, expressive language often represents the first stages of exploring new ideas and concepts that have not yet been fully clarified in the writer's mind. Poetic forms are similar to expressive, with words being arranged to provide a pleasing format for writer and reader, often involving metaphorical or figurative use of language.

Transactional language dominates the geography classroom. Teachers regularly engage in transactional writing and talking in a form that is clearly structured, ordered and professional. The purpose of using this type of language is clear – it is efficient in conveying information and 'getting things done'. Teachers also expect children to use transactional language when addressing them both orally and in writing, but often do not appreciate the steps that children must go through to produce such language successfully. The insistence upon transactional language can actually restrict the learning process:

> The demand for impersonal, unexpressive writing can actively inhibit learning because it isolates that which is to be learned from the vital learning process – that of making links between what is already known and the new information. It is through the tentative, inarticulate, hesitant, backward- and forward-moving, expressive mode that connections and links between old and new knowledge can be made. Then a student may be ready to set the understanding down in a formal transactional mode.
>
> (Slater 1983: 113)

Or:

> The demand for transactional writing in schools is ceaseless, but expressive language with all its vitality and richness is the only possible soil from which it can grow.
>
> (Rosen 1975: 190)

Geography demands transactional writing because of the very nature of the subject, but it must be realized that children have problems in producing such writing. Merely copying notes from the teacher, or filling missing words into gaps in a worksheet, does produce a form of transactional writing but may not help the pupil learn from the writing experience.

Research has recently moved our thinking forward to consider more closely the audiences which should receive these forms of writing, and the purposes for which they were written. Closely associated with this is the concept of genres which have been debated among certain English teachers in Australia and England.

AUDIENCE

Expressive language can be encouraged by getting children to write for (or talk to) different audiences from those which they normally encounter in their classroom-based work (Martin *et al.* 1976; Williams, 1981; Slater 1983; Carter 1991). The theory is that by getting pupils to write for realistic audiences (often other than the teacher) the immediacy of the teacher's assessing role will be downplayed, and the pupils will engage in more exploratory forms of writing.

The variety of audiences that pupils could write for are recorded by Britton *et al.* (1975), and later by Slater (1983), and can be summarized as follows:

- pupil to self;
- pupil to trusted adult;
- pupil to teacher, as partner in a dialogue;
- pupil to teacher, as examiner or assessor;
- pupil to pupil, or peer group;
- pupil to younger child.

The list can be extended by considerations of other audiences such as 'teacher as peer', 'teacher as layperson', 'teacher as working group member', and 'adult other than teacher' either within or outside school (Carter 1991).

The task for the teacher of creating both an original audience for children to write for, and establishing an understanding that this audience (rather than the 'teacher as assessor') is the main focus for their work, is difficult but not impossible. In classroom-based research carried out by Butt (1993), such audiences were created with the intention of helping children's writing in geography lessons to become more original, individual and creative. It was postulated that changing the audiences that pupils wrote for might change their thought, learning and understanding processes and ultimately improve their writing and talking in geography lessons.

Through pupil-centred discussion and the use of varied teaching resources, followed by writing for different audiences (such as an aid agency, a wood-gatherer, shanty town dweller, hospital consultant, television audience, MP, etc.), the children often displayed a deeper understanding of the geography being studied and a greater appreciation of values and attitudes. Butt (1993) devised a matrix for analysing the 'levels of geographical attainment children achieved' against their 'sense of audience', concluding that in many cases changing the audience has some effect on the learning process. Also of interest was a range of secondary effects such as the increase in work-related discussion, pupil questioning, perception of the audience's viewpoints, clarification of personal values, and use of the teacher as a 'geographical consultant'.

However, there were certain preconditions to audience-centred learning, namely:

- that a sense of trust and purpose needs to be established before good audience-centred writing will appear – boys did not reveal this sense of trust as readily as girls;
- that removing the idea of teacher as assessor in pupils' minds is important, but also extremely difficult;
- that audience-centred writing should be integrated into schemes of work, but not over-used;
- that audiences should be realistic and plausible;
- that if levels of pupil involvement, discussion and enquiry are allowed to increase through audience-centred work geographical attainment may also rise.

(Butt 1993: 22)

GENRES

Genre theory has moved the debate about language forms into considerations of the 'kinds and types' of language used in everyday life (Andrews 1992). The term 'genre' is regularly used in a wide variety of contexts, from descriptions of films and paintings to types of speech and literature. Within its narrower educational context genre theorists have used the term with reference to investigations into the styles of children's writing and textual forms and for debating the significance of the origins of writing processes (Kress 1989). They conclude that the genre and style of writing is closely related to the audience for whom one is writing and to the social context in which the writing takes place.

By extension genre theorists believe that children will not produce different forms of written language if they do not have access to various genres, or the chances to experiment with them. As Butt concludes:

> Thus genres have a fundamental role in language use, because they are closely linked to the audience one is communicating with and the ways in which information is received and understood by that audience. When teachers give children a writing task they must therefore be fully aware of its implied purpose and function, and the audience for which it is being prepared. . . . If the genre the teacher expects from the child is one that he or she has little or no experience of, then the writing task will most probably not be completed satisfactorily.

(Butt 1993: 16)

Genre theory has its critics though. Rosen (1988), Stratta and Dixon (1992) and others believe that such writing can flourish only if children are placed into realistic contexts with believable audiences. They also need to have the necessary language resources to complete their tasks: two not inconsiderable assumptions!

Before moving on from any discussion about pupil writing it is important to mention briefly the marking of such work. Without becoming too embroiled in deliberations about assessment within the National Curiculum, it is essential that teachers realize the impact that their style of marking has on the motivation of pupils. Teachers who tend to mark as 'examiners', where brief comments are often accompanied by a grade or mark, may have the effect on some pupils of forcing them to try to conceal their lack of understanding. Instead of 'learning through writing', where they will express their own thoughts and feelings, these children attempt to present writing which (in their experience) the teacher values.

In addition, over-enthusiastic correction of every mistake of grammar, spelling and punctuation can be extremely disheartening to some pupils and may dissuade them from writing at all. In general, the use of praise and positive teacher comments, where appropriate, may help to encourage the reluctant writer and start a discussion between the teacher and learner about the geography being studied.

READING

In geography lessons pupils have to be proficient in a wide range of reading skills. We expect them to acquire the ability to read worksheets, texts, instructions and technical information, as well as carry out specialized non-linguistic reading such as 'reading' maps (graphicacy), satellite images and systems diagrams. Nevertheless, pupils actually spend comparatively small amounts of time reading the written word in most geography classes.

Children often encounter difficulties when reading because texts rarely give clues to their meaning in quite the same ways that spoken words can. There is no intonation, inflection, questioning, gesture or stress in written geography (unless it is read out loud), especially when compared to the oral, visual and body language clues given by most teachers when speaking in class. However, the reader has the advantage that he or she can go back and forward over a text at the speed most appropriate to learning and understanding it, a process that cannot be achieved with the spoken word without the aid of a tape recording or unrestricted questioning. This does not always guarantee comprehension though, since some texts are simply too difficult for the reader to understand.

The length and complexity of sentences in texts and worksheets, together with unfamiliar and technical words, density of text, font size and abstraction of concepts can also make pupil understanding a problem. Indeed, sometimes it is possible to understand all the words in a sentence individually, but not as a whole sentence.

Robson's research (1983) has shown how pupils approach the task of reading and comprehending texts, and what kind of reading/reader is implied by the way in which the text is written. She finds that readability tests related to sentence lengths, syllable numbers and word counts are only partly of use in understanding children's reading difficulties as they do not see the central importance of the reader in the process. Interviews with teachers and sixth formers discovered that few of the students had the competence expected of the 'implied reader', that they were often frustrated by texts, and could not easily link together text, maps, tables, photographs and diagrams to benefit from the whole. Some understanding was gained by pupils, but this was usually localized or merely re-confirmed impressions about geography that had been gained from other sources. Reading therefore becomes selective and incomplete. In some cases teachers are unaware of their pupil's difficulties because they themselves can easily engage with, and understand, the text in a variety of ways.

DARTS

DARTS (or Directed Activities Related to Texts) are designed to help children develop their reading skills and understand texts more fully. The teacher chooses the aspect of the text upon which they want the pupils to concentrate and issues instructions to enable them to focus on the text's structure and meaning. This may involve underlining key words, deleting parts of a text for pupils to replace (using either their own words, or words supplied by the teacher), reforming a text under given headings, hypothesizing about the ending to a piece of text, or comparing more than one text and looking for similarities and differences.

In many DARTS pupils are asked either to re-create or re-organize text in a more easily understood form. In geography these activities might usefully be supplemented by the pupils creating a diagram or a table from the written information already provided. Alternatively, according to the nature of the text being analysed, the teacher may wish the pupils to underline aspects of content, arguments, opinions, advantages, disadvantages, or even create classifications. Often pupils can be encouraged to talk through their findings with a partner or in small groups, or even present a more formal version of the text's content to the rest of the class.

Some DARTS require pupils to sequence text that has been disarranged by the teacher. This helps pupils to concentrate on the structure of a text in relation to its meaning and flow of ideas (Fig. 15.3).

GEOGRAPHICAL TERMINOLOGY

Geography has its own specialist language and terminology which can create problems for pupils. However, the use of technical language is necessary to help advance the development of pupils' understanding of

1. Fermentation in a cool, damp room to make black tea.	2. The plants are pruned so they become bushes not trees.	3. Two leaves and a bud are picked from each plant.	4. Tea is sold in an auction, e.g. London.
5. Into our teapots.	6. The land is cleared and the soil broken up and fertilized, ready for planting.	7. For green tea the process stops here.	8. Different types of tea are blended together.
9. Tea is packed into chests ready for export.	10. The harvested tea is taken to a special building for withering.	11. Young tea plants are grown in nurseries.	12. Plants are covered by bamboo frames to shade them from the sun.
13. The tea is taken to a factory to be packeted.	14. Tea is taken by van to the shops and supermarkets.	15. Firing – to produce the black tea we drink.	16. The leaves are rolled to remove any remaining juices.
17. The plants are transplanted to fields on the hillsides.	18. Plants are sprayed to prevent disease.		

Figure 15.3 Example of a sequencing DART: tea
Source: Simons and Plackett 1984

geographical concepts. Many of the terms geographers use are homonyms, words which are similar to those with 'everyday' meanings but which have a special significance in geography. For example, pupils will be aware of words such as 'space', 'city', 'communications', 'market', 'labour', 'environment' and 'energy', but may be unaware of their particular and specialist meanings in geography. Learning the terms used in geography is important as a precursor to geographical concept development, but merely rote learning these terms does not imply that concepts are being understood (Milburn 1972). Therefore the teacher needs to set oral or written exercises to probe the pupils' understanding of these concepts.

CONCLUSIONS

As Carter (1991: 2) implies, children should be encouraged to use language in geography lessons for a wide range of audiences and purposes. It should be a vehicle to help them engage more closely with the geography they are learning, rather than hindering or frustrating their understanding. They may have to restructure or transform the written or spoken word to appreciate its meaning, as well as being given opportunities to reflect upon their own use of language. All of these tasks will occur only with the support and guidance of the teacher. They are central to achieving new learning.

If geography teachers constantly emphasize the use of language solely as a tool to control, discipline and assess pupils they will fail to achieve its potential in promoting learning. A variety of pupil-centred talking, writing and reading activities in geography provides the basis for the larger development referred to in this chapter.

REFERENCES

Andrews, R. (1992) 'Editorial', in *English in Education* 26(2): 1–3.
Britton, J. *et al.* (1975) *The Development of Writing Abilities (11–18)*, London: Macmillan.
Butt, G. (1993) 'The effects of audience centred teaching on children's writing in Geography', *International Research in Geographical and Environmental Education* 2(1): 11–24.
Carter, R. (ed.) (1991) *Talking about Geography*, Sheffield: Geographical Association.
Chomsky, N. (1968) *Language and Mind*, New York: Harcourt Brace Jovanovich.
DES (1975) *A Language for Life: The Bullock Report*, London: HMSO.
Hull, R. (1985) *The Language Gap*, London: Methuen.
Kress, G.R. (1989) 'Texture and meaning', in Andrews, R. (ed.) *Narrative and Argument*, Milton Keynes: Open University Press.
Marsden, W.E. (1995) *Geography 11–16: Rekindling Good Practice*, London: David Fulton Publishers.
Martin, N. *et al.* (1976) *Writing and Learning Across the Curriculum*, London: Ward Lock.

Milburn, D. (1972) 'Children's vocabulary', in N.J. Graves (ed.) *New Movements in the Study and Teaching of Geography*, London: Heinemann.

Piaget, J. (1959) *Language and Thought of the Child*, London: Routledge.

Roberts, M. (1986) 'Talking, reading and writing', in D. Boardman (ed.) *Handbook for Geography Teachers*, Sheffield: Geographical Association.

Robson, C. (1983) *Making Sense of Discourse*, unpublished MA thesis, University of London Institute of Education.

Rosen, H. (1975) in *A Language for Life: The Bullock Report*, London: HMSO.

Rosen, M. (1988) 'Will genre theory change the world?', *English in Australia* 88: 18–23.

Simons, M. and Plackett, E. (eds) *The English Curriculum: Reading and Comprehension*, London: English and Media Centre.

Slater, F. (1983) *Learning Through Geography*, London: Heinemann.

Slater, F. (ed.) (1989) *Language and Learning in the Teaching of Geography*, London: Routledge.

Stratta, L. and Dixon, J. (1992) 'The National Curriculum in English: does genre theory have anything to offer?', *English in Education* 26(2): 16–27.

Vygotsky, L.S. (1962) *Thought and Language*, Cambridge, MA: MIT Press.

Williams, M. (ed.) (1981) *Language Teaching and Learning: Geography*, London: Ward Lock.

Chapter 16

Learning through maps

Paul Weeden

Maps and plans are extremely useful ways of storing and communicating information about places and the people who live and work in them. There is a 'language' of maps, and pupils can be helped to understand and use it just as they can be helped with any other language development.

(Beddis 1983: 5)

Maps are an important form of communication, and for some authors graphicacy has been placed alongside numeracy, literacy and oracy as the fourth 'ace in the pack' (Balchin and Coleman 1965). This chapter looks at the centrality of maps to geography teaching and how maps are used as a communication system. An outline of the properties, elements and purposes of maps is illustrated by three examples of strategies children use to 'read' maps. The final section considers how theories of cognitive development inform progression in learning through maps.

THE CENTRALITY OF MAPS

Geography studies the relationship between people and the earth and in particular considers place, space and environment. In investigating places and geographical themes, geographers describe and explain the patterns and processes they observe in the world around them. Thus investigation of spatial patterns and the development of locational knowledge form distinctive and central parts of the discipline, with the map in all its forms being a vital tool in this process. What must be remembered, however, is that maps are merely one form of communication or evidence used by geographers and 'in the investigation of a place, all kinds of evidence, literary, statistical, cultural are examined' (Daugherty 1989: 30).

THE MAP AS A COMMUNICATION SYSTEM

Most geographical literature includes a variety of maps which need to be 'read'. The clarity of the message depends on the skill of the map-maker in

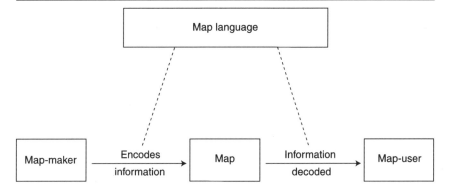

Figure 16.1 A simplified map communication system
Source: Gerber and Wilson 1989: 198

presenting the information and the user's ability to read and interpret the signals. The model of the map as a communication system (Fig. 16.1) demonstrates the need for a common understanding of map language otherwise there will be confusion and misunderstanding. As with any language the common conventions and the structure have to be learnt if the message is to make any sense. There is considerable evidence that children do this best through a structured programme involving practice both in the individual elements and in synthesizing them.

Decoding maps involves learning how to 'read' a map. Unlike reading a book there is no conventional method for reading a map (e.g. from left to right across the page), so skilled map-readers may use strategies such as initial random scanning to identify features or familiar names and then focus on their area of interest or they may look for larger recognizable patterns. Beginner map-users need clear guidance on where and how to start reading the map.

The Geography National Curriculum (DFE 1995) lists the making, using and interpreting of maps as the map skills that children should learn. The author suggests that these terms are loosely defined and proposes four strands of learning through maps – using, making, reading, and interpreting – defining these command words more precisely as:

- using maps – relating features on a map directly to features in the landscape;
- making maps – encoding information in map form;
- reading maps – decoding successfully the elements of map language;
- interpreting maps – being able to relate prior geographical knowledge to the features and patterns observed on the map.

THE PROPERTIES OF MAPS

If systematic learning through maps is to occur, both teacher and pupil should be aware of the essential basic properties of maps that determine most map skills development programmes. Gerber and Wilson (1989: 202), in describing a sequential mapping programme for secondary age children, propose four essential properties of maps that need to be understood – *plan view, arrangement, proportion and map language*. These properties should form the basis of mapwork skills development for any age-group and can be introduced individually and then integrated.

Plan view (perspective and relief)

Maps are drawn looking vertically down on an area, which enables the user to see features which may be hidden from them on the ground. The concept needs to be introduced and practised because the plan view is an unfamiliar viewpoint. Children are much more familiar with elevations, and initially commonly draw houses from this perspective. There is nothing wrong with this 'naive' map representation as a form of symbolism, but they should be encouraged to think about the 'picture' of the house from above. There are many opportunities for children to look down on things, such as high buildings, planes, aerial photographs and images on television, films or computer games.

Vertical aerial photographs illustrate some of the problems in representing height or slope on a map as the two-dimensional photograph often gives little impression of the third dimension of height. The representation of relief on a map is an important but difficult idea for children to deal with. Contours, the commonest form of relief representation, are also the commonest cause of confusion for most map-readers as they form complex patterns and are often obscured by other features or create 'noise' that is distracting.

Arrangement (location, direction and orientation)

Places or features on maps have a location that can be both absolutely defined (by a system such as grid references) and described in relation to other places (left of, north of, etc.). This enables map-users to locate specific places more easily and quickly on complex maps. Direction can be absolute (using a constant reference system – N,E,S,W) or relative to the user's position. The concept of absolute space means that objects or places stay in the same relationship to each other and are not affected by the position of the map-user (an important map-using skill is orienting the map to match the arrangement of observed objects)

Proportion (scale, distance and selection)

Maps reduce the size of objects on the ground so that the object can be represented on a small piece of paper. It is usually important that relative size is maintained, but in some cases important features are drawn larger than their true scale (e.g roads on Ordnance Survey maps). Distance can be measured using a scale, but involves numerical manipulation and often requires a series of complex procedures. Scale is therefore another area of difficulty for many map-readers. The reduction in size means some detail will be lost, involving the map-maker in selection of items to be included. Thus, while aerial photographs record everything seen at a particular time, maps are generalizations which, in improving clarity, can result in bias and omission.

Map language (signs, symbols, words and numbers)

Maps show information by the use of signs and symbols, and extra information is available through the use of words, letters and numbers which help decoding and interpretation. Skilled map-users learn not just to read the symbols but also to interpret the spatial patterns by drawing on their geographical knowledge.

When learning map language it is helpful to recognize that map symbols and information can be classified into three types – points, lines or areas. The symbols used can be classified on a continuum from pictorial to abstract with the more abstract symbols generally being more liable to misinterpretation. Figure 16.2 shows a map that employs a range of point, line and area symbols. The key helps in the interpretation of the symbols but in this case some symbols have been omitted because the features are named. The point symbols range from pictorial symbols such as the aeroplane representing an airfield to an abstract symbol for a sports centre. The line symbols range from representing features seen on the ground such as roads or rivers to more abstract features such as the city boundary. The area symbols on figure 16.2 are pictorial and concrete (wood, golf course) but other maps might represent more abstract features such as areas with high pollution levels in a city. Written information can range from letters (to represent schools), to words (names of important places), to numbers which can relate to features such as grid lines or spot heights.

To summarize, children should learn that maps usually:

- adopt a plan view perspective;
- arrange the features in the same relationship as they are found in real life;
- keep features in accurate proportion to their real size;
- involve the selection of information;
- employ a recognizable map language.

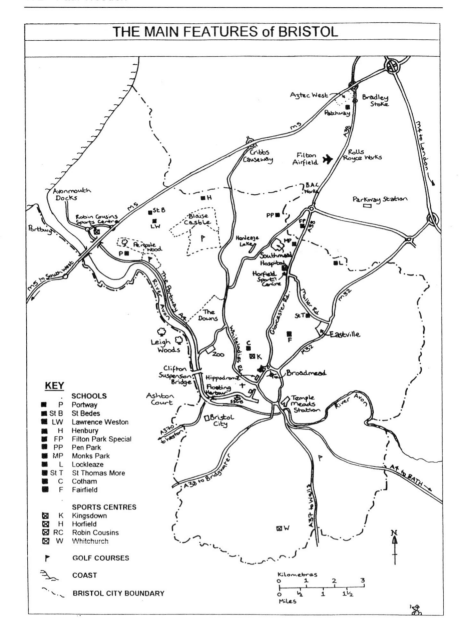

Figure 16.2 A map showing a range of symbols and information

Source: A. Wright, Cotham Grammar School, Bristol

Conventionally, maps also have a title, a key to define the symbols, an indication of orientation (direction indicator) and a scale line.

THE PURPOSES OF MAPS

The ability to encode and decode information on maps is useful not just in geography but also in everyday life. Maps are used in a wide variety of contexts which can be classified into four main functions (adapted from Catling 1988:168 and Wiegand 1993:19):

- location, enabling the user to find a place (e.g. in an atlas, on a street map);
- route-displaying, allowing the user to get from A to B (e.g. a road atlas, underground map or street map);
- storing and displaying information, allowing the user to isolate and sort information from a wide range of different items (e.g. OS maps), or to consider patterns and relationships of selected information (e.g. distribution maps);
- problem-solving, helping the user to solve problems by interpreting or inferring from the information provided (e.g. why a road does not take the most direct route or where to locate a factory). Skilled map-users have learnt to 'see' the landscape from the information on the map.

STRATEGIES CHILDREN USE FOR LEARNING THROUGH MAPS: THREE CASE-STUDIES

These case-studies illustrate the thinking strategies children use while working with maps. Each case-study is accompanied by a short commentary that considers both the thinking strategies used and indicates some problematic areas in working with maps.

Locational knowledge

Jane (year 4, age 8) is locating places and features she has been studying on a map of the British Isles. She remembers that England, Wales and Scotland are the names of the countries of Great Britain and that Scotland is above England, and Wales is a bump to one side. She knows that London is a city and that a city is smaller than a country. She uses the key to find out the symbol for a city. She remembers the approximate location of London having looked at a road atlas when she went there with her family. She knows a river is a wiggly line on a map and that London is on the River Thames. She unsuccessfully guesses where to locate Birmingham, her home town, as she only knows it is north of London.

Jane's thinking involved recalling from her memory the names of several places and features. To locate the places successfully she had to classify the different features and have some understanding of the terms country, city, river. Her recognition of the shapes and arrangement of features in the British Isles enabled her to synthesize this knowledge while the words in the key gave her extra clues in decoding the map. She had difficulty with locating her home town, Birmingham, partly because there are no recognizable features nearby and because her awareness of distance is poor.

The route from home to school

Thomas (year 6, age 11), when asked to draw a map of his journey to school as part of a topic on his locality, says, 'That's easy'. He starts by trying to visualize the journey and seeing whether he can fit it on the paper. Home is marked first in one corner of the map and the roads on the route drawn sequentially and topologically until he reaches school, which is squeezed into the far corner of the sheet. Considerable thought is required to clarify relationships and there are some mistakes, rubbings out and redrawings before the route is complete. When asked to add on further detail, he includes nearby roads, their names, pictorial symbols, a key and a direction arrow. He works out the direction of south, from his knowledge of the position of the sun at midday at his home, and is then able to work out the rest of the compass points.

Thomas, in his thinking, used daily experiences stored in his memory to problem-solve. This ability to recall his mental picture of the area combined with a clear understanding of map properties enabled him to work out logically the arrangement of familiar roads and to create a recognizable map. He had difficulties with distance, so the map was not drawn to scale (roads nearer home were overemphasized), and he ran out of space on the paper as he approached the school. He demonstrated the difficulties most people have in drawing mental maps, because of the need to recall and synthesize complex patterns and arrangements. However, he also showed how useful mental maps are for teachers in giving information about pupils' knowledge and understanding of map skills and places.

Interpreting patterns

David (year 11, age 16), when asked to describe and explain the patterns on a map as part of a GCSE examination question, starts by analysing the question. He decides the key word is redevelopment area, finds the symbol for this in the key, and locates the areas correctly on the map. He describes their arrangement (in a tight ring around the city centre) and draws on his knowledge of urban 'models' to recall the main features of this area. He also applies this knowledge by picturing a redevelopment area in his home town and remembers that the older buildings have been knocked down and rebuilt. He does not immediately use the scale to help him work out how far from the city centre the areas are; rather, he senses their proximity and only later confirms it. He recognizes the line around the city as a boundary of some sort and uses the key to identify it as the city boundary.

David's thinking involved a complex interaction of knowledge recall and synthesizing information from the map. His familiarity with maps enabled him to recognize the pattern of the redevelopment areas and to put them into a meaningful context. He moved quickly from description into the processing of his stored geographical knowledge and was able to read and interpret the information on the map in a sophisticated manner.

These case-studies illustrate how map language is used in the making, reading and interpretation of maps. Jane and Thomas show how they can draw on their own memories and perceptions of places, arrange their thoughts and synthesize information to complete the task. They are both familiar with the main properties of maps but demonstrate some of the difficulties of encoding information onto a map. In decoding the information on the map David illustrates clearly the difference between map-reading and map-interpreting. The symbols on the map can be read like the words in a book, but they have little meaning unless they can be combined to make 'sentences'. If the map-users have other geographical knowledge they can draw inferences and make interpretations – more akin to 'reading between the lines' in a written passage.

The case-studies demonstrate how learning through maps involves developing map skills in a range of contexts. They illustrate how pupils when using maps have to combine thinking about the maps themselves with their knowledge of geography, and that the best map-based activities will encourage work that is purposeful and appropriate to their age.

HOW THEORIES OF COGNITIVE DEVELOPMENT INFORM PROGRESSION IN LEARNING THROUGH MAPS

Geographical education has always been concerned with the systematic teaching and learning of map skills. There are many detailed accounts of apppropriate teaching and learning programmes, such as Boardman (1986), Catling (1988), Gerber and Wilson (1989), Foley and Janikoun (1992), Wiegand (1993) and Catling (1995). This section will not outline a programme of work but looks instead at some of the theories of cognitive development that inform our understanding of progression in map skills, and indicates how these theories can be related to learning.

Theories of cognitive development

Meadows (1993: 197–251) suggests there are three major current models of cognitive development: Piaget's model of stages, information processing models and Neo-Vygotskian models. The most influential of these for learning through maps has been Piaget, although there has been criticism of the way that Piaget's work has been misused by some educationalists who, by slavishly adhering to fixed stages, have underestimated children's abilities in using maps.

Piaget's model

Piaget's work is based on a biological model of adaptation. The child, or indeed the adult, is all its life actively trying to make sense of the world, just as any organism must try to adapt to its environment (Meadows 1993: 198). Piaget's model has been characterized by educationalists as suggesting that thinking develops in a series of stages, the sensori-motor, pre-operational, concrete operational and formal operational stages. These stages of development follow an invariant order and each stage can be associated with a certain mental age, so that a mental age of 8 typically goes with the concrete operational stage, while a mental age of 4 is associated with the pre-operational stage. This relatively simple model has been discussed and elaborated by authors such as Boardman (1983) and has led to a sequential programme for the development of map skills which has been adopted in many schools. It is clear from this experience that most children benefit from starting to learn about maps in a concrete manner in an environment they are familiar with (classroom, school, locality) and only at a later stage moving onto more abstract maps. However, it must be remembered that Piaget did not see his model of stages as a teaching model and it is now recognized as merely one way of thinking about cognitive development.

Information processing

Information processing models use the metaphor of the brain as a computer and there has been some work done simulating children's spatial abilities with computers (Spencer, Blades and Morsley, 1989: 19). The case-studies in this chapter illustrate how skilled map-users operate like computers and are able to make connections between observed patterns and stored knowledge. The speed of the information processing will depend upon experience, practice and ability. The links between this model and a teaching and learning programme for schools have not been explored in the literature.

Neo-Vygotskian models

Meadows (1993: 236) suggests that both Piagetian and information processing models emphasize the psychological structures inside people's minds while Neo-Vygotskian ideas have the premise that social interaction is paramount. If, as Vygotsky suggests, language has the power to shape mental development and social interaction is a prime way in which people learn – 'what the child can do co-operatively today she will be able to do individually tomorrow' (Knight 1993: 26) – then this has implications for learning.

In contrast to Piaget the Neo-Vygotskian model has an underlying belief that education can accelerate development, which leads to the concept of 'scaffolding' learning. For instance the concept of plan view can be introduced by looking down on objects arranged on a desk and discussing this view. Rhodes (1994: 111) has shown how in making choices about best routes for different transport networks, relief models and maps can be used by year 6 children, working in groups, to interpret relief and slope patterns.

In most cases these children are thinking at, or just beyond, their most advanced, current understanding (Vygotsky's 'zone of proximal development' (ZPD)) and engaging in learning through social interaction.

An important idea that emerges from these three theories, an idea of increasing importance in understanding how we think, is the concept of metacognition.

Metacognition

While some pupils may develop map skills by a process of osmosis through exposure to maps, learning for most is aided by clear and focused guidance, particularly if they are helped to 'think about their thinking' (metacognition). Knight (1993: 35) describes metacognition 'as helping chidren to be conscious of what they know and can do and then teaching them how to draw puposefully on that knowledge and to deploy it when working on problems'. Teachers can encourage pupils to think about their learning by asking, 'How did you reach that answer?', or challenging them to justify an answer. Orienteers do this when they discuss and analyse their routefinding after an event. Often there is a choice between a shorter direct route, that may be slower because it goes through dense woodland, and a longer faster route along paths. By analysing the advantages and disadvantages of each route the orienteers are increasing their familiarity with the range of information on the map and their ability to make successful interpretations. Discussion and disagreement can lead to metacognitive conflict and hence metacognitive advance (Meadows 1993: 81).

CONCLUSIONS

Geographers regard maps as tools that enable them to communicate knowledge and understanding of place, space and environment. In particular, maps enable a consideration of the spatial patterns that are central to geography. To develop their familiarity with maps fully, children should have the opportunity to use, make, read and interpret maps in a variety of contexts. Any programme of teaching and learning developed should introduce the four basic properties of maps (plan view, arrangement, proportion and map language) separately, but find ways of relating them to each other. Children can be helped with their understanding of map language if they recognize that map symbols can be points, lines or areas and are on a continuum of complexity from pictorial to abstract.

Children learn more effectively from maps if they have a clear idea of the purpose of the task being undertaken. These tasks can be linked to the four main purposes of maps (location, route-displaying, storing and displaying information, and problem-solving). In addition, successful interpretation of maps requires not just recognition of symbols and patterns but the synthesis of information from the map with other geographical knowledge.

Finally, our understanding of cognitive development suggests that children should work initially from direct experience (particularly with younger children or when introducing new or difficult concepts such as scale or relief) only later moving onto more abstract maps, and that they should be encouraged to think actively about their thinking (metacognition) since this aids the process of synthesizing and developing interpretation skills.

REFERENCES

Balchin, W.G.V. and Coleman, A.M. (1965) 'Graphicacy should be the fourth ace in the pack', *The Times Educational Supplement*, 5 November 1965.

Beddis, R. (1983) Introduction in T. Johnson, (ed.) *Maps and Mapwork – A Practical Guide to Maps and Mapwork in the Primary School*, Bristol: RLDU.

Blades, M and Spencer, C. (1986) 'Map use by young children', *Geography* 71: 47–52.

Boardman, D. (1983) *Graphicacy and Geography Teaching*, London: Croom Helm.

Boardman, D. (1986) 'Map reading skills', in D. Boardman (ed.) *Handbook for Geography Teachers*, Sheffield: Geographical Association.

Boardman, D. (1989) 'The development of graphicacy: children's understanding of maps', *Geography* 74: 321–31.

Boardman, D. (1991) 'Developing map skills in the National Curriculum', *Teaching Geography* 16: 155–8.

Catling, S.J. (1979) 'Maps and cognitive maps: the young child's perception', *Geography* 64: 288–96.

Catling, S.J. (1988) 'Using maps and aerial photographs', in D. Mills (ed.) *Geographical work in Primary and Middle Schools*, Sheffield: Geographical Association.

Catling, S.J. (1995) 'Mapping the environment with children', in M. de Villiers *Developments in Primary Geography*, Sheffield: Geographical Association.

Daugherty, R, (ed.) (1989) *Geography in the National Curriculum*, Sheffield: Geographical Association.

DFE (1995) *Geography in the National Curriculum*, London: HMSO.

Foley, M. and Janikoun, J. (1992) *The Really Practical Guide to Primary Geography*, Cheltenham: Stanley Thornes.

Gerber, R. and Wilson, P. (1989) 'Using maps well in the geography classroom', in J. Fien, R. Gerber and P. Wilson (eds) *The Geography Teacher's Guide to the Classroom*, Melbourne: Macmillan.

Knight, P. (1993) *Primary Geography, Primary History*, London: David Fulton.

Matthews, M.H. (1984) 'Cognitive mapping abilities of young boys and girls', *Geography* 69: 327–36.

Meadows, S. (1993) *The Child as Thinker*, London: Routledge.

Rhodes, B. (1994) 'Learning curves . . . and map contours', *Teaching Geography* 19: 111–15.

Spencer, C., Blades, M. and Morsley, K. (1989) *The Child in the Physical Environment*, Chichester: John Wiley.

Wiegand, P. (1993) *Children and Primary Geography*, London: Cassell.

Chapter 17

Ethnocentric bias in geography textbooks
A framework for reconstruction

Christine Winter

INTRODUCTION

> All teaching materials that deal in any way with images of the world bring with them a set of attitudes and assumptions, explicit or implicit, conscious or unconscious, which are based on broader cultural perspectives. These perspectives tend to be ethnocentric, i.e. they generally measure other cultures and groups against the norms of one's own, or racist in that one's own culture is considered to be superior and thus, by definition, others are inferior.
>
> (Hicks 1980: 3)

The warning about the dangers of ethnocentric bias in geography textbooks was signalled by Hicks, when he drew attention to the prevalence of European bias in the representation of people and places. In this chapter I contribute to this debate by describing a principled approach to analysing textbooks which allows teachers to gain a deeper understanding of the ideological position of the writer and thus to facilitate the detection of cultural bias in geography teaching materials.

Using the same principles, I give an account of a reconstruction of a curriculum unit in which an attempt is made to raise pupils' awareness of the subjectivity involved in representing knowledge about people and places in geography. I believe that this is required for three reasons. The first is that geography teachers need both to review textbooks critically in order to reject those which show evidence of ethnocentric bias and to select or develop materials which address such issues. The second reason relates to a view of the purpose of education as a means of encouraging pupils not to accept passively the geographical knowledge which is indicated in the curriculum but to challenge and ask questions about that knowledge. Finally, the increasing intervention of the state in the prescription and construction of the school curriculum brings to centre stage the need for teachers to enquire into theoretical, policy and practical issues relating to the values implicitly underpinning textbook interpretations of the curriculum.

EDUCATION FOR EMPOWERMENT

Before describing the framework for analysing cultural bias in geographical texts, I will give an account of the theoretical background underpinning the approach. The aim of education here is to develop pupils as autonomous, morally informed, critical agents who think for themselves, who ask questions and who are aware of and able to argue against inequalities. In this sense, engagement with geographical knowledge forms part of the process of education towards an empowerment which enables pupils to act upon and transform the world around them. The development of autonomy involves pupils in the process of learning how to challenge their existing thinking and the thinking of the culture in which they live, to move towards a more democratic, interdependent society in which the notions of freedom from oppression and tolerance of difference exist. Thus, this emancipatory ideal figures strongly in the thinking behind this approach.

A second part of the theoretical frame rests on the idea that geographical knowledge is not 'objective', indisputable and 'given', subject to organization according to universal laws, theories, models and systems in the positivist sense. Instead, it is chosen, organized and presented on the basis of subjective decisions by people who hold particular value positions. Indeed, the knowledge which is made available to pupils in the school geography curriculum is a social invention, having been selected and used with certain social interests implicitly or explicitly in mind. (Young 1971:31).

It is through a development in human geography called the 'new cultural geography' that the idea of knowledge as a social construction can be used to analyse critically the value positions underpinning the representation of people and places in the geography curriculum. This new paradigm rejects positivism i.e. the existence of 'true' knowledge about places and people, and embraces the idea that place knowledge is seen as an ambivalent concept, something that is known to us through our everyday lived experience, or constructed by us according to the way we 'see' or understand a place. This is in turn affected by the way in which the place is represented.

Social constructivism allows us to look more closely at the processes involved in constructing understanding about places and, at the same time, to challenge inequalities present within the 'truths' forming the organizing principles of our understandings in the past. We are thus challenged to look more closely at the ways in which places are represented in different textbooks and to understand the different ideological positions which underpin these. So, instead of accepting specific categories of places or a particular way of describing a place, we can deconstruct the text to reveal the inequalities which were previously 'taken for granted' truths. Jackson and Penrose write:

> If we can learn how specific constructions have empowered particular categories we can disempower them or appropriate their intrinsic power, to achieve more equitable ends.
>
> (Jackson and Penrose 1993:2)

By deconstructing texts, we can reduce their power to engender inequality and reveal the need to ask questions about their legitimacy.

A CASE-STUDY OF DECONSTRUCTING THE TEXTBOOK: TEACHING ABOUT PEOPLE AND PLACE IN KENYA

A popular series of textbooks used in schools at Key Stage 3 is the 'Key Geography' course (Waugh and Bushell 1992) written specifically for the Geography National Curriculum (DES 1991). In this example, the authors are seen as the mediators between the National Curriculum policy document and the textbook representation which they create. The authors' interpretation of the National Curriculum policy in relation to the Maasai people of Kenya forms the focus for the deconstruction.

The principles behind the deconstruction need to be explained. These are taken from McDowell's (1994:151) new cultural geography perspective and consist of the following four points:

- positionality, the ideological positions which underpin representations of places and people;
- provisionality, the changing nature of knowledge about places and people;
- contestation, the existence of conflicting views about places and people;
- social mediation, the idea that ways of thinking about knowledge are constructed by the thinkers themselves according to the way they 'see' or make meaning about a place.

These principles are used as a basis for analysing two pages in the *Key Geography: Connections* textbook (Waugh and Bushell 1992: 78–9). These pages are titled 'Kenya – what is the Maasai way of life?'.

In terms of position, a Eurocentric view is given in the text. Kenya is presented as an 'economically developing country' and by 'developing' the authors 'mean that it has less capital (money) and fewer services compared with a "developed" country like the UK'. Kenya is compared with the UK and found to be inferior on two points. A negative image of the country is portrayed and a deficit construction of the country presented. According to the authors, there are positive points about Kenya: 'The landscape of Kenya is very varied and beautiful . . . and although there are many different "ethnic" groups living in the country, there is little tension between them'. The positive points, of varied landscape and beautiful countryside are juxtaposed with information about ethnic groups, in which there appears to be an assumption that there might or should exist some tensions. To what extent does this derive from the conception of Africans as savage, warring, in need of European governance, a view held by the early geographers, the nineteenth-century explorers?

In describing the homes of the Maasai there is no attempt to encourage an understanding among pupils of the reasons for the particular configuration of the Maasai houses: 'tiny passages', 'huts barely reach the height of an adult Maasai', 'the inside is dark and full of smoke from the fire' and 'apart from an opening the size of a brick, there are no windows or chimneys'. Likewise, in dealing with clothes, work and diet, the authors present the Maasai as a museum piece, on view to the West because of their 'curiosity' features: the 'brightly coloured blankets' worn by the men and the 'lengths of cloth' by the women; the use of 'sticks' to clean teeth; 'animal fat and vegetable fat to clean themselves'; a diet of 'milk mixed with blood from cows' and the leaving of dead animals to be eaten by wild animals instead of burying them. These all serve as examples of a representation of the Maasai which can be traced to a view of Africans as influenced by the power of representation through European rule in the past.

In spite of the frequent reference to the idea of change in the National Curriculum policy document, the authors make no reference in the textbook pages to the Maasai places and people as undergoing change; instead, a picture of a static way of life is presented. There is no mention of the reduction in Maasai grazing grounds as a result of the appropriation of land by the European settlers; soil erosion caused by the overgrazing of pasture on reduced amounts of land; the employment of Maasai people as cattle-herders by European ranch-owners and employment in the tourist trade. Neither are the development of fixed villages with wooden homes, more sedentary lifestyles, tanked water supplies, schools and community health care projects mentioned.

The representation shows no evidence of a range of voices involved in the place being studied. The text is dominated by a white, male, western voice, with no views of the Maasai people about their places, history, stories and lives. If Maasai authors had written the two pages, what would they have looked like? How would they have represented themselves and their land? What do the Maasai women say about their places? And what about the other voices to be heard in a study of this place; the voices of the Kenyan government, the tourists, the cattle-ranchers and the safari travel firms?

In producing two pages of text about the Maasai, the writers have selected knowledge from their interpretation of the policy text of the National Curriculum document and from the ideology underpinning their thinking. The textual representation of the Maasai is a socially mediated one in which the 'truth' of the policy document is decoded, taken up and reconstructed. Engagement with the policy creates for the writers a conception of the possibilities of response in and through the language, concepts and vocabulary which this perspective makes available. As a result, the effect of policy in this case is to constrain the scope and opportunities available for thinking otherwise.

It has to be acknowledged that some may feel that certain of these ideas may present conceptual difficulties for teaching at KS3, particularly for, say a year 8 pupil who knows little about the Maasai, or even where Kenya is located in the world. It is important, however, for teachers and pupils to become aware of the dangers involved in representing places and people. The marginalization of such issues can easily occur in the course of planning a scheme of work given time and resource constraints.

'GOING BEYOND' THE NATIONAL CURRICULUM

The textbook pages under study here are based on the National Curriculum policy document, interpreted by the textbook authors. I have established the one-dimensional, static, unproblematical representation of Kenyan people and place to be found within the textbook pages. Why, then, does the National Curriculum policy document create an opportunity for the textbook writers to express an ethnocentric view? Is this, as Goodson suggests, part of the movement to establish a national identity founded on cultural hegemony (Goodson, 1994: 109)? If so, can we assume that the policy document and the textbook pages are underpinned by an ideology which does not discourage the construction of racist ideas about people and places? Jackson draws attention to the link between ideology and practice:

> Racist ideologies have severe practical consequences particularly when they become institutionalised through the power of the state. For racism in Britain and similar societies is a *dominant ideology*, not just a matter of individual prejudice and personal discrimination. On the contrary, racism refers to a set of ideas and beliefs that have the weight of authority behind them, they are enshrined in statutes and institutionalised in policy and practice.
>
> (Jackson 1989: 151)

At the same time, it has to be acknowledged that a range of perspectives on 'economically developing countries' other than the one discussed here is currently available to teachers through textbooks. These have been categorized by Hopkin using Hicks' earlier system as representing positions of 'status quo', 'liberal' and 'radical'. Hopkin (1994: 75) speculates that the textbooks which contain 'elements of alternative, less Eurocentric perspectives . . . probably fairly accurately reflect the spirit of National Curriculum goegraphy' whereas the texts representing a more radical paradigm 'have attempted to go beyond, and improve upon National Curriculm requirements' (1994: 86). Is it, then, the responsibility of textbook publishers, writers and teachers to 'go beyond and improve National Curriculum requirements' in order to ensure an unbiased view of an 'economically developing country'? In the following section I give an account of a reconstructed text which attempts to 'go beyond and improve National Curriculum requirements'.

TEACHING ABOUT PEOPLE AND PLACE IN KENYA – RECONSTRUCTING THE TEXT

The principles of positionality, provisionality, contestation, and social mediation which were used in deconstructing the textbook pages were drawn upon a second time in the process of reconstruction to guide the development of teaching materials for a curriculum unit of teaching and learning about Kenya for a class of year 8 pupils.

Positionality

In developing the curriculum unit the principle of positionality was considered to be important in terms of avoiding the presentation of a Eurocentric view of Kenya and also in terms of representing the relative power positions of the groups and individuals involved. It was clear that deficit images of Africa already existed in the minds of the pupils at the beginning of the unit, and an exploration of the sources and reasons for these images was planned as a starting-point, before moving on to alternative views of the country and the Kenyan people. This was achieved at the beginning of the unit in a 'brainstorm' of pupils' ideas about Africa, with little comment added by the teacher. It was followed in the same lesson by a simulated parachute landing in which the pupils imagined they had landed in Kenya. They were asked in pairs to discuss and write down the things they wished to find out about the country. Pupils were then encouraged to think about the sources of their existing knowledge and questions about Kenya and Africa. The activity was repeated at the end of the unit to discover how their responses had changed.

It was important to make available a range of pictures of the country and people which not only described but also offered a range of explanations for its situation. This was necessary to demonstrate that representations of a place and the reasons for its condition are subjectively created. By focusing on different voices involved in the topic of colonialism, in issues to do with environmental degradation and safari holidays, opportunities were planned for pupils to develop an understanding of the historical, political, economic, social and environmental influences at work in the country as well as an understanding of the power of images and words in constructing and representing knowledge. In the study of the Maasai, the materials focused on the life of a named family, with detailed descriptions of their lives and how they were changing.

Provisionality

In relation to the principle of the provisional nature of knowledge, attempts were made to incorporate the concept of 'change' in two ways: first through the materials demonstrating that peoples' lives and places undergo change and that this can be represented in the text of the unit, and, second, through the idea that whichever way change is represented in the text people construct their own knowledge and that knowledge undergoes change. The key point remains that the knower constructs her knowledge for herself in the social context in which she exists and any changes in that knowledge will be influenced by the particular context in which she operates. In preparing the curriculum unit, the notion of change was incorporated in terms of the representation and individual construction of knowledge as provisional.

Contestation

The dominance of the white, male, European voice in the text of the book and the absence of representations of other voices were difficult issues to address, given the restricted access to Kenyan places and people and the limited availability of appropriate resources. One way of challenging the knowledge about Kenya which pupils encountered through the study of rural Maasai places and people was to build into the unit visits from Kenyans studying locally. We were fortunate to be able to invite a Kenyan female (Kikuyu tribe) and male (of Asian descent) from the cities of Nairobi and Mombasa to the school to answer the pupils' questions about their lives (Pomeroy 1991). This gave the pupils access to the idea that a person's understanding about a place is influenced by their race, ethnicity, class, colour, gender and previous experiences of place. Pupils were encouraged to create the agenda by asking their own questions about Kenya. However, since the agenda is not only that 'belonging to' the pupils, but also that 'belonging to' the people of the country being studied, the agenda for the whole unit should ideally be constructed through a negotiated dialogue between Kenyan people, pupils and teachers. This way, Kenyan voices as well as pupils' voices would be heard and issues of importance to all parties would arise through the curriculum content.

Social mediation

The principle of social mediation of knowledge permeated both the content and the pedagogy of the unit. The selection of representations of Kenya was acknowledged as being made on the basis of the values underpinning my views about the place and the people by incorporating into the unit opportunities to demonstrate to the pupils that no one looks at places in a way which is neutral and objective but that there are several ways of constructing and representing knowledge about place.

THE DEARING REVIEW: AN OPPORTUNITY FOR CHANGE

The analysis of the textbook carried out in this chapter has a particular historical location which needs to be explored in order to tease out the implications of this work for the future. As stated earlier, the textbook studied here is a response to the 1991 National Curriculum Orders for geography, and these Orders have now been superseded by the Dearing Curriculum of 1995. Although there may be financial pressures in schools to retain textbooks which were written specifically for the 'old' curriculum, this new, slimmer, less prescriptive curriculum for geography gives teachers more freedom in selecting places for study and determining the approaches used. It therefore presents an opportunity to rethink an approach to place knowledge in which ethnocentric bias plays no part. In order to establish and maintain a high quality of content in the discipline of geography, it is important to avoid such sensationalization of geographical ideas and such emphasis on other people and places as inferior as described earlier. These are low-level, oversimplified and potentially dangerous representations.

At the same time, there is an opportunity to make geographical study relevant to the aim of education stated earlier, to make connections with and critically engage with moral and cultural understandings and focus on existing priorities in society. In treating geographical knowledge as unidimensional, unchanging, unproblematic and 'true' we limit the pupils' ability to think about alternative ways of looking at the world, and neglect to convey a sense of the relative positions of power involved in current geographical issues. As geographers, we are immersed in a discipline which deals with those very contentious issues which are of critical importance to pupils today. If we agree that the purpose of education in a democratic society should consist of something other than mere socialization into existing cultural traditions, then we should aim to develop in pupils the ability to think for themselves, to ask questions, to make decisions and judgements on the basis of their own rational reflections, supported by materials and teaching which uphold a notion of social justice.

CONCLUSION

In spite of the emphasis in this chapter on the dangers of bias in teaching materials, I hope that it will be read in an optimistic manner, and that it will act as a stimulus to thought in planning for teaching and learning about places in economically developing countries. Since the introduction of the National Curriculum in geography in 1991, the content focus in the curriculum seems to have centred on a technical approach to geographical knowledge and has led, in some schools, to a move towards a more transmissive teaching approach relying more heavily on the recall of facts. The approach described here, which uses the social constructivist framework combined with a particular view of the aim of education, is intended to encourage teachers and pupils to become more actively engaged in a critical consideration of the moral and political dimensions which are present within curricular knowledge. There is no doubt that these dimensions are complex and difficult, but in the light of the current widespread existence of racist and xenophobic attitudes, we should ask ourselves, 'What contribution can geographers make to the development of a "better world" (Fien and Gerber 1988)?'

REFERENCES

Department for Education (1995) *Geography in the National Curriculum*, London: HMSO.

Department of Education and Science (1991) *Geography in the National Curriculum*, London: HMSO.

Fien, J. and Gerber, R. (1988) *Teaching Geography for a Better World*, Edinburgh: Oliver and Boyd.

Goodson, I.F. (1994) *Studying Curriculum*, Milton Keynes: Open University Press.

Hicks, D. (1980) *Images of the World: An Introduction to Bias in Teaching Materials*, Occasional Paper No. 2, University of London Institute of Education.

Hopkin, J. (1994) 'Geography and development education', in A. Ostler (ed.) *Development Education: Global Perspectives on the Curriculum*, London: Cassell.

Jackson, P. (1989) *Maps of Meaning*, London: Routledge.

Jackson, P. and Penrose, J. (1993) (eds) *Constructions of Race, Place and Nation*, London: UCL Press.

McDowell, L. (1994) 'The transformation of cultural geography', in D. Gregory, R. Martin and G. Smith *Human Geography: Society, Space and Social Science*, London: Macmillan.

Pomeroy, J. (1991) 'The press conference: a way of using visiting speakers effectively', *Teaching Geography* 16(2): 56–8.

Waugh, D. and Bushell, T. (1992) *Key Geography: Connections*, Cheltenham: Stanley Thornes.

Young, M.F.D. (1971) *Knowledge and Control*, London: Collier Macmillan.

Chapter 18

Teaching and learning through fieldwork

Nick Foskett

THE VALUE AND PURPOSE OF FIELDWORK

For most geographers fieldwork is a key component of their enthusiasm for the subject and one of the strongest elements of their own personal biography. Read most reflections on school geography, too, and the role of fieldwork emerges as a central theme in curriculum planning. The first national geography curriculum in England and Wales, for example, indicated that 'fieldwork should not be an optional extra, [for] pupils are entitled to . . . regular, purposeful and integrated fieldwork' (DES 1990: 85). The revised geography National Curriculum that came into effect in 1995 requires that all pupils 'undertake fieldwork' (DFE 1995: 2), making it a statutory obligation on all schools in the state sector.

Smith (1987) has considered the aims of fieldwork in the context both of geographical education and of wider outdoor and environmental education, and concludes that 'field-based outdoor activity, whether residential or not, is a critically important approach to learning' (Smith 1987: 209). Specifically, he identifies the value of fieldwork in terms of three broad categories of experience – outdoor studies, outdoor pursuits, and personal and social development.

'Outdoor studies' relates to the intellectual (cognitive) development of the child. Fieldwork provides the opportunity to apply ideas generated in the classroom to the real world, to test hypotheses by empirical methods and to learn new knowledge and concepts from first-hand observation. In particular, though, it enables the development of skills, including subject-specific skills (e.g. field sketching), wider generic skills (e.g. data collection and recording) and intellectual skills (e.g. problem-solving). The importance of addressing development of the affective domain (i.e. that area of thinking that relates to feelings, attitudes and values) is also emphasized. Within a humanistic perspective the importance of personal perceptions of place and the development of personal geographies has been stressed (e.g. Massey and Jess 1995) and is often identified as the development of a 'sense of place'. Such a concept stresses the necessity of experience and participation in 'place', both in familiar and unfamiliar environments.

The second category of experience identified by Smith is the area of 'outdoor pursuits'. The emphasis on this dimension clearly depends upon the location and nature of the fieldwork, but there will always be, even in the school grounds, some element of personal physical challenge, the development of physical and practical skills, and enhanced awareness of safety issues from experiences outside the classroom. Smith underlines the role of fieldwork, too, in preparation for leisure, in that it increases pupils' awareness of their own and other environments and the potential role of outdoor activity for personal leisure activities.

Smith's third category of 'personal and social development' is the least tangible of the three areas identified, yet, perhaps, in the long-term education of most children, it is the most important and persistent. This stresses the development of self-awareness and awareness of the needs and skills of others in the context of working co-operatively in new environments.

Geography fieldwork, of course, is not uniquely able to deliver these dimensions of learning. The strength of geography in contributing to these areas, though, lies in the subject's historically accumulated experience of fieldwork and its ability to take the lead in planning these dimensions of education into the whole curriculum.

ALTERNATIVE APPROACHES TO FIELDWORK

Fieldwork may be considered as any activity that takes place outside the confines of the classroom which provides pupils with experiences, knowledge, understanding or skills that are part of the geography curriculum. We might consider these activities in terms of the location of the fieldwork and the teaching and learning strategies that may be used.

Fieldwork locations

The early history of fieldwork is rooted in the traditions of exploration and outdoor activity in distant locations (Brunsden 1986), creating an image that fieldwork activity is appropriate only in environments contrasting with those close to home. Early guides for teachers stressed this perception of fieldwork (e.g. Archer and Dalton 1968), and it was not until the late 1970s that writers such as Bailey (1976) and Arnold and Foskett (1979) began to stress the role and value of local environments for field study. Throughout the 1980s the expansion in fieldwork across the age and ability range in geography, combined with financial and pragmatic constraints, led to an increased focus on locally based fieldwork, so that by the mid-1990s Walford has suggested that 'it has become evident that for many school pupils in the future a fieldwork experience will be a local one' (Walford

1995: 112). By way of contrast, however, recent years have also seen the frontiers of school fieldwork expand so that work in Europe or Africa is now within the range of some school groups (Fenoughty 1992).

Table 18.1 shows a location spectrum for geography fieldwork, and indicates some of the salient characteristics of each location in terms of the flexibility, costs and planning horizons that need to be considered. The limitations on organizing fieldwork increase with the locational scale involved, yet it might be suggested that the educational benefits to children increase substantially as the locational scale increases – and the promotional benefits to a school of offering distant and challenging fieldwork locations may be significant!

Teaching and learning strategies

Most teaching and learning approaches that are appropriate within the classroom translate quite readily to the field environment, and working with children in the field opens up additional perspectives. We may identify a number of phases in the historical development of fieldwork which reflect differing perspectives on teaching and learning strategies. Prior to the quantitative revolution of the 1960s, two approaches dominated fieldwork. The expedition approach was based in the traditions of the adventure organizations such as the Scouts and Girl Guides, with fieldwork linked to outdoor activities, focused on walking, camping and mountaineering. The challenge lay in the physical demand of the activity and only in small part in the intellectual processes of geographical analysis. It was concerned with a descriptive, teacher-led study of landscape on a grand scale. The second tradition emerged during the 1950s and 1960s, based on improved transport availability, with pupils visiting and viewing geographical features considered in the classroom – what has been described as a Cook's tour approach. Its value lay in its concern for landscape and the integrating perspective that can be obtained by a wide-ranging but perhaps superficial visit. Such an approach, in providing an initial overview of an unfamiliar environment, still has value as a preface to other forms of fieldwork (e.g. Martinez and Patterson 1988).

In 1965, stimulated by the growing development of a quantitative and normative approach to geography, a joint conference of The Geographical Association, Royal Geographical Society and the Field Studies Council considered the purpose and methods of fieldwork. The conference was a bench-mark in the development of fieldwork, for its principal outcome was to stimulate an approach focused on active field investigation. The importance of skills development emerged strongly through this tradition in the 1970s, with a focus on data collection and hypothesis testing. This active engagement of pupils in their own learning was regarded as a positive step forward, yet the focus on data collection (e.g. land-use mapping) too

Table 18.1 A spectrum of fieldwork locations for geography

Location	Example	Characteristics	Case-Study*
School grounds	Litter survey Soil sampling	Within lesson; single task/focus; no/low cost; possibly 'spontaneous'	Lawes (1995)
School environs	Local shopping centre survey Local stream hydrology	Within lesson or part day Single task/focus; no/low cost	Arnold and Foskett (1979) Walford (1995)
Local region	Local town centre Local country park	Part day or whole day; single task/multi-task focus; transport costs arise	Bamber and Ranger (1990) Butt (1992)
Wider region	Regional city Nearest coast	Whole day; single/multi-task focus; transport costs significant; contrasting environment/locality	Mottershead and Suggitt (1992)
Distant locality	Upland Britain London	Residential (few days/week); multi-task focus; transport and residential costs substantial; long planning period; contrasting environment/locality	Adams and Croft (1985)
Overseas (Europe)	Alps Netherlands Iceland	Residential (week); multi-task focus; transport and residential costs high; long planning period; contrasting environment/locality	Fenoughty (1992)
Overseas (distant)	North Africa West Africa India	Residential (at least one week); multi-task focus; very long planning period; major risk assessment necessary; high cost; contrasting environment/locality	George (1992)

* References to the case-studies are contained in the bibliography

frequently emphasized the mechanics of measurement and recording and excluded adequate analysis and interpretation skills. Most geographers will question, for example, the value of the many hours they spent measuring pebble axes standing in rivers!

The main curriculum developments in geography in the late 1970s and 1980s (e.g. the Avery Hill Project) stimulated further development in fieldwork strategies. Their emphasis on enquiry-based learning focusing on people–environment issues stimulated an enquiry-based approach to fieldwork. Typical were the 'framework fieldwork' approach (Hart and Thomas 1986), and the 'fieldwork as process' model (Hawkins 1987) which saw fieldwork as field enquiry. The starting-point for such an approach would be the identification of management issues and problems in relation to the interaction of people and their environment in a specific locality (for example, the impact of a new motorway development in an Area of Out-standing Natural Beauty). From this a strategy for identifying causes, processes and consequences would be established by negotiation between pupils and teachers (for example, simple environmental impact assessment, and interviews with interested parties), leading to appropriate data collec-tion, data analysis and presentation and the identification of possible management strategies/solutions (perhaps through a mock public enquiry). Such an approach integrates concepts into a focus on environmental issues and engages intellectual, practical and affective skills (e.g. Bamber and Ranger 1990). It emphasized, too, the process of geographical enquiry, and provided an approach to fieldwork which supported pupils in indivi-dual work, an essential requirement where GCSE and A level syllabuses included individual fieldwork-based studies.

We may demonstrate this range of strategies in relation to Bartlett and Cox's (1982) continuum of teaching and learning (Table 18.2). It is impor-tant to stress that no single strategy is in itself the 'right' approach, for the selection of strategy depends upon a wide range of factors relating to content, educational objectives, the teaching environment and available resources, and the nature of the class being taught. Each strategy has a place in the practice of fieldwork, and a coherent fieldwork programme for a school will contain elements of each. The emphasis on enquiry, for example, which is found both in the National Curriculum and most GCSE and A level syllabuses does not exclude the value of exposition as a teaching approach, which may provide an excellent introduction to a highly individualized enquiry task, or explain a particular field technique or landscape feature.

PLANNING FIELDWORK

Comprehensive planning is essential for safe and effective fieldwork. The importance of planning in ensuring that the quality of teaching, the quality

Table 18.2 A continuum of teaching and learning strategies for fieldwork

Work increasingly pupil-centred ————→
Work increasingly teacher-centred ————→

Teacher activities	Exposition	Provides tight enquiry structure	Provides guidance on enquiry structure	Provides support/encouragement
Pupil activities	Reception/recording information	Follows instructions for individual work	Negotiation on methods/hypotheses to test	Develops own enquiry approach independently
Fieldwork approaches	←—— Expedition approach ——→			
	←—— Cook's tour approach ——→			
		←—— Data collection/hypothesis testing ——→		
			←—— Field enquiry ——→	
Example	Teacher exposition on corrie formation and field sketch on Cader Idris	Teacher-provided worksheet to be completed during teacher and farmer-led farm visit	Teacher leads pupils in developing hypotheses on urban land use; data collection method developed individually by small groups	Pupil enquiry on individual topic – designs own fieldwork strategy; (teacher acts as consultant)

of learning and the standards of achievement of pupils is optimized in the classroom is widely stressed (e.g. Capel *et al.* 1996), but in the field the increased risk makes this process *sine qua non*. Planning is essential at a variety of scales, too, ranging from the individual activity or lesson, to the place of fieldwork in a short scheme of work, to its development within a Key Stage and within the child's whole educational experience within the school.

Planning a fieldwork task

Planning an individual fieldwork task requires attention both to the issues of teaching and learning and the organizational aspects of the activity. In curriculum terms the principles of good lesson planning apply, with the need for clarity about aims, objectives and intended learning outcomes, the selection of appropriate methods (either for or with the children), the use of suitable resources and equipment, and careful attention to issues such as timing and sequencing of activities. An important emphasis is that fieldwork should always be integrated with classroom activities. It must be integrated with the scheme of work, with the key questions for investigation in the field emerging from previous tasks and the results and findings in the field being used to inform and direct subsequent work. Differentiation must also be considered carefully. Fieldwork offers good opportunities for differentiation by outcome, but the use of small groups working on similar or different tasks in the field enables differentiated tasks to be incorporated.

The range of fieldwork activities and tasks that may be used is very extensive, and a substantial literature exists which provides detail on specific skills and methods. The present paper does not allow space to deal in detail with these approaches, and the reader is encouraged to examine the case-studies referenced in Table 19.1 together with appropriate literature on fieldwork techniques (e.g. Lenon and Cleves 1984).

The individual fieldwork task itself fits into a broader organizational framework, which will be very demanding of time in planning. First, following initial discussions with the headteacher and head of department (or curriculum co-ordinator) in school, the fieldwork location and task must be pre-visited and tested to assess the practical aspects of the task, safety, and organizational arrangements. Second, the financial and logistical dimensions of the work, including the organization of transport and domestic arrangements (accommodation, meals etc.), and the arrangement of access to locations, must be planned in the context of a full budget analysis. Third, a range of legal, bureaucratic, communication and pastoral care issues must be considered, which includes such tasks as providing details of the arrangements to parents and seeking both their permission and their financial contribution for pupil participation, checking the school's/LEA's insurance

Table 18.3 Outline planning checklist for fieldwork organization

Planning stage	Planning activity	Approximate timing ahead for day visits/ residential work
Obtaining permission	1. Preliminary discussion with head of department/headteacher	As early as possible, probably in previous academic year, but at least 1 term/1 year
	2. Consult school/LEA policy documents	
	3. Consult professional association guidelines	
	4. Seek formal approval from head/governors/LEA	
Pre-visit/background reading	5. Planning and site visit	1 term/6 mths
Costing	6. Calculate budget and check charging policies	1 term/6 mths
Insurance	7. Check insurance arrangements	1 term/6 mths
Transport	8. Arrange transport	6 wks/3 mths
Pre-visit documentation	9. Provide information to parents/obtain parental permission/medical information	6 wks/3 mths
Preparation for activity	10. Prepare resources, pupils and colleagues	1 wk/3 wks
	11. Make safety arrangements (e.g. first aid kit, emergency contact lists)	1 wk/2 wks
Managing the activity	12. On the day – monitor weather, pupils, safety, assess for contingency plan	Continuously during fieldwork
Follow-up	13. Pupil follow-up and product	Immediately
	14. Evaluation of activity and planning	No more than 2 wks after

cover in relation to off-site activities, checking LEA and school policy on pupil–teacher ratios and teacher qualifications and experience, and checking health-related issues in relation to individual pupils. Finally, the in-school arrangements for covering staff absence, setting work for groups and communication pathways for dealing with emergency issues must be addressed. The Geographical Association (GA) has produced a guide to the organization of fieldwork, which includes a planning checklist (The Geographical Association 1990). Table 18.3 shows the main planning categories suggested by the GA, and gives some indication of the time-planning framework that might be appropriate.

Fieldwork and outdoor activities in school have attracted substantial media attention in the light of recent accidents involving field parties. As a consequence, teachers must be aware of a number of legal dimensions in relation to fieldwork, and of their own responsibilities. Some of these relate to statutory limitations and responsibilities, for example in relation to charging pupils for participation in fieldwork (DES Circular 2/89), where no charge can be made for any activities which take place in school time, although voluntary contributions from parents can be invited. Others relate to policy frameworks for schools and LEAs where policies in relation to the experience and training of leaders, pupil–teacher ratios, and insurance must be in place. Details of these requirements are included in the government booklet *Safety in Outdoor Education* (DES 1989), and adherence to the guide-lines in that publication should be regarded as a legal obligation upon teachers organizing fieldwork. In particular, the emphasis on safety must be paramount in fieldwork, and the importance of appropriate leadership training for staff and of vigilance, risk avoidance and conservative decision-making in the field must be stressed. As a result of recent legislation (the Activities Centres (Young Persons) Safety Act, 1995, and the Adventure Activities Licensing Regulations, 1996), Activity Centres offering fieldwork under certain specified circumstances must be licensed. This does not apply to teachers or schools leading fieldwork, or to Centres offering accommodation only, but teachers organizing fieldwork should check whether any Centre they use falls within the scope of this legislation, and, if so, whether it is licensed. Failure to check this might be regarded as a breach of a teacher's statutory 'duty of care'.

Planning a fieldwork programme

The planning of a Key Stage scheme of work or the coverage of a GCSE or A level syllabus includes a consideration of progression and the logical sequencing of work for pupils. Fieldwork within a geography department should demonstrate a similar pattern of structure and development. While the integration of fieldwork into individual schemes of work should ensure that progression in fieldwork parallels that in the rest of the curriculum, an overt broad plan in terms of fieldwork progression may be helpful. We might envisage that progression will involve the following changes:

- an increase in distance from the school, with early experiences within the school grounds and the local environs, and later experiences involving fieldwork elsewhere in the region or in more distant locations;
- an increase in duration, from early experiences of fieldwork in single lessons to half days whole days, and short or long residential experiences;
- an increase in complexity of the fieldwork, from simple descriptive and observational tasks, to issue-based enquiries;
- an increase in the demand of fieldwork skills themselves, where older pupils, for example, will be able to use more sophisticated analytical techniques, including statistical tests and computer-based databases or spreadsheets;
- an increase in pupil autonomy in the design and practice of fieldwork, with the intention of developing by year 11 or year 12/13 the skills to undertake an individual fieldwork task.

Table 18.4 shows a fieldwork plan for a secondary school which demonstrates some of these key principles.

FIELDWORK AND INFORMATION TECHNOLOGY (IT)

The importance of information technology within the geography curriculum and the contribution that geography makes to the development of IT skills has been emphasized many times (e.g. Kent 1992). Two dimensions of the use of information technology emerge strongly through fieldwork, and provide a number of important opportunities for developing IT skills (Lucas 1993). First, the generation of data creates opportunities for the use of databases and spreadsheets for data analysis and for the use of word processing and drawing software in the preparation of reports and displays. This will normally need to be undertaken in the context of classroom-based follow-up, but the availability of laptop computers makes field-based data input possible. Second, the use of data loggers and environmental sensors makes the measurement of many environmental factors simple (e.g. river pH, temperature), and collects data in a form that enables them to be loaded directly into databases in classroom-based computers. It is clear that the value of IT in fieldwork lies in the scope it provides for rapid handling of data, which enables the focus of the fieldwork to be on the enquiry process, the in-field skills and the interpretation and application of findings, and not on mechanical data processing.

Table 18.4 A geography fieldwork plan for a secondary school

Year	Term	Location	Duration	Fieldwork tasks
7	Term 1	school grounds	3 lessons	mapping school grounds
	Term 2	school grounds	daily rota	weather readings
8	Term 2	local shopping centre	afternoon	shopping survey/sphere of influence
	Term 2	regional out-of-town centre	afternoon	impact of out-of-town developments
9	Term 1	local stream	afternoon	hydrology/pollution study
	Term 1	school grounds	lesson	litter survey
	Term 2	coast	whole day	marine processes/cliff management issues
10	Term 1	school grounds	lesson	soil sampling/quadrat sampling
	Term 2	town centre	half day	urban structure
	Term 2	school grounds	daily rota	weather readings
	Term 3	London Docks	whole day	urban redevelopment (teacher-planned enquiry for GCSE assessment)
11	Term 1	South Wales	weekend	industrial location and change/tourism management/coastal ecosystems
	Term 2	local	=3 days	fieldwork for GCSE project
	Term 2	local country park	2 lessons	recreation management
12	Term 1	Lulworth and Portland	1 day	coastal processes/tourism/economic change
	Term 3	school grounds	daily rota	weather readings
	Term 3	Cevennes	week (half-term)	issue-based topics in agriculture, landform management, industry, settlement studies
13	Term 1	local	=5 days	fieldwork for A level individual study
	Term 1	local	1 day	EIA/planning exercise on proposal for site of waste incinerator

CONCLUSION

Fieldwork in the geography curriculum has been under external threat during the last decade as issues of safety, cost and the internal managerial and curriculum pressures in schools militate against it. There is increasing pressure to use local fieldwork that is accessible within walking distance and, preferably, within single or double geography lessons. However, the value of fieldwork is still clearly recognized by most geographers, and its position, albeit at a potentially nominal level, within the curriculum is assured. With effective planning and management and a commitment to the educational and personal benefits to pupils of fieldwork, geography teachers can ensure that it remains as one of the most significant learning experiences that pupils have during their school career.

ESSENTIAL READING

Department of Education and Science (1989) *Safety in Outdoor Education*, London: HMSO.
The Geographical Association (1990) *Geography Outside the Classroom*, Sheffield: The Geographical Association.

REFERENCES

Adams, K. and Croft, R. (1985) 'Fieldwork in regional disparity', *Teaching Geography* 10(2): 78–80.
Archer, J.E. and Dalton, T.H. (1968) *Fieldwork in Geography* London: Batsford.
Arnold, R. and Foskett, N.H. (1979) 'Physical geography in an urban environment: two examples' *Teaching Geography* 5(2): 60–3.
Bailey, P. (1976) 'Is anyone doing local fieldwork?', *Teaching Geography* 2(1): 4–6.
Bamber, C. and Ranger, G. (1990) 'Values enquiry in practice: investigating a local controversial issue' *Teaching Geography* 15(2): 60–2.
Bartlett, L. and Cox, B. (1982) *Learning to Teach Geography*, Melbourne: John Wiley.
Beaumont, T and Williams, J. (1983) *Project Work in Geography*, London: UTP.
Brunsden, D. (1986) 'The science of the unknown', *Geography* 72(2): 193–208.
Butt, G. (1992) 'Education through industrial visits: a link with Rover, Long-bridge', *Teaching Geography* 17(2): 78–80.
Capel, S., Leask, M. and Turner, T. (1996) *Learning to Teach in the Secondary School*, London: Routledge.
Department for Education (1995) *Geography in the National Curriculum*, London: HMSO.
Department of Education and Science (1990) *Geography for Ages 5 to 16*, London: HMSO.
Fenoughty, T. (1992) 'Organising an overseas fieldwork expedition', *Teaching Geography* 17(3): 132–4.
George, B. (1992) 'A school exchange: fieldwork in an Indian village', *Teaching Geography* 17(2): 61–5.
Hart, C. and Thomas, T. (1986) 'Framework fieldwork', in D. Boardman, *Handbook for Geography Teachers*, Sheffield: The Geographical Association.

Hawkins, G. (1987) 'From awareness to participation: new directions in the outdoor experience', *Geography* 72(2): 217–21.

Kent, W.A. (1992) 'The new technology and geographical education', in M. Naish, (ed.) *Geography and Education - National and International Perspectives*, London: Institute of Education.

Lawes, B. (1995) 'Orienteering for beginners!', *Teaching Geography* 20(3): 122–4.

Lenon, B.J. and Cleves, P.G. (1984) *Techniques and Fieldwork in Geography*, London: UTP.

Lucas, R. (1993) 'I.T. and fieldwork', *Teaching Geography* 18(1): 38–9.

Martinez, M. and Paterson, A. (1988) 'Going back to "look and see"', *Teaching Geography* 13(3): 130–1.

Massey, D. and Jess, P. (1995) *A Place in the World?*, Oxford: Oxford University Press/The Open University.

Mottershead, D. and Suggitt, S. (1992) 'Spatial variation in stream water quality: a scientific approach', *Teaching Geography* 17(2): 66–70.

Smith, P.R. (1987) 'Outdoor education and its educational objectives' *Geography* 72(2): 209–16.

Walford, R. (1995) 'Fieldwork on parade', *Teaching Geography* 20(3): 112–17.

Chapter 19

Using information technology and new technologies in geography

Diana Freeman

INTRODUCTION

It is now accepted that all teachers need to have an understanding of the way in which Information Technology (IT) can enhance teaching and learning within their subject. Geography is a subject in which IT can make a genuine and worthwhile contribution and it is therefore even more important that geography teachers know how to harness the benefits of IT for their students. This chapter explores how teachers may put IT into practice.

We can no longer ignore the fact that we are living through an Information Revolution whose consequences for society will be just as great as the Industrial Revolution in the nineteenth century. The beginnings of this revolution were established in schools around fifteen years ago and are continuing. The average secondary school has a resource or library area with CD-ROMs and perhaps other electronic means of communication via the Internet. Personal computing is coming into the classroom and the field via small laptop computers which are used for report writing and data collection. Computer networks in schools are more sophisticated and computers more prolific, allowing students access to databases, word processors, spreadsheet programs and other resources that increase their productivity and achievements. Apart from the general availability of IT at school level to fulfil the requirements of the National Curriculum, there are pressures from the world outside the classroom. Professional geographers such as town planners and meteorologists use new technology as an integral part of their work.

How can teachers of geography benefit from these resources in order to enhance their students' learning? Although the context and concepts that make up the essence of school geography remain relatively constant, the skills and techniques that underpin and contribute towards geographical understanding change more rapidly with the times. Changes in technology pervade the pedagogy and methodology of geography – we can now gain access to instant pictures of the world from electronic sources, process statistical information and map digital data on computers, and use them as a means of communicating the results of these actions. There are two main branches of these new techniques: first, 'information technology', a student's computer literacy or IT capability and, second, 'new technologies in geography', i.e. those new techniques, such as remote sensing and Geographic Information Systems (GIS), which help geographers specifically. This chapter will show some of the ways in which both these branches contribute to teaching and learning geography in school.

INFORMATION TECHNOLOGY (IT)

Since 1995, IT has been a subject in its own right, set down in the Statutory Orders for IT in England and Wales, but IT is also strongly cross-curricular and is expected to be taught through the medium of other subjects (DFE 1995b). The revised Geography Orders (DFE 1995a) also contain statements about the use of IT to enhance and enrich geography. Every subject Order has a statement on IT, such as that included in the Geography Orders.

> Pupils should be given opportunities, where appropriate, to develop and apply information technology capability in their study of geography.
>
> (DFE 1995a: 1)

However, the geography curriculum goes further and itemizes some areas where IT could be used to advantage.

Geographical skills

Key Stage 1

Pupils should be taught to use secondary sources e.g. CD-ROM encyclopaedia, to obtain geographical information.

Key Stage 2

Pupils should be taught to use IT to gain access to additional information sources and to assist in handling, classifying and presenting evidence, e.g. recording fieldwork evidence in spreadsheets, using newspapers on CD-ROM, using word processing and mapping packages.

Key Stage 3

Pupils should be taught to use IT to gain access to additional information sources and to assist in handling, presenting and analysing geographical evidence, e.g. automatic weather stations to collect weather data, spreadsheets to record environmental impact scores, CD-ROMs to obtain census data, desktop publishing packages to produce a leaflet on a local issue, simulation packages to investigate a flood hazard.

In the IT Orders the emphasis is on students becoming capable users of IT tools and information sources to solve problems, to analyse, process and present information, and to model, measure and control external events. All these areas, with the exception of using IT to control events, are relevant to the geography curriculum.

If we look more closely at the IT requirements, it becomes even more apparent that IT can make a genuine contribution to geographical learning. There are two main aspects of IT which fit closely with the overall theme of enquiry learning and geographical skills.

Communication and handling information

- using software to create good quality presentations for particular audiences, integrating several forms of information;
- systematically searching a range of sources to obtain accurate and relevant information;
- collecting and amending quantitative and qualitative information for a particular purpose, and entering it into a data handling package for processing and analysis;
- interpreting, analysing and displaying information, checking its accuracy and plausibility.

Controlling, measuring and modelling

- using IT equipment and software to measure and record physical variables;
- exploring a given model with a number of variables and creating models of their own, in order to detect patterns and relationships;
- modifying the rules and data of a model, and predicting the effects of such changes.

It is apparent from these extracts that there is a close correlation between geographical and IT skills. They complement each other. Using IT as a tool for learning is entirely appropriate for a resource-based, enquiry-led subject such as geography.

How can Information Technology support teaching and learning geography?

Looking at IT from the perspective of geography, there are certain key elements that may be distinguished in which IT plays an integral part.

IT is a tool for enquiry learning

IT helps geographers assemble, organize, analyse and present information in words, maps, diagrams and tables from both primary and secondary sources. This requires an understanding of information skills, enquiry learning methods and data handling skills on computer. When these are combined they make a powerful and compelling argument. For instance, a hypothesis about the use of a shopping centre may be enhanced by carrying out a questionnaire survey to discover people's shopping habits. If this information is entered into a database on computer, questions may be asked which will produce results quickly and easily on graphs and tables to accept or reject the original hypothesis. Once the data are on computer, many more questions can be asked, and graphs and tables selected carefully in order to investigate thoroughly the problem.

IT is a resource for obtaining secondary source material

Up-to-date information in newspapers, pictures, statistics and reports, including first-hand experiences, from around the world is available on CD-ROM and via the Internet. These materials widen students' experiences and provide the basis for carrying out investigations. Keeping up with the mass of statistical information and acquiring first-hand reports on, for instance, hazards or weather phenomena, has always been a problem to geography teachers. Rapid electronic communications now available in schools ease this situation.

IT helps in measuring physical events and situations

Datalogging devices, such as automatic weather stations or other environmental monitors, are more accurate and reliable, and offer more regular continuous data, than traditional methods. Students may still carry out fieldwork using traditional methods, but have the added advantage of the comparison with automatic readings. For instance, automatic weather stations operate in all conditions at all hours of the day and night. Although students should know how different instruments are used to measure meteorological data, they would not be expected to do this continuously throughout the year.

IT as a tool for enquiry learning in geography		
Collecting information	*Analysing information*	*Presenting results*

Primary sources –
Automatic:
datalogging: weather
stations, environmental
monitoring.
 	
Manual: data
collection and data
entry, e.g. with
laptops in the field.
	Databases (asking
	questions, looking for
	relationships).
	
	Spreadsheets
	(making calculations,
	making predictions).
	
	Modelling programs
	(looking for patterns,
	predicting).
		Using previous
		packages and word
		processors, desktop
		publishing and multi-
		media packages to
		present results as:
		  graphs,
		  tables,
		  maps,
		  pictures,
		  multimedia
		  presentations
		  including
		  sound,

Secondary sources – Using CD-ROM, Internet and databanks to obtain statistics, remotely sensed images, maps and other geographic information.	GIS packages (asking questions, looking for spatial patterns and relationships).	video.

Figure 19.1 How IT supports enquiry learning in geography

IT is used to model real-world situations

Geographers are familiar with models of the water cycle, population growth, industrial development and urban patterns of growth. IT offers an opportunity to use and create dynamic models. It is easier to learn the principles of, for instance, industrial development if there is a computer model which may be altered and discussed. Students can set up 'What if. . .?' examples to try out different scenarios. This helps them look for environmental and spatial patterns and relationships and acquire more understanding of the principles by which the model operates.

IT helps in communicating and presenting information

Whether the results of a geographical enquiry are generated in words, maps, diagrams, photographs, sound or video, computers offer a means of presenting information for a variety of different audiences. This information may also be communicated electronically to students in other parts of the country or even exchanged with other countries.

The ways in which IT can support enquiry in geography are shown in Figure 19.1. The process of enquiry learning generally requires students to test a hypothesis. In order to do this they need to collect information relevant to their enquiry, process and analyse this information, then present their results. Figure 19.1 also shows which software or IT equipment is appropriate to use at different stages in an enquiry.

Information handling skills and data handling skills

Geographers use information handling skills as a regular part of hypothesis testing. There are some elements of information handling that may be accomplished to advantage on computer. This is known as data handling. Successful enquiry learning combines these two techniques so that computers are used as tools to help the enquiry process.

The table overleaf shows how information handling and data handling contribute to the enquiry learning process.

Some suggestions for introducing IT into geography topics

Weather studies

- Collect weather data: use an automatic datalogging weather station to collect data and store it in a data file to use again.
- Use a spreadsheet to draw graphs of recent weather and match them with the forecasts and maps in the newspapers.
- Keep the data for typical or unusual weather. Find recent satellite images on the Internet or through the MetFax service to compare with the data.
- Print a graph of weather data for each month of the year.
- Save the weather data to use with a database program. Question the data to show differences between seasons, e.g. which days were above or below a certain temperature?
- Ask questions to show relationships between weather, e.g. does it always rain when the wind is from the West?
- Compare weather data with other schools in your own area or in another part of the country.

If your school does not have access to an automatic datalogging weather station, data and suggestions for using it for weather studies are in the package *Geography and IT – Investigating Weather* from NCET and the GA.

Environmental assessment

- Carry out an investigation on a local environmental issue.
- Carry out a survey using your own criteria for a number of locations. Score your criteria from 0 (very bad) to 6 (very good). Enter the

Data collection	
Information-handling skills	*Data-handling skills*

Posing a hypothesis
Developing a questioning attitude
Identifying sources
Discriminating between sources
Organization
Observation, measuring
Map interpretation
Interviewing, questionnaire
  surveys
Record-keeping, collating
	Structuring data
	Designing data capture sheets
	Entering and checking data on
	  computer
	Encoding data
	Storing data files on disk
	Keyboard skills

Data retrieval and interrogation	
Information-handling skills	Data-handling skills
Hypothesizing Accurate definition of a question Modifying a question Combining questions Selecting and rejecting results	Browsing Searching Matching data Framing a question in computer terminology Sorting data
Data display and analysis	
Information-handling skills	Data-handling skills

An understanding of the
  application of diagrammatic,
  statistical and cartographic
  techniques.
Making a précis or report of the
  results of searches
	An understanding of the methods
	  for displaying data in graphs,
	  tables, maps and statistics on
	  computer

Data evaluation	
Review of all methods of collection, retrieval and analysis Criticism of the outcome Discussion, self-assessment Application of subject criteria to the enquiry: modification or acceptance of the hypothesis	

Figure 19.2 How information-handling skills used in geography teaching combine with data-handling skills on computer for enquiry learning

information into a spreadsheet and work out class averages and discuss them.

- Plot this data onto an educational GIS and ask questions to make new maps.
- Devise a questionnaire survey for people's views on their own environment. Use a database program or a word processor to make forms for the interviews. Enter the data into a database and ask questions to find out people's preferences. Draw graphs to show the results.

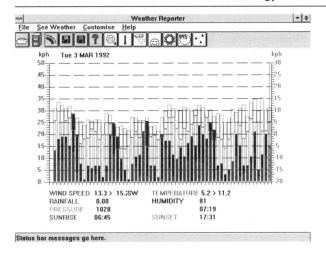

Figure 19.3 Data at your school site collected by an automatic data-logging weather station

Figure 19.4 Satellite images may be collected from your school's satellite receiving station or obtained from the Meteorological Office's MetFax Service, CD-ROMs or the Internet

World population distribution and growth

- Find out about the statistics and case-studies of sparsely and densely populated areas from CD-ROMs.
- Model population growths on spreadsheets or dynamic modelling systems.

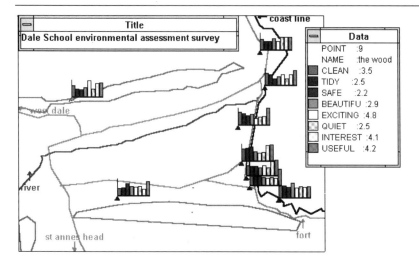

Figure 19.5 When Dale School carried out an environmental assessment survey they plotted the results on a map using a GIS program

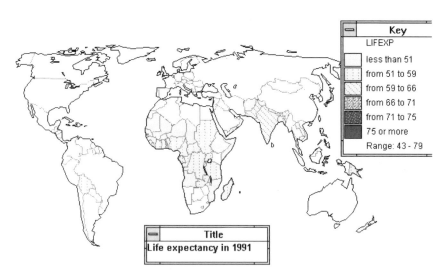

Figure 19.6 World map showing countries with an average of less than 60 years life expectancy in 1991

- Make world maps showing population distribution and other factors affecting population growth with a GIS or CD-ROM atlas.
- Ask questions in a database about differences in population growth and density in different countries.

Checklist for integrating IT in geography lessons

There are a variety of factors that contribute to successful integration of IT into geography lessons. Here is a checklist of those which need to be taken into account:

- What is the geographical context: year group, theme and place(s)?
- What is the IT context: communicating, data handling, modelling, monitoring?
- What are the students' IT experiences?
- Objectives: what will the students achieve in knowledge, skills and concepts in geography and IT?
- Resources: what software/CD-ROM and IT equipment or other IT resources will be needed to support the lesson?
- Where will the lesson take place: geography room, library, resources room?
- What is the most appropriate learning style: directed or open, structured questions or free searches?
- How will the class be organized: individual, pair, group or whole-class work? Do the teacher or students choose the pairs or groups?
- What type of management of teaching: parallel sessions (IT and an alternative), a circus of different activities, whole class using IT at the same time?
- What IT support materials are needed?
- What geography curriculum materials are to be used?
- What other support staff are available: librarian, IT teacher, technician?
- What are the intended and unintended outcomes of the lesson?
- How will the lesson be evaluated and assessed: by teacher and students?

Some strategies

Talk to your IT co-ordinator. Most schools have a teacher who has a responsibility for ensuring that the requirements of the IT Orders are delivered. They will be able to discuss the types of software packages in the school and the students' experience with those packages. Many IT co-ordinators wish to use IT in the context of subject lessons and are very willing to work in a team to do this. It may be that geographical activities are able to be incorporated into IT lessons, and thus gain additional time for geography teaching.

Talk to your librarian or resource manager: it may be possible to combine work on, for instance, searching on CD-ROM, with a geographical task.

Try to work out a plan to use IT for at least one main theme per year group, such as weather studies or fieldwork. There should also be opportunities to use IT for obtaining secondary resource material, perhaps as an extended homework project.

Geography context	IT element
With Y7 doing a shopping survey. Collecting data on a functions survey. Analysing information to explore shopping hierarchies from a questionnaire and functions survey.	Collecting data, entering data onto computer, interrogating the data and displaying it in a variety of ways.
River survey with Y10. Collecting data on river flow and river cross-section.	Using a laptop computer for collecting data and entering it into a spreadsheet to work out cross-sectional area and discharge.
Y9. Exploring a global development database to compare levels of economic and welfare development, to identify patterns and relationships between different indicators.	Interrogate a large database, display the information on graphs or maps.
Y10. Examine the effect of recent changes in a traffic scheme in the local area by means of a questionnaire survey to assess their impact on shopkeepers and residents.	Collecting data and entering them into a database, interrogating the data, and displaying the results.
Y6. Measure and record local weather using datalogging equipment or using instruments in order to describe conditions over a period of time.	Collecting data and entering them into a database, interrogating the data, and displaying the results.
Y10. Using hourly weather data and a synoptic chart, relate the weather conditions at a particular time to a synoptic pattern.	Use a spreadsheet to analyse and display data. A weather satellite system, or MetFax, could provide the synoptic information.
Y11. Using a CD-ROM of UK census data, identify geographical patterns within the home region.	Interrogating a large database and displaying the information on thematic maps.
Y10. Compare two contrasting regions in Europe using a simple database/GIS package.	Interrogating and displaying data to obtain information on thematic maps.
Y8. Using a simple database/GIS package to display spatial information as an aid to decision-making about the environment impact of building houses in a woodland area.	Interrogating and displaying data to obtain information on thematic maps.
Y11. Calculate location quotients to compare proportions of the working populations engaged in different employment sectors for a range of countries.	Using an existing set of data on a spreadsheet to calculate location quotients.
Y9. Carry out an environmental impact assessment to explore people's perceptions of their local area with a view to improving their environment.	Use a database or spreadsheet to enter and analyse the information.
Y5. Use a computer Atlas or CD-ROM to research some information about a place.	Retrieve information stored on a computer.

Figure 19.7 Some contexts for introducing IT into geography activities

Geography context	IT element
Y9. Industrial location – a decision-making exercise on possible locations of a new hypermarket or hotel.	Use a simulation program e.g. Choosing Sites or a spreadsheet to model the most appropriate location based on different criteria.
Y10. Predict and explain changes in the population of a region or country.	Use a simulation package or a spreadsheet to assess the consequences of changing the birth rates and death rates of a population.
Y7. Journey to school – the relationship between distance, method of transport and time taken.	Use a spreadsheet to enter data and sort it into order. Look for patterns in the data.
Y11. Exploring changes in a large inland drainage basin based on differing environmental and human factors.	Modelling information on a spreadsheet to explore and predict the outcome of changes in rainfall, evaporation and water extraction on water levels.
Y10. Explaining the main components and links in the hydrological cycle.	Using a modelling program or simulation to explore the elements within the hydrological cycle. Alter variables and assess the changes that have taken place.
Y10. Creating a qualitative model to locate a new airport.	Use an expert system to enter locational rules to enable an outcome to be elicited.
Y8. Explain the causes and effects of flooding using flood hydrographs.	Using a spreadsheet to model the pattern of rainfall and river flow during a storm.
Y11. Assessing the effects of proposed developments on a derelict site in the local area.	Using a spreadsheet to calculate the costs of building and revenue for different scenarios.
Y12. Assessing the effects of a development in the local area and the environmental impact of building in an area of scenic beauty.	Using a spreadsheet to calculate the environment impact of building on a site.
Y8. Investigate an environmental issue within an economically developing country as a simple role-playing exercise e.g. in the Sahel.	Using a simulation to explore patterns and relationships.
Y9. Using a newsroom simulation as a stimulus to investigating an issue from different standpoints. For example, defending the rain forest.	Using a word processor or DTP package to present geographical information from different viewpoints for an audience.
Y11. Working in expert groups to research an element within a topic, then bring the elements together into a composite report, after drafting and re-drafting the ideas. e.g. different plans for changing the rural landscape.	Using a word processor or DTP package to present geographical information from different viewpoints for an audience.
Y9. Prepare a fieldwork report on a local issue e.g. construction of a bypass.	Combine information from a word processed report and graphs from a spreadsheet.

NEW TECHNOLOGY IN GEOGRAPHY

Geographers in the commercial and business world are using new methods and techniques which are transforming the way they work. Access to stored information about the land and its people and new methods of processing this information are making the tasks of mapping, environmental assessment, planning and resource management much easier. For instance, Mexico has one of the most modern census data processing systems, and satellite mapping provides important land use data in the Sahel in West Africa.

There are two main aspects of new technology in geography – remote sensing and GIS (Geographic Information Systems) – which may be used in classrooms to help geographical understanding and incidentally show how geography is at the forefront of innovative uses of IT.

Remote sensing

Images obtained from satellites or aerial photographs help geographers understand more about earth and its atmosphere. This aspect of new technology is part of our lives – we are used to seeing remotely sensed images on television every evening in the weather forecast.

Rapid response to environmental change and mapping distant lands are possible only because there are images beamed to earth daily from satellites. There are two main types of satellites that distribute this information: orbital and geostationary. Orbital satellites follow a predictable track when they circle the earth but a receiving system can collect information only when it is within range of the satellite. Schools that have such a receiving system will accept 'live' meteorological data for a short period during the school day.

Geostationary satellite systems, such as Meteostat, hover above a fixed position on the earth and move in relation to the earth. Images from Meteostat are available at any time. If schools do not want to go to the expense of buying and maintaining their own satellite receiving station, they may take advantage of the fact that many universities, and organizations such as NASA, put recent images on the Internet and update them regularly. The Internet is a prime source of weather information such as satellite images and weather statistics.

Global positioning systems also rely on linked geostationary satellites to give several bearings onto a place on the earth. The small hand-held device (GPS – Global Positioning System) gives a readout as a grid reference or latitude and longitude wherever you may be on the earth.

Landsat and Spot satellites send back sophisticated data about the earth as wavelengths outside the visible light spectrum. This is decoded on computer to produce land use maps, geological mapping and topological mapping. At present there is so much information coming to earth from Landsat or Spot, that the original data have to be processed on a mainframe computer. However, there are organizations that make pre-digested raster images available, and affordable GIS software that manipulates and processes them.

Geographic Information Systems (GIS)

GIS is 'a powerful set of tools for collecting, storing and retrieving at will, transforming and displaying spatial data from the real world for a particular set of purposes' (Burrough 1986: 6). From GIS' beginnings in the 1970s, computer GIS packages are now the fastest growing type of software in the world. GIS is used for planning and decision-making by governments, local authorities, oil companies, public utilities and other organizations which need to use and present information on maps. For instance, GIS is used by freight companies and emergency services to route vehicles efficiently, by food stores to site new supermarkets, or by the European Union to check that farmers are adhering to their claims for Common Agricultural Policy funding.

There are a growing number of different GIS packages which process maps and data, but they all have these main features:

- Data input – loading maps in computerized form from surveys or remote sensing. Some GIS can also use information from surveys and census that link to places on the maps.
- Data management – asking questions about the maps and data, selecting what to show on the maps.
- Data transformation and display – making new maps from the selected data or showing data in diagrams on maps.

There are two main types of GIS which process raster or vector data. Raster data is information about a map stored as a series of cells on a computer screeen. Each cell has information about that part of the map. For instance, a map of land use may have a particular colour to describe a type of land use. A raster map has information about every cell on the map and so takes up a great deal of storage space on a computer. Remotely sensed images may also be used as raster maps. A meteorological satellite image may contain one item of information about each cell, such as the amount of water vapour in the atmosphere, while a Landsat image has more complex wave band data for each cell. New maps can be made by selecting which wavebands to show on a map to portray different types of land use or topography.

Vector maps are drawn as areas, lines or points from a set of instructions held in a map data file. Vector maps have been carefully digitized, often from paper-based maps. Additional information may be attached to areas, lines or points on the map, for instance, areas could represent regions, and have additional data on demographic or social statistics, while lines may make a network of roads with times of travel or distances attached to them.

GIS is changing the way maps are made and sold. The Ordnance Survey (OS) has now completed digitizing large-scale mapping for the whole of Britain, but the maps will not be sold as published sets. Most OS agents have a computer terminal linked to OS headquarters and can print out a large-scale plan (a Superplan) on demand, centred on a particular grid reference. (No more juggling with two sheets because your study area is over the join!) The OS large-scale digitized map data are also available to schools to use with suitable GIS software.

OS map data, plus your own data collected from fieldwork can be processed on educational GIS. Using maps is a fundamental geographical skill. Today's students need to be familiar with the way digitized map data can be a basis for their enquiries.

Fieldwork of the future?

It is possible that fieldwork of the future will be augmented by new technology aids such as Global Positioning Systems, laptop computers, remote environmental monitoring systems and Geographic Information Systems on computer. In the year 2010 will a geography teacher be adding these notes to fieldwork instructions for students?

Use your GPS (Global Positioning System) to follow this course around the study area.

At each field, enter your position and the landuse at that point into your laptop. Check that the environmental monitor at each station has gathered hourly data on stream flow, pH, nitrate levels, rainfall, temperature and light levels since yesterday, and download the data into your laptops.

When you get back to the centre, transfer all the data into the GIS, plot them on maps and graphs ready to discuss in your groups for after dinner this evening.

HOW WILL WE KNOW IF WE HAVE GOT IT RIGHT?

However IT is used, we need some indication of the effectiveness of this method of learning in geography. Here are some questions which may help to clarify what has taken place in your classroom, whether IT has been only one of a number of resources, or an essential and integral part of a topic.

- Are you using IT for a real purpose?
- Are you using IT to further your students' geographical understanding?
- Is incorporating IT an efficient use of both your time and the students' time?

- Have you a clear aim and understanding about what learning is/should be taking place when students use IT?
- Have you talked to your students about their views on IT and asked for their evaluation of the use of IT in geography?

REFERENCES

Burrough, P. A. (1986) *Principles of Geographical Information Systems for Land Resources Assessment*, Oxford: Oxford University Press.

Department for Education (1995a) *Geography in the National Curriculum*, London: HMSO.

Department for Education (1995b) *Information Technology in the National Curriculum*, London: HMSO.

National Council for Educational Technology (1994) *Remote Sensing: the Welsh Office Satellites in Schools Initiative*, Warwick: National Council for Educational Technology.

National Council for Educational Technology (1995) *Geography – Approaches to IT Capability*, Warwick: National Council for Educational Technology.

Ordnance Survey (1995) *Ordnance Survey Digital Map Data Catalogue*, London: Ordnance Survey.

School Curriculum and Assessment Authority (1995a) *Key Stage 3, Information Technology: the New Requirements*, London: School Curriculum and Assessment Authority.

School Curriculum and Assessment Authority (1995b) *Key Stage 3, Information Technology and the National Curriculum*, London: School Curriculum and Assessment Authority.

Chapter 20

Teaching about the local community
Using first-hand experience

Rachel Bowles

INTRODUCTION

The principle of actively observing the local area and using personal knowledge to understand its geography has a long tradition. In 1931 the Hadow Report stressed the importance in geography of outdoor activity and experience (Marsden 1994). Garnett (1934: 20) pointed out in her guide for teachers and students in training that 'nothing but the real thing, scientific truth, should be offered to children of any age'.

By 1986 HMI was declaring that 'pupils should not be primarily passive recipients of information, but should be given adequate opportunities to carry out practical investigations, to explore and express ideas in their own language . . . and to reflect upon other people's attitudes and values' (HMI 1986: 32). In 1991 the principle was formally stated in the National Curriculum Programmes of Study: 'Enquiry should form an important part of pupils' work in geography . . . . Work should be linked to/take account of pupils' interests, experience and capabilities and lead to investigations based on fieldwork' (DES 1991: 31, 35).

In 1995 the Revised Orders still expect opportunities for investigation that are 'based on direct experience . . . and fieldwork in the locality of the school' (DES 1995: 2).

It must be understood that the current National Curriculum states the minimum requirements. The simplicity of the current statements is to be regarded as a key to more detailed opportunities. Teaching about the local community involves the whole child. Combined with the interpretation of photographs and maps, direct investigation helps bring order to the child's own 'sense of place' which in turn brings about a degree of attainment in geographical understanding.

USING A CHILD'S KNOWLEDGE

Research has shown that a child has a great fund of knowledge and understanding supporting a 'sense of place' which has developed with growing cognition of its own surroundings. The good teacher has always used and built upon the knowledge already known by the child. Today, in order to comply with the new Orders the teacher must recognize this knowledge and the understanding of place that arises from a child's immediate concerns with the features and activities within the local area.

The rest of this chapter suggests how best this may be achieved, first, by considering the geographical viability of the area known to the child, and second, by using an enquiry approach to motivate children to find out about the geographical features of local and distant communities.

THE OFFICIAL REQUIREMENTS

A considerable part of the National Curriculum is concerned with the study of places with precise attention given to at least three localities during Key Stages 1 and 2. One of these localities is to be within the school's vicinity and the study of this area is to be progressive through to Key Stage 3.

By Key Stage 3 it is expected that the primary child will have completed a thorough coverage of the geographical features of the local area sufficient to appreciate these features at different scales and to develop more precise enquiries of selected features of the area.

THE ACTUAL LOCALITY: CHANGE IN SIZE BETWEEN KEY STAGES

The Orders give a clear directive to regard the locality as an area 'which is based on and around a community' (Catling 1995). At each stage the locality core is the primary school and in every community the core includes the school. Further, the definition expects the size of the locality to differ between Key Stages 1 and 2.

THE CHILD'S VIEW OF THE LOCALITY

Matthews (1992) points out that 'children's ability to acquire and handle environmental information as they encounter geographical space is a process not convincingly understood'. Nonetheless, every child has a perception of its own environment built upon personal knowledge and skills. Matthews reviews the large body of research which has investigated the diverse influences upon a child's direct experience. Gender, culture, class and the nature and planning of the environment all play their part in the development of a child's image and understanding of its immediate locality. Such factors must not be underestimated when, for practical purposes, the teachers of geography set out to discover the child's view of the locality in order to inform their own teaching priorities when developing a scheme for teaching in the community at any Key Stage.

WAYS OF ASSESSING THE LOCALITY AREA

A teacher, new to both class and area, could use core subject time, particularly in English, to find out about the way a class views the local surroundings. The final objective could be a 'talking map' for describing the area to another school. The means would be writing about their favourite place in the home area and the stimulus a sequence using sounds, photographs and map to generate conversation about favourite places in the locality. The geography would be the request that the favourite place be given an address and a sketch map be made to show its location. Whatever the quality of the final map it will graphically reveal a degree of knowledge or lack of knowledge of the community both by individuals and group.

Alternatively, a database could be developed using survey sheets with several classes and the school staff. The surveys should investigate where to go for everyday goods and places, special goods and places and include columns for the nearest, farthest and best places. The final results when graphed and mapped offer evidence not only of the range of places visited but also the focus or foci of the locality.

GROWTH OF THE IDEA OF LOCALITY

Investigations in schools in a variety of areas suggest the following progression in children's ideas of their local area:

- Children will relate to places which they visit most frequently with their families. This is their 'local area', an area with which they can compare other areas.
- The core of this locality is consistent with every age-group and is usually determined by walking distance to school, the nearest post office and general stores.
- The size of the core area is coincident with the concept of the whole locality if it also contains all the needs of the community for special as well as everyday needs. This usually means a choice of supermarket and stores, fresh food and other markets and a variety of entertainment.
- In most schools the idea of locality expands with maturation. This is excepting community characteristics such as the 'village' concept found in inner city schools and the cultural demands of ethnic communities.
- The greatest extent of the idea of locality comes with the upper junior child who has a secure base of frequent visits for specific purposes within a certain area (Bowles 1995).

STAGES OF GROWTH

There appear to be two phases in the growth of a child's idea of locality and with it a sense of community and place. First, there is absolute certainty about the core character of the area known to it. This shows itself as a willingness to describe features without prompting, to debate another's view of those features and to begin to enquire into the reasons for them – human or physical. It is the area visited most frequently. Second, there is acknowledgement of a fringe area within which he or she has secure knowledge of certain features but keeps each discrete. Thus the inner city KS1 child knows older members of the family go 'up to town', but only becomes loquacious when specific features such as toy shops are mentioned. The KS2 child will give a fuller picture of the extent of this larger area, define its limits be it major road, river or hills, and can be prompted to raise questions about its character. For the older child this is its recognized locality within which he or she makes frequent journeys.

THE ACTUAL LOCALITY: VARIATIONS IN EXTENT AT KEY STAGE 2

School catchment area

At Key Stage 2 the size of the locality area could differ from school to school depending upon the home location of the school population. One relevant example is the denominational school which has a catchment area larger than the neighbourhood local authority schools.

Regional location

Other reasons for variable locality size between schools are bound up with the infrastructure of the region. Figure 20.1 shows the considerable difference in length of regular journeys made by inner urban and rural children.

In inner city areas most needs for school, work, shopping and leisure activities such as swimming and music are within walking distance or a short bus ride of home. Car ownership, which can liberate the suburban and rural dweller, is often not possible through lack of parking or garage space. The size of the children's known locality for this kind of area does not change between KS1 and KS2 (Bowles 1995).

In rural areas these needs are supplied from a much wider area. The Key Stage 1 child may not look beyond the confines of the village or cluster of villages for experiences. The Key Stage 2 child needs access to regional hospitals, libraries, swimming pools, music lessons, choice of clothes and entertainment. To fulfil these needs may require travel up to 20 miles (32 km) to the nearest centre. Moreover, the variety of needs tends to be spread among a variety of centres within a 20-mile (32-km) radius of home – the idea of region as locality therefore comes early to these children (Bowles 1994).

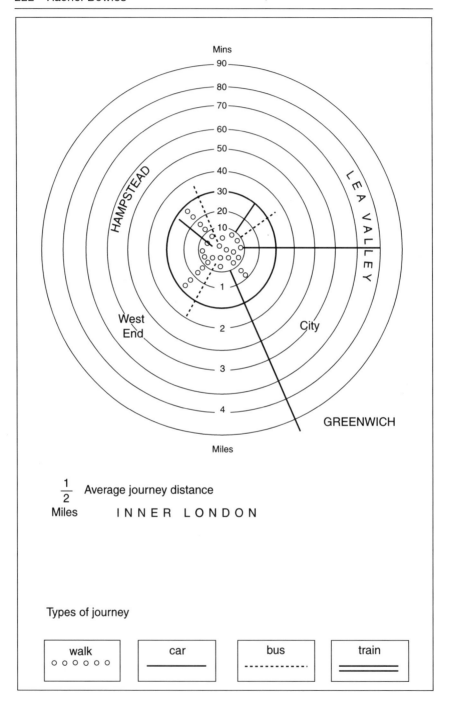

Figure 20.1 Regular journeys of children in their locality

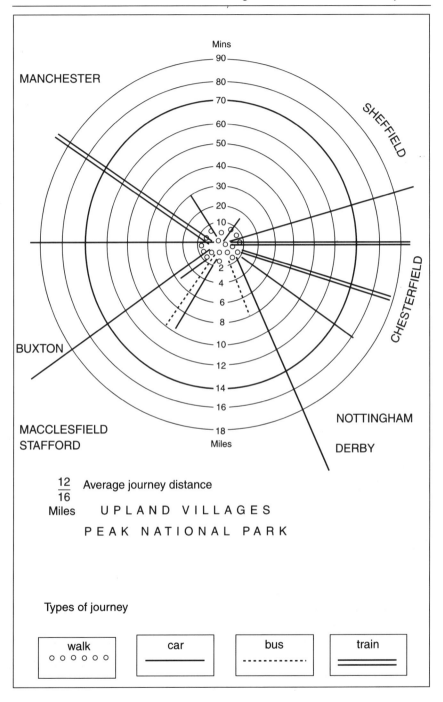

MANCHESTER

SHEFFIELD

CHESTERFIELD

BUXTON

MACCLESFIELD
STAFFORD

NOTTINGHAM

DERBY

Mins
90
80
70
60
50
40
30
20
10

2
4
6
8
10
12
14
16
18
Miles

$\frac{12}{16}$ Average journey distance
Miles

U P L A N D   V I L L A G E S

P E A K   N A T I O N A L   P A R K

Types of journey

walk	car	bus	train
○ ○ ○ ○ ○ ○	——	·············	═══

CONTENT OF THE LOCALITY AREA

When the preliminary investigations outlined above are complete, the general boundary of the area frequented by the class or the school population should be marked out on the local map. It will be a guide for planning the school geographical activities at each Key Stage and for each class according to its ability. This map should be available for all the staff, not just the geography co-ordinator.

It is not the size of the area which is important, rather the content of physical and human features, the way they are arranged within the area, and how far they offer opportunities to develop children's knowledge and understanding of places. Consider whether the area frequented by the children is large enough to enable the development of concepts of scale and spatial distribution, and whether it extends awareness and develops their interest in the surroundings. Consider too whether it is possible to recognize and investigate changes, whether there is sufficient diversity and character to begin to develop an interest in people and places beyond the children's immediate experience and whether it is possible to develop responsible attitudes to the cross-curricular concerns of citizenship, economic and industrial understanding, environmental and earth science education.

In simple terms the locality within which the child spends most time should be the geographical locality. In central urban areas this is insufficient for a rounded geographical education, while in rural areas this could be too extensive. However, in suburban districts the area is probably adequate. The criteria to be met are that there should be a variety of distinctive features both physical and human – a stream, contrasting buildings, variety of land use, evidence in the landscape of change and historical growth – and that there should be elements of the environment common to every community – church, meeting place, small and large shops, workplaces, playing areas, major connections with other places.

DEVELOPING UNDERSTANDING OF THE COMMUNITY

If teachers are to develop the children's local perceptions from the early years onwards there must be some understanding by the teacher of the school locality before any planning can begin. No study ought to begin without an understanding of the scale of building, the variety in age, character and functions of the buildings, be they homes or businesses, and a realization of the landforms and watercourses which have influenced, and still influence, the way the locality is changing.

The CCW Advisory Paper 11 puts these practical concerns in perspective:

> Understanding communities is not unlike the process of understanding literature. Just as we understand a book only after we have read all the chapters and only understand each chapter more completely on reading

the whole book, so too with communities. We can only hope to approach an understanding of communities, be they local, national or international, by constant reference to the larger communities of which they are part and the smaller communities of which they are comprised. Consequently, pupils at all stages should be aware of the various contexts within which community life occurs.

(CCW 1991: 10)

In other words it is not enough to look at the immediate area about the school, yet it is from that area that information can be drawn to indicate that it is part of a much larger community. An indication of the possible geographical principles to be observed within the community can be found in daily personal geographies. Where local people live, how they travel, what difficulties they encounter, where and at what they work are answers to part of the geography of the community. An enquiry approach adds rigour to such random geographical observations and it is this approach which is endorsed by the National Curriculum.

BASIC QUESTIONS FOR ENQUIRY

Storm (1989) pointed out that for every locality and for every level of enquiry five fundamental questions should be asked. Supplementary questions can be quickly envisaged, and in each instance below some possibilities are indicated:

1   What is this place like? (Is it urban? rural? Is it a village or part of a larger settlement? How can we investigate it at first hand?)
2   Why is this place as it is? (Is it the result of providing homes for commuters? for workers in local industries? Has it seen changes in purpose? Can these be recognized? Is it practicable to collect and record data about it?)
3   How is this place connected to other places? (Is it a route centre? a resting-place along a major route? isolated? part of a complex network? Which route maps shall we use? Where are the safe places to observe and record the nature of the connections?)
4   How is this place changing? (Are more than buildings being altered? Is the economic function changing? How quickly are the changes happening – in months? years? or is it static? Who can tell us? What investigative procedures can be established?)
5   What would (does) it feel like to be in this place? (Are there contrasts? What is unusual? How does it compare with other places? Why should people visit from other places?)

The five main questions and the supplementary ones provide a framework for collecting evidence and for enquiry. This framework subsequently becomes a conceptual structure which acts as the guide to direct the unsystematic, but pertinent and detailed, observations of the children. All teachers, in addition to the co-ordinator, should ask such questions about the locality.

Two further fundamental questions are added by Foley and Janikoun (1992), 'Where is this place?', and 'How is this place similar to, or different from, another place?'

Not only do these questions in total draw attention to the great variety of geographical knowledge but also to the range of contexts within which change takes place.

ENQUIRY, GEOGRAPHICAL CONCEPTS AND KNOWLEDGE

Figure 20.2 tables these questions and variations with examples of associated geographical concepts, knowledge and activities. These are generic questions intended to be asked about any locality. The concepts are statements which may or may not be true in particular localities. Deviations from the concept necessitate further questions and investigation. The final column suggests, in brief, the knowledge to be gained, the skills to be enhanced and the activities to enable these to happen.

These are questions to be asked when organizing the whole school curriculum. Catling emphasises that 'the important consideration is which questions might be appropriate to follow through at the different points in the curriculum when localities are studied' (1995: 22). It does not mean that a concept should not be revisited. For example, looking at different single houses for Homes at Key Stage 1 is but a preparation for recognizing houses of a certain type when investigating how and when the residential areas of a town have changed. This is progression. Within this sequence other supplementary questions will provide differentiation.

ORGANIZATION OF THE ENQUIRY PROCESS

Concepts are built up steadily, using skills begun in the early years and knowledge acquired in the process of previous enquiry. The range of this knowledge is the starting-point of the process. There are several stages:

1 Recognition of a focus for study relevant to the levels of cross-curricular attainment in the class, knowledge of and past work in the local area with or without a specific issue in mind. Development of the focus as a question or a statement.
2 Organization of the collection and recording of data. Fieldwork sites need to be checked for safety and given supervision. Questionnaires,

record sheets and maps have to be devised (IT) and co-ordinated with cross-curricular work with core subjects which handle data.

3 Analysis and display of data – to do this may require a rota of children to enter information on to a spread sheet or database, or individual groups may enter up information using a key on a master map.

4 Interpretation and presentation of the findings and seeing how far they support the original statement. Where appropriate, community experts should be involved to supply further information and different view-points. The use of role-play to produce a 'public enquiry' to show to the rest of the school and to parents can be invaluable (Bowles 1994).

5 Conclusion and evaluation. Where appropriate the enquiry results should be sent to the relevant community authority, or at the very least added to the school archives for use in other areas of the curriculum or in other years. The other questions raised by the enquiry should be considered, becoming in turn another enquiry focus.

LENGTH AND BENEFITS OF ENQUIRY

The sequence above has assumed the use of the enquiry process over a six-week period which would be appropriate for a thematic or issue-based focus. A short enquiry investigating the location and purpose of the oldest buildings in the community could be based upon photograph and mapwork lasting for one period.

Geography in the local community is a two-way collaboration. The children, their families and community experts, amateur and professional, have a wealth of knowledge and experience gathered over the years, i.e. unrealized geography. This knowledge, particularly in a cosmopolitan community, should be used wherever possible to widen geographical horizons. In return the school develops skills of graphicacy, research and data handling using familiar material in a systematic form which in turn contributes to the formation of future responsible members of the community.

Geographical work emphasizes the value of evidence from a wide spectrum, the need to avoid bias and intolerance, to be suspicious of simple explanations, to be concerned for the quality of environment and to value and conserve the resources therein.

BEYOND THE LOCAL COMMUNITY

To achieve breadth in these values and attitudes, several communities should be investigated on different occasions in parallel with looking at the local community. Fieldwork could be extended with a planned sequence of half day and full day visits and where possible a residential visit, each of which is concerned with an enquiry comparable with one undertaken locally. At the very least there could be twinning with a variey of different

NAME OF LOCALITY OR LOCALITIES: ANY COMMUNITY OF SIMILAR SIZE

Questions	Concepts/ideas	Knowledge/skills/ activities
LOCATION Where is the community?	Location in region and country influences character.	Comparisons with other communities. Maps and atlas work.
Why is the village/town/ suburb here?	Village/town location influenced by physical and historical factors.	Map, photograph, fieldwork to locate human and physical features.
FEATURES What is the village/town/ suburb like?	Distinctive community features show change of functions over time. Landscape influences character.	House types, land use, slopes and rivers, evidence of growth and change; map, photograph and fieldwork skills.
SERVICES Where are our community services found?	Some communities have to travel great distances for simple services.	Location of healthcare, shops, markets, post offices. Development of map and directory skills.
How are essential services (water, energy, sewage supplied?)	Water storage is essential for supply. What supplies energy? wood, gas, electricity, oil?	Investigate differences between isolated and town supplies. Environmental consequences.
CONNECTIONS How do we get there?	Different modes of transport make different networks, different environmental and community demands.	Minor and major journey systems in school, local area, country. Environmental considerations.
WORK What kind of work is here? Is farming significant? Why does some industry need special sites?	Farms are affected by climate, geology. Farms are businesses. Extractive industry is resource based. Manufacturing industry can adapt and use available labour.	Place in community of farming, extractive, manufacturing service industries and new industries. Photograph, map, directory skills. Environmental considerations.
WEATHER Is our weather different? upland/ lowland/tropical/ seasons	Altitude and aspect affect weather; regional climate affects lifestyle. Weather hazards influence community life.	Skills in weather recording and analysis. Understanding extreme weather conditions. Forecasting effect of weather upon community life.

LEISURE What is it like to be here? Where do people play?	The place of open space in a community. Commercial and community needs often conflict.	Range and impact of recreational needs at different scales. Environmental issues and local needs.
ISSUES How is this community changing?	New building and industry affect communications, population and environment.	Identify effect of new features by observation, recording and analysis. Identify issues arising.
CONTEXT Why are villages/ towns/suburbs as they are? What are their functions?	Location affects function and development of function. Change can be recognized in buildings and spatial patterns.	Comparisons between communities of buildings and industries. Photograph, map and atlas work.
ENVIRONMENT Why is this place liked/disliked? Why should some areas be protected?	Special landscapes attract conflicting activities and views. Competition of community and national concerns.	Countryside issues of farming, industry and tourism. Urban issues of pollution, traffic. Role-play 'enquiry' for attitudes and values.

Figure 20.2 Questions to be asked about a locality

communities to obtain breadth in understanding similarities and differences in landscape, buildings, land use, weather, work, leisure and current issues. In turn themes could be developed with actual examples and resources from all the communities.

RESOURCES FOR COMMUNITY STUDY

A comprehensive resource kit has five core features:

1 Maps – local national survey maps, historical maps, everyday maps.
2 Photographs and drawings – historical and current to show change and character.
3 Written materials – past and present, factual and fictional descriptions; selected census returns and newspaper reports; selection from directories past and present.
4 Audio resources and people – taped interviews with essential community people who visit the school; reminiscences and interviews on local issues.
5 Artefacts and statistics – samples of clothes and materials, food labels, products of industry, music, local geology, weather statistics and statistics relating to family, children, local population.

An evaluation of the success of teaching about the community could be to see how many of the above items are regarded as important enough to pack and send in exchange for similar items from another community. Real success would be for the children to send the products of interpretation and use of the items as a true reflection of the geography of their community.

CONCLUSION

A community, both people and place, is a source of raw geographical data. With careful selection, opportunities can be provided to develop fieldwork and enquiry skills, use and develop core skills associated with map, photograph, text and data, and contribute to practical work in core subjects. Consideration of similarities and differences with other communities extends the education of the whole child as a responsible community member.

REFERENCES

Board of Education (1931) *Report of the Consultative Committee on the Primary School* (Hadow Report), London: HMSO.

Bowles, R. (1994) *Eyam: An English Village*, Leamington Spa: Scholastic.

Bowles, R. (1995) 'How well do you know your locality', *Primary Geographer* 23 (October): 16–18.

Catling, S. (1995) 'Choosing and using places', *Primary Geographer* 21 (April): 21–3.

Curriculum Council for Wales (1991) *Community Understanding* CCW Advisory Paper 11.

DES (1991) *Geography in the National Curriculum (England)*, London: HMSO.

DES (1995) *Geography in the National Curriculum*, London: HMSO.

Foley, M. and Janikoun, J. (1992) *The Really Practical Guide to Primary Geography*, Cheltenham: Stanley Thornes.

Garnett, O. (1934) *Fundamentals in School Geography*, London: Harrap.

Her Majesty's Inspectorate of Schools (HMI) (1986) *Geography from 5 to 16*, Curriculum Matters series no. 7, London: HMSO.

Marsden, B. (1994) *Primary School Geography*, London: David Fulton Publishers.

Matthews, M.H. (1992) *Making Sense of Place*, Hemel Hempstead: Harvester Wheatsheaf.

Storm, M (1989) 'The five basic questions for primary geography', *Primary Geographer* 2 (Autumn): 4.

Chapter 21

The European dimension in primary education

John Halocha

OUR PLACE IN EUROPE

A glance through the post-Dearing National Curriculum Geography Orders for Key Stages 1 and 2 may encourage the reader to ask why a chapter called 'The European Dimension in Primary Education' has been included in this book. There appear to be few direct references to it in the Orders. Although they have been simplified and the content reduced, primary teachers still have many decisions to make about the design, content and teaching of the curriculum they provide for their children. Their time is limited and there are still numerous demands which have to be accommodated within each school day. This chapter has been written to help busy primary teachers involved in the development of their school curriculum consider current issues and opportunities in order to make informed decisions for planning a European dimension within their teaching. It has three aims:

- to offer a clear introduction to, and discussion of, key concepts related to this aspect of education;
- to stimulate staff discussion of ways forward for the school by giving some examples of activities already successfully developed by practising teachers;
- to provide initial access to up-to-date ideas and information in other publications, and suggest contacts and links with various agencies to help teachers and their colleagues develop work appropriate for the children.

Each reader of this chapter will come to it with a wide variety of experience and understanding of what they think Europe is and how it affects their everyday life. The author's uncommon surname has Polish roots. His father arrived in Britain during World War II and joined re-formed Polish regiments based in Scotland. National boundary changes at the end of the war placed his home town in the USSR. Also, as his whole family had 'disappeared' during the war, he made the decision to settle in England. He married an English woman. This very brief family history illustrates some of the many processes which have occurred throughout time and which are still taking place in Europe today.

Superimposed on our personal experiences are current political and social trends and values related to the debate on Europe. At the time of writing, Eurotunnel and French nuclear testing are realities. Individuals and political parties hold various views on the extent to which Britain should be connected with other parts of Europe. We make decisions about the food our families buy from other countries. We read about evidence linking pollution from Britain causing environmental problems in Scandinavia. We take many holidays in European countries, often travelling in cars bought from them. Even though there are few formal references to the European Union in the National Curriculum, our children cannot fail to experience many links with Europe in their everyday lives and probably hear many arguments both for and against them. Many will have first-hand experiences and links upon which we can build and extend their understanding. If they are to become active citizens able to assess key trends in Europe and make informed decisions, then primary teachers have the important role of creating the foundations of knowledge and understanding which will help them to acquire these skills. What are some of these key concepts and skills?

SOME FOUNDATIONS FOR UNDERSTANDING EUROPE

It is very easy to make assumptions about where 'Europe' is and what it contains and what it does not. If we use the term 'European dimension' too generally, we run the risk of making assumptions about what Europe actually is. Some geographers will offer a range of definitions based on physical features. Politicians may base their arguments on the member states belonging to the various economic groupings which have grown up in the last fifty years. At primary school we need to lay foundations which allow children to begin to understand that 'Europe' is a constantly changing concept and that many of the criteria we use to define it and the countries 'inside' and 'outside' are arbitrary. Historical examples ranging from grandparents' maps of Europe before World War II to the reference to 'Europa' in a map developed from research by Ptolemy in Alexandria in the second century AD can be used to illustrate these points. Their views will be affected by the resources they use. A range of map projections will show how the area and shape of countries can be distorted. Try to obtain a world map from Australia or New Zealand, in which Europe is printed near one edge. This type of resource can help to counterbalance a Eurocentric view of the world. A satellite image of Europe will not show any political boundaries and can lead to a discussion of how and why national boundaries develop and change. 'The Changing Map of Europe' published by

Pictorial Charts Educational Trust to accompany the BBC schools radio series 'In the News' is a useful resource which is regularly updated.

Another concept which can be introduced is that of 'a country' or 'a region'. These exist for many reasons. They are cultural constructs which allow people to identify with shared values and which can have economic benefits, but borders can also exclude other peoples and nations, – thus there are both positive and negative features to them. However, if the debate is taken to extremes, one can end up arguing for total global uniformity. Children therefore also need an introduction to the ideas of rich cultural heritage and diversity, at national, regional and local levels. These relate to other concepts such as migration, resources and environmental issues. Political borders can have strong effects on the migration of groups of people, ranging from those looking for work to war refugees – examples of both can be seen within Europe today. However, many environmental problems ignore borders and can be used as a foundation on which to introduce ideas about shared responsibilities between nations. This is also related to another important concept about using the 'European Dimension' in school. It is part of a much broader continuum of understanding about the world, which children can be encouraged to develop. The teachers' ability to introduce these contrasting concepts within a range of scales from local, through to national, European and global will influence their pupils' ability to begin to understand the complex processes at work in our constantly changing world.

While political borders do exist, many issues are global and 'interdependence' is becoming an increasingly important concept for children to develop. This also provides starting-points for work on citizenship, human rights and responsibilities. At a very practical planning level, an example may be given for Key Stage 2. 'Rivers' is a required thematic study. It can be studied within a European context and teachers have considerable flexibility in order that it 'may be studied separately, in combination with other themes, or as part of the study of places' (DFE 1995: 89). By taking, for example, the River Rhine, children could develop enquiries into where the river is, what it is used for, what happens along it and in it, which countries it flows through and how it may be changing. Effective planning would also include aspects of the 'environmental change' theme at Key Stage 2. All these questions encourage good geographical enquiry and will most likely raise issues of pollution, conflicting uses and of how various groups of people have to make decisions about the worlds' resources. Citizenship, human rights and responsibilities have a natural and relevant place in geographical studies. These ideas and approaches to their teaching are developed in Osler, Rathenow and Starkey (1996).

As children gain confidence in working with ideas such as citizenship, they will begin to examine some of the values and attitudes found in various parts of Europe. An ability to understand other points of view, value diversity, and yet observe underlying similarities are important skills to be developed. Children should begin to understand the nature of stereotypes and how they can affect our views of other people and cultures. Geography may not appear to be a subject through which aesthetic awareness may easily be developed, but if one thinks of the wide range of landscapes and natural phenomena and of the excitement generated when studying other cultures, then possibilities do surface. The development of an aesthetic awareness and a sense of 'awe and wonder' within the whole school curriculum are looked for in OFSTED inspections – geography offers many opportunities for children to experience these. It takes time for teachers to grow sufficiently confident to include more value-laden aspects within their teaching, but with careful whole-school planning and a clear school policy to support them, the European dimension offers many ways into these important areas.

The next section of this chapter looks at some of the ways in which this work may be planned into the primary curriculum and how a school policy might be developed.

PLANNING A EUROPEAN DIMENSION

The revised Orders have returned some professional teaching decisions to teachers. One of the strengths of the Geography Orders is that they are worded in such a way as to give teachers considerable choice about both the content and methods of curriculum design they create. In the Key Stage 1 section on 'Places' the Orders state that 'two localities should be studied: the locality of the school and a locality, either in the United Kingdom or overseas . . . ' (DFE 1995: 87). The thematic study section states that 'the quality of the environment in any locality, either in the United Kingdom or overseas, should be investigated' (DFE 1995: 87). Both these provide excellent opportunities for the European dimension to be introduced to young children. At Key Stage 2 it is clearly stated that children's studies of rivers, weather, settlement and environmental change 'should include the United Kingdom and the European Union' (DFE 1995: 89). Other Key Stage 2 statements focus on countries beyond Europe and it is therefore possible to develop a balanced range of experiences for these children to include an area larger than the school's vicinity, a contrasting UK locality and thematic studies in European contexts, in addition to the wider world. When teachers plan Key Stage 2 activities, it may be possible to build on the Key Stage 1 experiences and localities to assist with progression and continuity.

The Orders provide the chance to relate issues and enquiries to various scales of study. Returning to the River Rhine example in the previous section, this could mean perhaps extending the discussion of our use of rivers beyond the local and European context by providing opportunities for children to compare what they find happening on and around the Rhine with examples based on the Amazon. This type of planning approach also allows relevant links to be made to a global perspective of the theme being studied.

It may take time for a European dimension to become established within the work of the school. Williams (1994) suggests that a school may go through a number of stages during the introduction of a European dimension. The author's own experience of working with primary schools on developing European activities strongly supports this broad pattern. Our studies have also indicated the need for two other processes to be present, especially when working to develop links with schools in other countries.

The first is the importance of starting on a very small scale and gradually building on success. As other staff and children begin to see the positive work taking place, general enthusiasm and a desire to participate develops. In a recent project the author introduced a school in Italy to one in Oxfordshire. The first small activity was for the children to plan what they would want to photograph in their school and village on a 36-exposure film, as their initial contact with the Italian children. From that one small exchange of photographs, very strong and exciting links and activities have grown.

The second factor for success is the high level of commitment which develops when staff in the linking schools are able to meet and build personal relationships. In the schools mentioned above, a teacher from the English school was able to visit the children, teachers and locality in Italy, while their headteacher visited Oxfordshire. When this type of exchange of resources and evidence gets under way an extensive range of resources is soon created. It is, for instance, often hard to get large-scale maps of precise parts of other countries – a link with a local school should soon make this easy. Also, when children become involved in explaining their locality to other children, this work can be related to many aspects of their own locality studies. It gives them another reason for looking at their locality critically and may help the teachers in the assessment of their understanding of key geographical concepts. The opportunities for children to visit their link schools in other countries are often limited in reality by economics, the age of the children and the distance in some cases, but teachers can visit. The ways of achieving this are covered in a later section.

Once such activities are under way, it may be possible to formalize them within a school policy. Indeed, this would be a positive step where the evidence of practice can also be identified in OFSTED inspections of the school. A school in Wales begins its policy statement with 'During years 5 and 6 we aim to instil in children the concept of being "young Europeans" and all that this entails' and goes on to identify a series of objectives.

There are a number of ways in which the contents of a policy on the European dimension may be included within the planning activities of a school. Many schools now have programmes of topics or themes which will be covered by the various year groups in each term or part of a term. As a school examines its whole-school plans, it may be possible to identify times where a strong European focus may be appropriate. For example, if the teacher intends to develop a block of work on rivers, the skills, places and themes elements of the geography curriculum could be well integrated into work which focused on a river in Europe. This form of planning will create certain times of the year when children can focus their attention in depth on European issues within a predominantly geographical study.

There is, however, another way of building the European dimension into whole-school planning at the primary level. There may be units of work which focus on Art or Music within the National Curriculum. Examine the plans to see where there may be opportunities to plan in a European dimension when geography is not the main focus. In this way, children can begin to experience a more continuous exposure to European themes.

Finally, it may be appropriate to examine the whole-school plans in relation to the range of activities which take place beyond the school. Field visits do not take place only in the geographical areas of the curriculum. If the teacher is able to identify when the various events take place during the time the children are at school, it may be possible to develop a coherent set of experiences for them. This can help with continuity and progression and encourage staff to think about the skills and concepts which are being developed and extended during such visits. This mapping of progression can also help to show parents why it has been decided to build in such activities. Parents are often asked to make a contribution towards the costs and clear objectives can help the case for this. Work in the immediate locality, day visits to a contrasting UK locality and perhaps even four days in another country could all be considered. Again, from an external point of view, such clarity of purpose and sense of progression can only be good when the school is under scrutiny.

USING THE RESOURCES IN THE SCHOOL'S OWN LOCALITY

One activity which might be developed during the planning process is the making of an audit of school resources to assist in teaching a European dimension. These resources might consist of those which the teacher already has and those whose potential needs to be explored. An example of the first would be to see if there are already materials such as up-to-date and non-stereotypical teaching materials in the school library. These might include books, posters and videos. Any contact already present but perhaps not being used should be assessed. The second approach is to look really closely at the school's own locality to see where there is potential for developing new resources with a European perspective. Are there parents who regularly travel within Europe and who may be able to create links and acquire resources? Are there untapped resources right in the school, such as one witnessed recently by the author where a learning support assistant was a fluent Greek-speaker and had close contacts with a locality in Greece – the school is currently developing her contributions both in a geographical locality study and in the Key Stage 2 history requirements for the study of aspects of ancient Greece. Are there families in the school from other parts of Europe? They may well have relations in their home country who could help with resources or establishing links with a local school. The school may not yet have a fax machine but is there a local business who would allow use of their machine for the cost of the phone calls? The Oxfordshire school already mentioned as having links with Italy does not own a fax machine but is in very frequent contact by using the one at the local garage a few minutes down the road. Is there a road haulage company in the locality which specializes in European freight transportation? Might they be interested in supporting your geographical enquiries with help from the drivers during their journeys? Once located, this type of resource can be included within broad curriculum planning in many ways as well as acting as a link between the locality studies around the school and children's enquiries about the wider world. Also, once these local resources can be located, they lead on to access to up-to-date materials from the country being studied – so much more accurate, stimulating and relevant than many of the materials in standard textbooks, which rarely have enough information about the precise localities in which the children are interested. Being able to track and investigate the year's journey of a long-distance lorry driver who has been into school, will be far more relevant to the children than reading a book about transport in Europe.

One of the most successful ways of developing the European dimension within the curriculum is through direct contact with a primary school in another country. A growing number of schools in Britain have developed very successful links, but many teachers still feel uncertain about this approach, often because they are unsure how to make the first steps. If the school audit of actual and potential resources does not find a link with another country, a number of other approaches can be considered. The first is to get in touch with The Central Bureau, Seymour Mews House, Seymour Mews, London W1H 9PE. The Central Bureau is an educational charity, funded by the Department for Education and the European Union. It exists to promote international education through exchange and interchange. There are many financial resources available to teachers to help create links with other schools, to support study visits by teachers and manage teacher-exchange schemes. The Central Bureau administers these schemes and can advise individual schools on making links and bidding for funding for European projects. They have many publications and currently offer a video entitled 'European Awareness in Primary Schools' which provides many actual examples, practical ideas and starting-points.

Many LEAs now have either an adviser or an officer with a particular responsibility for the European dimension within the county or borough. The local education office will be able to provide details of any personnel they may have working in this field. This officer in turn will be able to make contact with any locally available resources and schools already working in Europe. They should also be able to supply up-to-date information about applying for money from European funding programmes.

The school's town or city may be twinned with another place in Europe. If it is, there should be an officer in the council with a brief to manage this link and who can discuss the ways in which help may be available. Even if they do not know many schools in the linked place, it should be possible for them to make contact with the education authority in that area and perhaps even with someone interested in making links between schools.

Universities and colleges of higher education have projects and exchanges funded by the European Union. If the school is near a higher education campus it may well be worth getting in touch with their European affairs tutor or manager. They may be able to arrange links. One of the most successful ways of doing this is if the institution has a teacher training department or school of education. Tutors often have personal contacts with tutors in other European teacher training establishments and therefore direct access to contact with schools around Europe. It may be worth contacting geography and modern language departments initially, but all have potential. If the school has students on school experience programmes then these ideas can be discussed with the visiting tutors, who should be able to help contact colleagues working in the field. The other advantage of this approach is that students and tutors undertake exchanges in Europe and may be able to act as couriers for resources and messages as well as helping with language translations at 'the other end' of the link.

One of these ideas should help the teacher to contact a school or group of schools interested in working with them. Of course, there is nothing wrong with having links with schools in a number of countries. There are two main considerations in this respect: the first is that the work which can be developed in each of the links should be relevant and appropriate to the overall curriculum planning; the second is that there must be the desire and resources to sustain a number of meaningful links. There is nothing more upsetting for children than not getting replies to their letters, or more frustrating to teachers who may have put much effort into arranging for their children to write. As already mentioned, small but genuine personal commitments at the outset form the basis of a successful scheme. Some current European funding projects actually require groups of schools from four or five countries to link together. The school needs to show in its bids that it has thought through how the scheme will work.

A chapter of this length cannot discuss the details of activities to be developed with the children. Geographical Association publications are a valuable source. The pack 'Europe in the School: The School in Europe' published by Shell Education Service (Bell and Dransfield) contains many practical ideas. The Central Bureau produces many guidance sheets, booklets and other support materials. In-service courses on the European dimension are available in many areas.

MAKING THE MOST OF TECHNOLOGY

Effective communication is one of the keys to a successful link. It is important to choose the most effective method for what is being attempted. This needs to be discussed with the children and assessed for its relevance to work within the English Orders. The language skills developed in a child preparing to send an A4 size fax with specific information or questions are considerable. Photography is an excellent means and also raises questions about choosing and reading images. They should be up to date, making the use of some other published materials less relevant. Video is excellent but time-consuming. Its use must be planned well in advance with clear ideas of why images which move and have sounds need to be sent. Also, the television system of the link country must be checked to ensure each can play the other's tapes.

It is worth clarifying what Information Technology means within the revised Orders. In addition to computers, CD-ROM, etc. it also includes the use of camcorders, dataloggers, fax machines and other equipment used in the collection and exchange of information. Planning relevant ways of using these within European enquiries could soon increase the profile of technology in the school. There are also less obvious but equally relevant uses of technology: the Meteorological Office now provides a free service to schools where up-to-date weather charts, satellite images and data can be received at school (or the local garage!) on a fax machine. Teletext services and perhaps even satellite broadcasting provide up-to-date information on Europe. A primary school may not have access to the Internet but its local secondary school could well have the equipment. By developing contacts with their IT and modern languages staff, a teacher can find valuable support and help reinforce the work already being done in primary/secondary liaison arrangements.

Although a successful link will supply most of the necessary resources, it is useful to note selected other sources. Some educational suppliers offer valuable resources for the study of Europe. MJP Geopacks have a superb range of large colour satellite images of Europe which are ideal to use with primary children. The Geographical Association has a variety of publications on the European dimension and articles with a European focus often appear in their journal *Primary Geographer*. Book and resource reviews in the educational press can lead to some up-to-date and suitable printed materials. The *European* and the European sections of other newspapers can provide useful information. The BBC and ITV produce an excellent range of programmes for primary geography. Teacher training establishments should have a European dimension within their courses. In some this means that student teachers become involved in researching and producing materials, in which case it may be possible for a school to work with such students in developing resources of value to everyone involved.

There are a number of crucial issues and concepts which need careful thought when a European Dimension is being developed in a school. Integrating such work into whole-school plans is important. A knowledge of the contacts and resources already available can give the confidence to make a start. The hard work will be well worth the effort if future generations of children throughout Europe have the opportunity to make contact with each other. They will start to learn about and respect each other's way of life, while also beginning to understand that we are all linked together, perhaps more closely than previous generations ever were, as we begin to tackle some key questions which have not only European but global dimensions.

REFERENCES

Bell, G.H. (1991) *Developing a European Dimension in Primary Schools*, London: David Fulton Publishers.

Catling, S. (1992) *Placing Places*, Sheffield: The Geographical Association.

Council of Europe (1989) *Using the New Technologies to Create Links between Schools Throughout the World*, Strasbourg: Council of Europe.

DFE (1995) *Key Stages 1 and 2 of the National Curriculum*, London: HMSO.

Fountain, S. and Selby, P. (1988) 'Global education in the primary school', *Aspects of Education* 38: 21–42.

Osler, A., Rathenow, H. and Starkey, H. (1996) *Teaching for Citizenship in Europe*, Stoke on Trent: Trentham.

Wiegand, P. (1992) *Places in the Primary School*, Lewes: Falmer Press.

Williams, M. (1994) 'Researching the European Dimension in school geography', in A. Convey and C. Speak *A European Dimension in the Teaching of Geography*, Sheffield: Geographical Association.

Chapter 22

Towards a critical school geography

John Huckle

In our working lives as geography teachers we should never forget or abandon those ideals which draw so many of us to the job in the first place. School geography has the potential to develop young people's understanding of their 'place' in the world and so help form their identity. It can enable them to perceive the structures and processes which help and hinder their development, and can also foster the commitment to social justice and democracy, and the conserving, participatory and critical forms of citizenship, whereby they can seek to conserve or change those structures and processes and thereby help to create a better world. The International Charter on Geographical Education (IGU 1995) provides a comprehensive statement of such ideals and they are reflected in the aims for geography in the National Curriculum for England and Wales (DES 1990).

The reality is that such ideals are increasingly neglected or put to one side as geography teachers' work, along with that of other teachers, is de-professionalized or proletarianized. Teachers are increasingly required to adopt the role of technicians who deliver prescribed and pre-packaged content, assess and stratify pupils by reference to standard norms, spend more and more time serving an educational bureaucracy, and cope with a growing minority of alienated and disruptive pupils. New working conditions and forms of accountability increase teachers' workloads and erode their professional, economic and political status (Harris 1994). Young geography teachers are therefore more likely to work with disillusioned and cynical older colleagues than they were ten or twenty years ago. They are more likely to be affected by the high levels of stress and low levels of morale which pervade some staffrooms and they are more likely to have inadequate resources, facilities or encouragement to teach geography in an enlightened way. Schools and teachers are variously affected by recent attempts to redefine, restructure and repoliticize schooling, but in general it is becoming harder for geography teachers to work in ways which reflect progressive and radical ideals.

Nevertheless, this chapter urges geography teachers to cling to such ideals and seeks to introduce them to the theory and practice whereby they find contemporary expression. It traces the history of the radical or critical tradition in geographical education and suggests how it can be revived and updated using advances in academic geography and curriculum studies. It outlines the aims, content and pedagogy of a critical geography for a society undergoing profound change and hints at the political skills and alliances which geography teachers will need to develop if they are to gain greater control of their work and develop a true professionalism.

DEVELOPING AN HISTORICAL PERSPECTIVE

What counts as school geography (its content, teaching methods and assessment) is largely, but not wholly, determined by dominant groups and interests in society. The links between powerful economic, political and cultural interests and the everyday realities of geography classrooms are complex and are mediated by such agencies as National Curriculum working parties, textbook publishers, examination boards and PGCE courses, but school geography is socially constructed and continues to play a role in the economic and cultural reproduction of our advanced capitalist society. It helps to produce young workers and citizens with 'appropriate' knowledge, skills and values and so contributes to changing forms of social regulation whereby the state, and other institutions, maintain social order and ensure the reproduction of both the means and conditions of production.

Our society's need for a school subject which would foster nationalism, imperialism and a positive view of the world of work, while teaching useful knowledge and skills to future clerks, merchants and soldiers, largely explains the entry of geography into the school curriculum in the late nineteenth century and its subsequent revival and growth in the universities to meet the demand for qualified teachers (Capel 1981). Old geography textbooks reflect the racism, ethnocentrism, sexism and paternalism which pervaded the early teaching of the subject (Marsden 1989), and it was not until the 1970s and 1980s that this legacy was thoroughly exposed and real efforts made to counter stereotyping. Geography and history were favoured as social subjects for inclusion in the curriculum at the end of the last century and they have sustained their privileged position despite periodic challenges (Goodson 1983). The majority of pupils continue to be deprived of sufficient economics, politics, sociology and cultural studies to develop a real understanding of geography, and the provision for social or citizenship education in our state schools is inadequate to sustain, let alone improve, our current deteriorating level of democracy.

While school geography's legacy of stereotyping has been exposed there has been less attention to the changing ideologies, or ideas which contribute to social regulation, which have pervaded the geography curriculum.

Existing studies (Gilbert 1984) suggest that changing ideological emphases have left generations of pupils largely impotent as agents of social change. Nationalistic and imperialistic ideology taught them an unquestioning respect for nation and empire. Environmental determinism and natural regions taught them to accept a society shaped and limited by nature, while economic determinism taught them to accept the social relations of capitalism as normal and inevitable. The separation of the physical and human geography taught them a false separation of nature and society, while the subject's view of progress reinforced the modern faith in science, technology and bureaucracy. Too much school geography continues to draw solely on empiricist and positivist philosophies and so describes rather than explains the world. It fails to recognize power, conflict and agency, or to consider social alternatives, and can be seen to suggest to pupils that there are no real alternatives other than to accept the world largely as it is. Anyone doubting this assertion might try asking students who have recently passed A level geography, what they understand by capitalism, green politics, or the state.

Enough of such pessimism. Capitalist schooling, and an essentially capitalist school geography, were opposed from the outset. Elementary education for the working class was only conceded when people's popular efforts at self-education proved too threatening to the establishment and when its need for a more literate citizenry and technically competent work-force proved overwhelming (Shotton 1993). In 1885 the anarchist geographer Peter Kropotkin advocated an anti-militarist, anti-imperialist and anti-capitalist education through geography which would examine issues from the point of view of the working class, foster social harmony and mutual aid, and involve pupils in the everyday life of the community (Kropotkin 1885). Such messages have since been periodically applied, revived and updated by a minority of geography teachers who, like other radical educators, have drawn on Marxism, anarchism, progressivism, humanistic psychology and liberation pedagogy (Wright 1989), Radical education 'flowered' briefly in the late 1960s and early 1970s, along with the new Left and the new social movements, and some predict that it will resurface again in the late 1990s or early 2000s as the political pendulum swings back towards democracy, social justice and the empowerment of the individual through collective action.

CURRENT EDUCATIONAL REFORM AND THE NATIONAL CURRICULUM

The conditions of sustained economic growth and social democracy which gave expression to radical ideas in the late 1960s were not to last. The onset of an economic crisis and the need to restore levels of capital accumulation resulted in the rise of the new Right and the onset of a long period of economic, social and educational restructuring which continues to have profound effects on teachers' lives. The transition from an organized to a disorganized regime of capital accumulation, and from Fordist to Post-Fordist labour processes, required changes in the mode of regulation together with new forms of schooling (Flude and Hammer 1990; Whitty 1992). The state's expenditure on education for the majority of pupils would continue to fall in real terms and market forces would play a greater role in allocating pupils to more diverse kinds of school. While opting out, local management of schools, and open enrolment were designed to restratify schools and pupils, National Curriculum testing, examination league tables and OFSTED inspection reports were designed to provide indicators to guide the decisions of those parents who have real choice. The National Curriculum is essentially a minimal provision or entitlement. It does not have to be taught in private schools but its similarity to earlier academic curricula hints at its social control function and suggests that it is not suitable for advancing a liberal interpretation of the 1988 Education Reform Act's curriculum objectives: that education should promote the spiritual, moral, cultural, mental and physical development of pupils at school and of society.

The rise of the new Right owed much to its ability to sense people's disillusionment with those forms of social regulation which accompanied organized capitalism and to promote an alternative social vision to that associated with the welfare state. Thatcherism developed a mode of regulation and ideology in tune with disorganized capitalism and its economic, political and cultural imperatives were to shape the content of the National Curriculum. Too much education was once more seen as a dangerous thing and the curriculum again pressed into service to tighten social regulation and control. There were tensions between those who emphasized traditional, economic and progressive values (Ball 1990), but the outcome was a curriculum which seeks to rekindle nationalism, individualism and moral certainty, and prevent a coherent and critical understanding of society and social change. The cross-curricular elements do seek to address the Act's curriculum objectives, but they are non-statutory, not related to one another, not free from ideology (Ahier and Ross 1995), and are likely, following the Dearing Review, to disappear yet further from the perceptions and priorities of most schools and teachers.

After a brief romance with positivism and the 'new' geography in the 1970s, school geography was challenged in the early 1980s to assess post-positivist philosophies (behavioural, humanistic, welfare and radical geographies) and incorporate these into the curriculum so that it would better meet pupils' and society's needs (Cook and Gill 1983; Huckle 1983; Johnston 1986). The response was somewhat limited, for the government's educational agenda soon threatened the very survival of school geography and its status as a foundation subject could be assured only by promoting its more conservative characteristics. At a time when academic geography engaged with diverse philosophies and social and cultural theories in order to explain the contribution of space, place and geography to the profound social changes which were taking place (Cloke *et al.* 1991; Thrift 1992), the school subject's professional establishment turned its attention to a re-interpretation of the school subject which seemed to be little informed by these developments and parallel developments in social education (Bailey 1991; Wise 1993). The construction of the geography National Curriculum was not without its critics and dissenters but the final product gives little indication of the relationship between geography and society and does little to advance teachers' and pupils' understanding of the threats and promises presented by disorganized capitalism (Morris 1992). It fails to indicate what 'enquiry' really entails or what 'understanding' the themes really involves, and while some teachers and textbook writers have inter-preted it in progressive and radical ways (Hopkin 1994), it has generally been a conservative influence (Roberts 1991).

Such reforming of school geography between 1985 and 1995 drove an increasing number of radical geography teachers to seek support from the 'adjectival' educations which had grown alongside the new social move-ments from the late 1960s (Dufour 1989). Environmental, development, peace, human rights, and futures education seemed more prepared than school geography to draw eclectically on the natural and social sciences so that pupils could explore how the world works and how it might be changed. They were more prepared to examine social structures and processes and adopt a genuinely democratic and empowering pedagogy, and seemed more in touch with the realities which confronted and inter-ested pupils from day to day. Supported by development and environmental non-governmental organizations, and by other agencies seeking to promote equality through education, the adjectival educations have developed a wide variety of curriculum material (Hicks and Fisher 1985; Huckle 1988; Pike and Selby 1988) which has influenced geography teaching (Fien and Gerber 1988; Serf and Sinclair 1992). Many radical teachers continue to promote integrated humanities as a vehicle for linking these educations to cross-curricular themes but it can be argued that a proliferation of adjectival educations, often embracing competing liberal, radical and utopian agendas, has slowed the emergence of a genuinely radical social (and socialist) education which integrates all their concerns (Lauder and Brown 1988; Chitty *et al.* 1991). Like a radical geographical education, such education should now be based on an understanding and application of critical theory.

CRITICAL THEORY

In the 1980s, when structural Marxism and socialism lost some of their authority and appeal, radical educators increasingly turned their attention to critical theory and the ideas of the German philosopher Jurgen Habermas (Gibson 1986; Young 1989). Such theory draws on both Weber and Marx and shifts the focus from labour and the social relations of production to social interaction and the nature of language and morals. Habermas' principal claim is that interaction has become distorted by the rise of positivism and instrumental reason which promotes science as universal and value-free knowledge and so fosters a distorted and incomplete understanding of our relations with one another and the rest of nature. His critical theories seek to reveal this distorted or incomplete rationality and empower people to think and act in genuinely rational and autonomous ways. They deal with legitimation crisis, knowledge constitutive interests, and communicative action, and can be applied to the development of a critical theory of geographical education.

Habermas argues that the modern state must manage the economy while maintaining the support of the majority of the electorate. It attempts to do this through technocratic systems which are pervaded by instrumental rationality, but economic problems are thereby displaced first to the political and then to the socio-cultural sphere. An inability to maintain simultaneously capital accumulation, full employment, social welfare, and a safe and healthy environment, contributes to a legitimation crisis along with a motivational crisis as people lose faith in state institutions and liberal democracy. The state then develops new kinds of regulation and consultation in an attempt to restore legitimacy and motivation, but opposition parties and movements in civil society may use such innovations to reveal the limits of technocracy and the continuing need for decision-making and problem-solving governed by genuine rationality, democracy and moral principles. Legitimation crisis provides some explanation for many young people's disillusionment with society and politics and hints at the foundations of a relevant citizenship education through geography which would enable them to consider the diverse beliefs, values and strategies of those groups seeking more radical and participatory forms of democracy.

In deciding what kinds of knowledge and geography might best contribute to a new radical agenda, teachers should be guided by Habermas' notion of knowledge constitutive interests. He suggests that human beings have three distinct categories of interest which shape their social construction of knowledge. While their technical interest in the control and management of their physical environment leads to empirical and positivist knowledge, their practical interest in understanding and participating in society through communication with others leads to interpretive or hermeneutic knowledge. Both are of value in relevant contexts but both can act as ideology, for positivism treats the social world as if it were part of the physical world (with given structures and processes), while hermeneutics recognizes the difference but is also too inclined to accept the social world as it is. Both encourage people to overlook the true form of their relations with the rest of human and non-human nature (their state of alienation) which can only be revealed through critical theory.

Critical theory serves people's emancipatory interest in being free from alienation and the constraints of ideology and distorted communication. It recognizes the difference between the physical and social worlds but unlike hermeneutics, it critiques and seeks to improve the latter by, for instance, making it more egalitarian, democratic and sustainable. Such theory should inform all geographical education which seeks to develop autonomous and self-determining individuals, yet school geography has been slow to consider and incorporate critical theory as Unwin (1992) reminds us in his comprehensive account of the history of geography in terms of Habermas' knowledge constitutive interests.

The theory of communicative action provides the means whereby we can test the validity of critical theory and develop a critical pedagogy. It maintains that all speech presumes an ideal speech situation in which participants are required to sustain and defend four kinds of validity claim and in which only the force of better argument decides the issue. What they say should be meaningful, true, justified and sincere, and in a truly democratic society it will be possible to redeem all such claims and so arrive at a consensus in ways free from distortion, manipulation and domination. The process of actively constructing and reconstructing theory and practice through rational discussion and democratic politics leads to communicative action based on shared understanding rather than to strategic action based on instrumental reason. It leads to universal knowledge and values, serves to validate critical theory, and may be described as praxis or participative action research. Such enquiry provides geography teachers with a form of socially critical pedagogy, or democratic problem-solving, in which they and pupils employ different kinds of practical and theoretical knowledge to decide what people can, might and should do. It is through such pedagogy that empirical, hermeneutic and critical knowledge is combined and pupils come to recognize their true interests and identities.

Critical approaches to education based on Habermas' work have been criticized by those who claim that he clings too strongly to a modern notion of a universal rationality, knowledge and values, and can be seen to reduce politics solely to a matter of communication. His theory is essentially modernist in clinging to a single grand theory or narrative of emancipation, and idealist in locating the causes and solutions to our current crisis in modes of discourse. He assumes that undistorted communication necessarily corresponds to universal needs and knowledge claims, gives too little attention to the power which sustains technocracy and instrumental reason, and puts too much faith in the new politics of social movements rather than the old politics of class. The recent work of Giroux and others (Aronowitz and Giroux 1991; Giroux 1992) on border pedagogies suggests that it is possible to develop a critical pedagogy between modernism and post-modernism which is anchored in political economy. This would be more sensitive to notions of power, language, context and difference and would be far more modest in its claims to be able to empower others.

PRIORITIES FOR A CRITICAL SCHOOL GEOGRAPHY

Returning to our ideals as geography teachers it would seem important to make more use of critical theory and pedagogy to help young people find their identity and place in the world – to find out how, why, with what, and where they belong, and to develop their sense of longing and belonging within a range of communities or collectives. This requires us to develop curricula which help pupils answer the following types of questions:

- How are people and geography (places, spaces, and people–environment relations) being constituted by society?
- What roles can people and geography play in constituting society?
- How should people understand and connect with history, the economy, the state, civil society, and the rest of nature, as they affect their lives and local and distant geographies?
- What provides people with their identity, longings, sense of belonging and meaning in life?
- What social and cultural resources can people use to extend their imaginations, to construct places and communities where they can live sustainably with each other and the rest of nature, and to develop their identities and sense of belonging and meaning in life?
- What longings and belongings should I develop, and what kinds of society, geography and community allow me to express my identity and desires?

Addressing such questions through socially critical pedagogy requires inputs of critical knowledge concerning the economy, the state and civil society, contemporary culture, and people–environment relations. Pupils should develop a basic understanding of the nature of organized and disorganized capitalism (modernity and post-modernity) and the manner in which they shape, and are shaped by, geography. They should understand the processes of economic restructuring and globalization, should assess their impact on workers and communities in diverse locations, and should evaluate the roles of appropriate technologies, labour relations, the market, regulation and planning, in moving Britain, Europe and the global community towards more equitable and sustainable levels of economic welfare.

As far as the state is concerned, school geography should develop a multidimensional and multilayered form of citizenship which prompts a critical engagement with economic, political, social and cultural rights and responsibilities at local, national, regional and international scales (Lynch 1992). Pupils should explore how governments can protect and extend people's rights and responsibilities but should recognize that post-modernity puts strains on the nation state and conventional forms of politics and prompts greater attention to civil society and social movements based around race, gender, the environment, community and identity. Classroom activities should explore the complementary nature of the old emancipatory politics and the new life politics and help pupils to understand how their search for meaning and identity is made more urgent, challenging and exciting in a post-modern world.

It is the realm of culture and cultural studies which presents critical school geography with its greatest challenge and potential. Disorganized capitalism is increasingly a cultural economy of signs and spaces in which the information and communication structures of consumer society replace social structures in shaping people's lives (Lash and Urry 1994). Young people increasingly form their identities from the raw material of media and consumer culture and adopt a post-modern attitude which is sceptical of all authority, revels in artificiality, accepts a fragmented and placeless existence, regards security and identity as purely transitory, and welcomes an aestheticization of everyday life in which politics becomes the politics of style, presentation and gesture. Post-modernism threatens fragmentation, relativism and the erosion of community, but it also offers the possibility of using new cultural technologies, products and attitudes to redefine identity, community and pleasure, as a means towards radical democracy. School geography should acknowledge that young people face a world with few secure signposts yet display much commitment and imagination in using popular culture to construct meanings and identities. Our lessons should educate their sensibilities and interests by exploring how texts of all kinds represent places and environments and shape the geographical imagination, how the meaning of texts can be constructed and reconstructed to serve different interests, and how different senses of longing and belonging are produced in different places, among different groups, at different times (Gilbert 1995; Morgan 1995).

Our relations with the rest of living nature, in a world increasingly pervaded by manufactured risks, are the focus of such phenomena as green consumerism and protest over live animal exports. These reveal the increased significance of identity and cultural politics for young people and suggest that a relevant school geography should merge physical and human geography under the umbrella of political ecology, should develop citizenship within the context of the old and new politics of the environment, and so allow pupils to explore the kinds of technology and social organization which may allow us to live more sustainably (Huckle 1993).

A RETURN TO PROFESSIONALISM

School geography is in urgent need of reform. After a decade or more of largely pragmatic development at the bidding of politicians and dominant interests within the subject community, it is now time to acknowledge that the subject has distanced itself from change in society and from those developments in academic geography and curriculum theory which could be used to enable us better to meet our ideals. We need to return to professionalism in geographical education and debate the new social, theoretical and pedagogical challenges with rediscovered energy and enthusiasm (Marsden 1995). New times have brought much de-skilling and de-professionalization, but they also offer the prospect of developing more flexible and responsive curricula for schools with more empowering structures and cultures (Hargreaves 1994).

New technologies provide a means of transforming modern institutions for schooling into post-modern institutions for education. The open geography classroom with real and virtual links to the community and wider world, in which computer-assisted learning frees teachers to teach and pupils to learn, is an exciting prospect. How soon it arrives, and in what form it arrives, largely depends on wider political struggles over the future of disorganized capitalism and the nature and funding of schooling. Establishing a critical school geography requires radical teachers to continue to turn existing curriculum frameworks in more empowering directions and to argue their case, by example, in such settings as department meetings, OFSTED inspections, Geographical Association and union branches, and meetings organized by community groups and political parties. They should form alliances with those elements of the new Left and cultural industries which are using critical theory and pedagogy to promote radical democracy and should seek to popularize their subject and its potential for social education within the local community. A strand of critical school geography has continued to develop in recent difficult times and its fortunes in coming decades partly depend on a minority of geography teachers winning more of the arguments, gaining more support, and so helping to secure the conditions in which their ideals can become reality.

REFERENCES

Ahier, J. and Ross, A. (eds) (1995) *The Social Subjects within the Curriculum, Children's Social Learning in the National Curriculum*, London: Falmer Press.
Aronowitz, S. and Giroux, H. (1991) *Postmodern Education, Politics, Culture and Social Criticism*, Minneapolis: University of Minneapolis Press.
Ball, S. (1990) *Politics and Policy Making in Education*, London: Routledge.
Bailey, P. (1991) *Securing the Place of Geography in the National Curriculum of English and Welsh Schools: A Study in the Politics and Practicalities of Curriculum Reform*, Sheffield: Geographical Association.
Capel, H. (1981) 'Institutionalization of geography and strategies of change', in D.R. Stoddart (ed.) *Geography, Ideology and Social Concern*, Oxford: Basil Blackwell.
Chitty, C., Jakubowska, T. and Jones, K. (1991) 'The National Curriculum and assessment: changing course', in C. Chitty (ed.) *Changing the Future, Redprint for Education*, London: Tufnell Press.

Cloke, P., Philo, C. and Sadler, D. (1991) *Approaching Human Geography, An Introduction to Contemporary Theoretical Debates*, London: Paul Chapman.

Cook, I. and Gill, D. (1983) 'An introduction to "Contemporary Issues in Geography and Education"', *Contemporary Issues in Geography and Education* 1/1: 1–4.

DES (Department of Education and Science and the Welsh Office) (1990) *Geography for Ages 5 to 16, Proposals of the Secretary of State for Education and Science and the Secretary of State for Wales*, London: HMSO.

Dufour, B. (ed.) (1989) *The New Social Curriculum*, Cambridge: Cambridge University Press.

Fien, J. and Gerber, R. (eds) (1988) *Teaching Geography for a Better World*, Edinburgh: Oliver and Boyd.

Flude, M. and Hammer, M. (eds) (1990) *The Education Reform Act 1988: Its Origins and Implications*, London: Falmer Press.

Gibson, R. (1986) *Critical Theory and Education*, London: Hodder and Stoughton.

Gilbert, R. (1984) *The Impotent Image, Reflections of Ideology in the Secondary School Curriculum*, Lewes: Falmer Press.

Gilbert, R. (1995) 'Education for citizenship and the problem of identity in postmodern political culture', in J. Ahier and A. Ross (eds) 1995.

Giroux, H. (1992) *Border Crossings, Cultural Workers and the Politics of Education*, London: Routledge.

Goodson, I. (1983) *School Subjects and Curriculum Change*, London: Croom Helm.

Harris, K. (1994) *Teachers: Constructing the Future*, London: Falmer Press.

Hargreaves, A. (1994) *Changing Teachers, Changing Times, Teachers' Work and Culture in the Postmodern Age*, London: Cassell.

Hicks, D. and Fisher, S. (1985) *World Studies 8–13: A Teacher's Handbook*, Edinburgh: Oliver and Boyd.

Hopkin, J. (1994) 'Geography and development education' in A. Osler (ed.) *Development Education, Global Perspectives in the Curriculum*, London: Cassell.

Huckle, J. (ed.) (1983) *Geographical Education, Reflection and Action*, Oxford: Oxford University Press.

Huckle, J. (1988) *What We Consume, The Teachers Handbook*, Richmond: WWF/ Richmond Publishing Company.

Huckle, J. (1993) *Our Consumer Society (What We Consume, Unit 3)*, Richmond: WWF/Richmond Publishing Company.

IGU (International Geographical Union) (1995) 'International Charter on Geographical Education', *Teaching Geography* 20(2): 95–9.

Johnston, R. (1986) *On Human Geography*, Oxford: Basil Blackwell.

Kropotkin, P. (1885) 'What geography ought to be', *Nineteenth Century* 18: 940–56.

Lauder, H. and Brown, P. (eds) (1988) *Education in Search of a Future*, London: Falmer Press.

Lash, S. and Urry, J. (1994) *Economies of Signs and Space*, London: Sage.

Lynch, J. (1992) *Education for Citizenship in a Multi-cultural Society*, London: Cassell.

Marsden, W. (1989) '"All in a good cause": geography, history and the politicization of the curriculum in nineteenth and twentieth century England', *Journal of Curriculum Studies* 21(6): 509–26.

Marsden, W. (1995) *Geography 11–16, Rekindling Good Practice*, London: David Fulton Publishers.

Morgan, J. (1995) 'Citizenship, geography education and postmodernity', paper presented to the conference *Geographical Education and Citizenship*, organized by the History and Philosophy Study Group of the IBG-RGS, Oxford University, 21.10.95.

Morris, J. (1992) ' "Back to the future": the impact of political ideology on the design and implementation of geography in the National Curriculum', *The Curriculum Journal* 3(1): 75–85.

Pike, G. and Selby, D. (1988) *Global Teacher, Global Learner*, London: Hodder and Stoughton.

Roberts, M. (1991) 'On the eve of the Geography National Curriculum: the implications for secondary schools', *Geography* 76(4): 331–42.

Serf, J. and Sinclair, S. (1992) *Developing Geography, a Development Education Approach at Key Stage 3*, Birmingham: Birmingham Development Education Centre.

Shotton, J. (1993) *No Master High or Low, Libertarian Education and Schooling in Britain 1890–1990*, Bristol: Libertarian Education.

Thrift, N. (1992) 'Light out of darkness? critical social theory in 1980s Britain', in P. Cloke (ed.) *Policy and Change in Thatcher's Britain*, Oxford: Pergamon Press.

Unwin, T. (1992) *The Place of Geography*, Harlow: Longman.

Whitty, G. (1992) 'Education, economy and national culture', in R. Bocock and K. Thompson (eds) *Social and Cultural Forms of Modernity*, Cambridge: Polity Press.

Wise, M. (1993) 'The campaign for geography in education: the work of the Geographical Association 1893–1993', *Geography* 78(2): 101–9.

Wright, N. (1989) *Assessing Radical Education*, Milton Keynes: Open University Press.

Young, R. (1989) *A Critical Theory of Education*, London: Harvester Wheatsheaf.

Part IV

Chapter 23

Principles of pupil assessment

David Lambert

INTRODUCTION

Many aspects of the geography teacher's professional life are said to be dependent on effective professional judgement. There is probably no activity to which this principle can be applied more obviously than assessment. Educational assessment refers to the processes by which judgements of value are made by teachers on the learning of others. It is a highly skilled activity requiring confidence as well as competence – confidence, that is, which allows the teacher to adjust earlier judgements and to recognize and value the positive at least as much as the negative, and competence to make appropriate decisions about what to assess and how to do it. The aim of this chapter is to set out the principles upon which professional judgements of this sort can be based. Table 23.1 on page 256 provides a summary of assessment terminology, referring to concepts which are used in this chapter and with which teachers need to be familiar.

ASSESSMENT: GETTING TO KNOW PUPILS

The assessment of pupils in school often seems, perhaps simplistically, to be interpreted as primarily a technical matter. It is seen, by pupils, teachers and parents, as an inevitable and essential part of the education process, something done by teachers (or other agents of the education system such as examination boards) to pupils using a variety of 'devices' and 'instruments' which provide appropriate outcomes – usually in the form of some quantifiable data such as marks or grades.

The purpose of this chapter is to examine critically such assumptions by providing an account of the nature of educational assessment. To achieve this we need to examine the purposes of assessment and certain principles which underpin assessment practice, which themselves are dependent on a prior understanding of purpose. For anyone engaged in educational assessment, the identification of purpose – the reason it is being undertaken – is of paramount importance.

Table 23.1   A glossary of the principal features of educational assessment

Feature	Meaning	Feature	Meaning
Formative assessment	assessment to support future learning during a course of study	Summative assessment	assessment undertaken at the end of a course of study
Formal assessment	includes a degree of standardized procedure, as in tests	Informal assessment	based on observation and conversation with pupils
Formal records	often numerical, consisting of marks, grades etc.	Informal records	qualitative information carried in teachers' heads
Marking pupils' work	one part of the overall knowledge building process; in practice can be little more than monitoring work done	Criteria referencing	pupils' work is judged in relation to explicit criteria which identify progress by describing levels of attainment
Norm referencing	pupils' work is judged in comparison with the performance of other pupils	Ipsative assessment	pupils' work is judged solely in the context of the individual pupil's previous performance and circumstances
Validity in educational assessment	usually refers to the content or strategy adopted: is this assessing what I think it is assessing?	Reliability of assessment	usually a reference to the influence of external factors on outcomes: how well standardized are the questions, procedures and marking?
Fitness for purpose	assessment information has several purposes to which it may be put; does the adopted assessment method provide data in the right form?	Achievement	a broader concept than attainment: includes non-academic goals such as motivation, social and personal skills
Attainment	usually described as a 'Level' in relation to specified 'Attainment Targets'	Teacher assessment (National Curriculum)	a summative judgement made near the end of the Key Stage based upon the pupil's overall performance and progress
Performance	a range of tasks, exercises etc. provide the evidence on which judgements relating to attainment are based	'Ability'	a complex idea; over-hasty extrapolations about general 'ability' on the basis of limited evidence drawn from pupils' performances are best avoided

Source: Lambert 1996

In 1993 the National Commission on Education (NCE 1993: 205) published research which indicated that nearly half year 7 and year 9 pupils never talked individually to their teachers about their work. In some ways this is a surprising statistic, but perhaps it serves to illustrate the point made in the preceding paragraphs that, rather than involving a process of dialogue, assessment may have become all too often a one-way channel, something which is done to others.

An idea to emphasize ahead of a more detailed consideration of purpose, however, is the common-sense notion that in essence good assessment is nothing more, or less, than a 'getting to know' exercise, that as a result of making assessments we should know more about – and achieve a greater understanding of – the pupils we teach. Ultimately, the chances of achieving this laudable goal are almost certainly enhanced by self-consciously entering some kind of dialogue with the pupils. To put this another way, teachers as assessors essentially operate in the role of teachers as learners, not so much learners of techniques or of particular competences (though teachers need an abundance of both) but of pupils in their various circumstances in geographical educational settings. We can come to understand individual pupils, for example, as potential examination candidates and as people, and the more we know about them in these roles the better we are able to prepare them for examinations, for future educational and employment chances and choices, for deciding where they stand in relation to an environmental issue etc. Since it would be foolish to imagine that we ever reach a point when we finally 'know' our pupils – they are after all individuals who are growing and changing before our very eyes – it follows that teachers should constantly be ready to learn.

If we follow this argument further we immediately confront a number of key questions. We need to ask:

- What kind of knowledge of pupils do we need?
- How best can we set about gathering this knowledge?
- How do we record it?
- How can we use it and who do we tell what we think we know?

As we began to argue earlier, the particular way we respond to these questions depends on our prior clarification of purpose. What we identify to be the primary purpose of an assessment exerts a fundamental influence on how we respond to these questions.

THE PURPOSES OF ASSESSMENT

There are generally agreed to be four major roles of assessment in education. The first two apply to the assessment of individual pupils, while the third and fourth are concerned with the assessment of groups of children.

This in itself is an important distinction to make for reasons which should be clear in what follows.

Diagnostic or 'formative' assessment is the process whereby information on pupils is gathered with the expressed purpose of evaluating strengths and weaknesses so that future learning needs can be identified and organized efficiently. Knowledge and understanding of pupils is built up over time through the rational use of informal (e.g. conversation) and more formal (e.g. class tests) methods of assessment. Assessment processes that teachers claim are formative need, as a matter of principle, to possess consequential validity. This describes a condition whereby the act of assessment can be measured up against its impact. That is, the validity of the assessment is dependent on whether or not it causes or supports improvement (has positive consequences). Formative assessment of this sort is normally 'private', a matter that remains between the teacher, pupil and parents. It does not yield information which becomes 'public'.

Assessment can be used to grade pupils for the purpose of selecting them for employment or continuing education. Results are 'public' and consequently the assessment has a 'high stake' attached to it – the results really matter. In this scenario the attitude of the pupil differs from their approach to formative assessment. For example, it is not in the pupil's interest to expose potential weaknesses, assuming they might learn from taking risks and the teacher's subsequent corrections, if only the final grade matters. The impulse instead is to play safe and maximize the score. The format of the assessment and how it is administered also differs from what is appropriate for diagnostic assessment, because public, high-stake results need to be reliable (see Table 23.1). Standardization, such as established by the imposition of 'examination conditions', is a way to maximize reliability.

Assessment of pupils provides data used for institutional accountability; results are used by institutions, and others, to make statements about their effectiveness or how well the pupils and their teachers have 'performed'. Results, derived from examinations such as the GCSE or from National Curriculum 'teacher assessment', are 'public' in the sense that they can be aggregated and published in the form of league tables. When this happens it is tempting to make crude comparative judgements about the effectiveness of schools, simply on the basis of the 'output' measure of results. It is for this reason that schools (and individual teachers within schools) feel publicly accountable on the basis of unfair evidence, because outputs are inevitably dependent, in part, on the quality of inputs (i.e. the talents and circumstances of the pupils when they first enter the school). There is consequently much interest in the so-called 'value added' analysis of results leading to the adjustment of scores in a way that will enable like-with-like comparisons to be made. Though this is a straightforward idea, it is one which technically may be very difficult to put into practice nationally.

The assessment of pupils can be used for evaluative purposes, at a system level. Evaluation implies a process involving a judgement of worth being made but one which leads to an informed strategy for improvement (i.e. assessment, plus some form of action). At a system level we may, for example, wish to judge the impact of the National Curriculum programme of study on learning outcomes nationally, or compare different approaches to the learning and teaching of geography, or the role of fieldwork in enhancing environmental awareness. The significant point to realize in relation to such a 'research' function of assessment is that detail on individual pupils or named schools is not necessary. Furthermore, if the government of the day wishes to evaluate the success of the education system (and specifically their reforms of it), it is not necessary to assess all pupils. A large national sample of pupils would suffice, as well as being far more cost-effective!

Analysing assessment according to its function, as attempted above, provides the means to understanding some of the controversy which characterizes much of the assessment debate. We can, for example, imagine (and have probably been part of) discussions on the relative merits of 'norm-referenced' and 'criteria-referenced' assessments (see Table 23.1). We may agree that the latter possess considerable advantages in helping to focus the objectives of learning, and, in principle, criteria referencing is educationally more sound when set against norm-referenced tests which inevitably 'fail' a proportion of pupils regardless of the overall standards. In the final analysis, however, any form of assessment may be used for any of the above purposes and a discussion of forms, styles and methods can resemble little more than a technical distraction from the main issue: how is the assessment to be used? The function of assessment determines how pupils respond and how their teachers prepare them for it.

This fundamental issue was avoided rather than confronted by the rather hastily devised National Curriculum assessment framework (TGAT 1988). A single framework, it was claimed, could serve a multiplicity of purposes. The failure of this system was therefore inevitable as the burden on pupils and teachers to assemble information for the conflicting aims of the bureaucracy (accountability and evaluation), the education system (summative grades) and teachers (formative and diagnostic) became intolerable. The framework was reformed and simplified in 1994 (the 'Dearing review'), although it remains to be seen whether the resulting 'political fix' has enough integrity to work satisfactorily (see Daugherty 1995). In geography there is now little prospect of external standardized tests, even at the end of Key Stage 3, and yet what has become known as teacher assessment (see Chapter 25) is intended to become the basis of establishing national standards in geography.

PRINCIPLES OF FAIRNESS

It is important that the assessments undertaken with pupils maintain a sufficient level of trust to be believed. Public examinations, such as A level and the GCSE, have created a high level of confidence resulting from elaborate and expensive standardization procedures and safeguards. For example, the School Curriculum and Assessment Authority (SCAA) has an agreed Code of Practice for the conduct of examinations. Questions are trialled and scrutinized by panels of experts, scripts marked under conditions supervised by experienced 'Chief Examiners', coursework checked by teams of appointed moderators and the whole system is subject to periodic, exhaustive inspection by SCAA. It is imperative that the public results from these examinations can be judged reliable – that standards between examination syllabuses, and from year to year, are believed to be consistent – and, generally speaking, such confidence has been achieved.

Apart from standardizing systems and procedures, one way reliability, and validity, can be improved is by attempting to specify in advance what the assessment objectives are. This frequently takes the form of statements categorized under the so-called 'elements of learning':

- knowledge – recall of information;
- understanding – the application of knowledge;
- skills – practical and intellectual;
- values – clarification of own and those of others.

This is useful, not only because it helps support a more analytical approach to organizing learning in the geography classroom, but because it can become the basis for identifying and communicating among teachers and pupils the criteria for judging the success, or progress, in learning.

Using criteria to reference assessment is not always easy, but is an essential part of a strategy to ensure fairness in assessment practice. Studies show that the use of criteria increases the openness of assessment – crudely, both teachers and pupils can create, through dialogue, a better concept of what constitutes success. This in itself improves fairness, but the fact that the criteria can also be used to evaluate the validity of assessments, from individual questions to entire strategies, is an antidote to the unwitting bias that has all too often been built into assessment practices in the past. A practical outcome of such developments is that assessment practice is now far more varied than ever it used to be, and coursework in public examinations is the official acknowledgement of this, and an institutionalization of the importance of providing assessment with a broader base. Though research evidence in such matters is rarely conclusive, evidence seems to support the view that coursework assessment in the GCSE may have raised the general level of attainment of girls.

It is also worthwhile recording that the ideas described briefly here are gaining international acceptance, usually under the generic term authentic or performance assessment (see Torrance 1995). New approaches such as these are not only considered to be 'fairer', but are also thought to be more appropriate than simple, old-fashioned 'pencil-and-paper' tests for assessing more ambitious intellectual capacities such as analysis, synthesis and evaluation, which underpin problem-solving and decision-making.

MARKING PROGRESS

The move to make assessment more criteria-referenced has become accepted good practice. The National Curriculum experience (with the original 183 'Statements of Attainment' in geography) taught us that criteria can become unusable if they are allowed to proliferate or become too closely tied to specific content. The 1994 curriculum, with its eight 'level descriptions', looks more manageable, and what seems to have occurred is that 'good practice' has become a basic principle, i.e. that assessment at all levels should relate to broadly framed criteria. This has implications for the way marking is handled by teachers. Importantly, the use of criteria has the potential to help teachers spot pupil progress and describe to pupils how they may make further progress.

The previous paragraph brings us back to the principle of fitness for purpose (see Table 23.1), which encourages us to confront the question of whether our professional actions are appropriate. For example, when we turn to the pile of exercise books are we clear about why we have collected the work in and what we are looking for? The purpose may be one of the following, or indeed something else:

- to check that it has been done?
- to find out whether the pupils have grasped the material?
- to judge how far the children have progressed in relation to this or that concept?
- to make an overall assessment of pupils' attainment, or progress, over the last half term?

Our response to these questions governs what we look for in the exercise books and, in turn, how much time we need to spend with the books and what sort of record we make of our assessment. A final, vital question to bear in mind is the extent to which the pupils themselves are let in on this process. What are the pupils' expectations? Do they expect a mark, a grade, a comment, corrections or just a big tick? (If it is the last on this list we might ask both teacher and pupils what purpose, if any, this serves!)

The point here is that the main reason for making use of an assessment opportunity (such as marking a pile of books) is likely to vary. Monitoring our activity helps us distinguish different purposes in order to piece

---

Sunrise Comprehensive School
Marking Policy

Monitoring
The marking of books takes place fortnightly.
It is largely a checking activity resulting in a tick or a cross in the mark book and/or a short comment for the pupil.
Teachers will also use this opportunity to gain an impression of how the class are coping, any conceptual difficulties, information that can feed back into teaching.
Any individual pupil causes for concern can be briefly recorded in your 'day book'.[1]

Assessment
Once every half term the books are examined as a whole, in the round, against subject specific level criteria.
Resulting grades are recorded in the mark book and given to the pupils.
Lessons at this time are organized in such a manner that a number of pupils can be given detailed feedback, either in small groups or as individuals; over the academic year all pupils may expect at least two face-to-face feedback sessions of this type.

[1] The day book is an idea borrowed from primary teachers. It is not the same as the mark book and certainly different from the scheme of work or your lesson plans. It is also not a diary, though this is perhaps the closest analogy. It is simply a hard-backed exercise book with a number of blank pages allocated for each class you teach. You keep it with you all the time and it becomes the place to locate short notes to yourself, or *aides memoire*, about significant events or insights concerning just those individuals who may particularly concern you, or for whom numbers in your mark book lack real meaning.

Figure 23.1 Part of a marking policy which distinguishes purpose

together a rational and manageable assessment policy. For instance, see Figure 23.1.

In summary, marking can increasingly be seen as a component of an overall assessment strategy which has at its heart a concern to observe and to judge progress. Criteria can serve the function of describing progress and help pupils understand what it means for them. Criteria used in this way to support day-to-day marking may be based upon the statutory level descriptions which were devised largely to guide statutory 'teacher assessment'. Still, whatever form marking takes it is clearly useful to have its aims and purposes set out in departmental policy. Ideally, of course, such departmental policy will relate smoothly with whole-school assessment policy.

ASSESSMENT AND RECORDING

Just as the assessment of pupils – getting to know them – utilizes a range of methods from the formal to the informal, the way we record this informa-

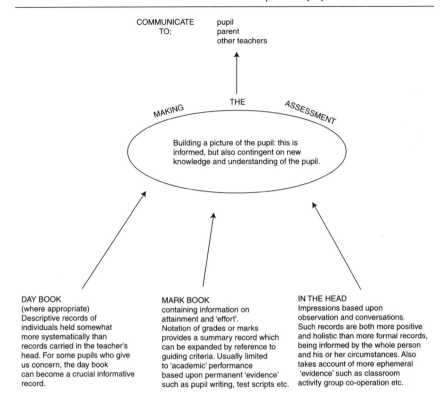

COMMUNICATE
TO:
pupil
parent
other teachers

MAKING   THE   ASSESSMENT

Building a picture of the pupil: this is
informed, but also contingent on new
knowledge and understanding of the pupil.

DAY BOOK
(where appropriate)
Descriptive records of
individuals held somewhat
more systematically than
records carried in the teacher's
head. For some pupils who give
us concern, the day book
can become a crucial informative
record.

MARK BOOK
containing information on
attainment and 'effort'.
Notation of grades or marks
provides a summary record which
can be expanded by reference to
guiding criteria. Usually limited
to 'academic' performance
based upon permanent 'evidence'
such as pupil writing, test scripts etc.

IN THE HEAD
Impressions based upon
observation and conversations.
Such records are both more positive
and holistic than more formal records,
being informed by the whole person
and his or her circumstances. Also
takes account of more ephemeral
'evidence' such as classroom
activity group co-operation etc.

Figure 23.2 Records at the disposal of a teacher. The purpose of records is to enable a fair and reasonable picture of the pupil to be communicated to others

tion also varies according to its source and its quality. Figure 23.2 summarizes this.

A useful way to think about the elements of a recording system, such as that shown in Figure 23.2, is not as a record of discrete or finite assessments but as records of interim judgements that provide a basis for making composite, multifaceted and 'synoptic' assessments. The distinction being made here is similar to the distinction made between formative and summative assessment: the interim judgements are part of the formative process involving much interaction between the teacher and pupils, while the teacher's growing knowledge of pupils can, at intervals, be summated to provide a rounded, overall judgement (or synopsis) of each one. Such assessments are required for a variety of purposes including writing reports and records of achievement, parents' evenings and case conferences. To have a rich knowledge of children based upon sources ranging from examination scripts to classroom observation enables teachers to use their information flexibly, tailoring it for the particular purpose. It is for this reason that the central component of Figure 23.2, 'making the assessment' is couched in tentative terms. All assessments are informed (by your records) but also contingent – not only in the light of further information which may force a change of view, but also in terms of the audience. Other teachers, the Head, parents, the pupil, each require different kinds of assessment which your records, ideally, should enable you to supply.

The reminder that Figure 23.2 provides, therefore, that our assessments of pupils are always developing, serves to highlight that assessment is perhaps best conceptualized as an art form rather than a mechanical or primarily technical activity. For this reason also, it is worth emphasizing that one further 'record' to which teachers have access is the pupils' work itself. There is probably no more powerful and useful 'record' of achievement to pass on to the next teacher than the pupils' exercise books.

The obvious reason why we do not simply horde pupils' work as the record on which to base assessment is the sheer inefficiency that this implies. We need summaries and interim judgements and we need to be able to avoid having to go back constantly to the 'raw data'. On the other hand, if teachers can develop ways to ground assessments in real work – the outcomes of pupils' endeavours to get to grips with the learning we plan for them – then how much more useful and informative will their assessments become. Such thinking is the origin, at least in part, of the notion of departmental portfolios which are described in more detail in Chapter 25.

CONCLUSION

In discussing the nature of educational assessment this chapter has argued for an approach which recognizes and promotes the basic human-ness of assessment processes. It is essentially an activity which assists teachers (and others) in getting to know pupils. The reason that teachers, employers or anyone else should wish to get to know pupils depends on their main motives. Teachers have a duty to promote educational goals and need assessment knowledge of a certain kind in order to support their work with pupils (Gipps 1995). This is not to argue that there are no other justifiable reasons to assess pupil learning, but it is important for the education service as a whole to recognize that for an assessment system to maintain intellectual integrity it cannot serve several conflicting purposes simultaneously. Clarifying purpose enables appropriate choices to be made in assessment policy and practice.

REFERENCES

Daugherty, R. (1995) *National Curriculum Assessment: A Review of Policy 1987–1994*, London: Falmer Press.

Gipps, C. (1995) *Beyond Testing: Towards a Theory of Educational Assessment*, London: Falmer Press.

Lambert, D. (1996) 'Assessing pupil attainment', in A. Kent, D. Lambert, M. Naish and F. Slater (eds) (1996) *Geography in Education: Viewpoints on Teaching and Learning*, Cambridge: Cambridge University Press.

NCE (1993) *Learning to Succeed: a Radical Look at Education Today and a Strategy for the Future*, National Commission for Education, London: Heinemann.

TGAT (1988) *Task Group on Assessment and Testing: A Report*, London: DES.

Torrance, H. (ed.) (1995) *Evaluating Authentic Assessment: Problems and Possibilities in New Approaches to Assessment*, Buckingham: Open University Press.

Chapter 24

Assessment in the primary school

Patrick Wiegand

For most primary school teachers, geography comes fairly well down the list of assessment priorities. This is a consequence of two principal characteristics of primary education: the generalist role of most teachers and the integrated nature of much teaching.

Most primary teachers have responsibility for the whole curriculum for a group of children. It is not surprising therefore that their first priority tends to be given to statutory assessment. The National Curriculum requires compulsory testing and reporting in English, mathematics and science at regular intervals and in some detail. Foundation subjects such as geography present far less demanding obligations. At the time of writing, this seems likely to amount, some years hence, to the simple requirement to match each pupil to a broadly phrased short paragraph or 'level description'. In most primary classes this is likely to involve teachers in no more than choosing which of two or three paragraphs apply best to each individual child. There have, nevertheless, been some thoughtful approaches to this task (Butt *et al.* 1995).

School subjects in the primary school, other than 'the basics', are more often than not taught as 'topics'. This long-established tradition in British primary education seems to be surviving the essentially subject-structured National Curriculum and, indeed, official assessment guidelines are often based on the assumption that this is how teachers will proceed. Work on the immediate locality of the school, for example, will often include both geographical and historical study. This makes much sense from a practical point of view because geographical skills, although distinct, are not easily separable from other skills needed by the developing child. This is especially the case when it comes to assessment, and many busy teachers will find themselves concentrating on children's mastery of generic skills rather than on distinctly geographical achievements.

The integrated nature of much primary teaching and the absence of any rigorous requirement to assess in detail does not, however, mean that we can avoid the assessment issue. Assessment is a necessary and integral part of planning for teaching. This chapter will focus on assessment which is small scale, diagnostic, formative and, above all, do-able. In primary geography we have relatively little experience of norm-referenced tests, that is those which gauge the performance of an individual child against what might be expected for other children of a similar age. There has never been the national investment that we have seen in, say, maths or science (for example in the work of the Assessment of Performance Unit) or the standardized tests available for assessing reading. What we do, however, have experience of (see especially Blyth 1990; Blyth and Krause 1995) is the use of diagnostic techniques which are continuously undertaken by teachers, provide information about children's strengths and weaknesses and inform what happens next in the teaching programme.

Such teacher assessment is not without its difficulties. Children's mastery of skills and knowledge is complex and appraising their progress is time-consuming. Individual teacher assessment can be notoriously unreliable. We are all easily misled by the 'halo effect' of neatly presented written work or socially skilled children's conversation into thinking that a particular pupil's understanding is greater than it in fact is. Perhaps we also tend to focus too readily on what children cannot do rather than on what they can. Pupil performance needs to be gathered from as wide a range of sources as possible. Teacher observation needs to be focused and systematic, rather than random or fleeting. The results of such observations, including what the children have said, written, drawn and appear to be able to do, need to be recorded. There are advantages and disadvantages with each method of doing this. Tick charts are quick but often seem to suggest that, once learning has been demonstrated, it is there for good. We know this not to be true. Diaries and individual pupil record sheets are more flexible but may not help us readily to make comparisons from one pupil to another. Portfolios of children's work may simply substitute the collection of data for reflection on individual achievement.

What follows are some case-studies of assessment in practice in primary geography. They are a partial and incomplete picture of the full range of potential approaches but serve to illustrate ways in which teachers can identify understanding and incorporate such evidence into their planning.

PLACE KNOWLEDGE: UNDERSTANDING WHERE WE LIVE

A teacher of 6 to 7 year-olds is planning a unit of work about 'where we live'. She knows that many of the children in her class can repeat (parrot-like and in one breathless gulp), their home address and she knows that her colleague last year did some work on the immediate locality of the school. She asks the children in her class to address an envelope to their parents, using the opportunity of a termly school newsletter. She records with a tick in her record book which children can write their address correctly. She then asks children in groups to identify where they live on a map of the British Isles and to locate on an atlas map the various elements of their addresses. She notices that many children do not use terms such as Great Britain, the United Kingdom and the British Isles with accuracy and that some appear to have difficulty differentiating between the town in which they live and their county. She notes in her diary that while many children appear to understand that their county is 'an area', others make comments such as 'it's like a town' or 'it's further away'. She prepares some materials to help their understanding of these spatial relationships. The activities include arranging labelled cut-out card shapes to show 'me', 'my classroom' and 'my school', so that these elements are seen to fit one inside each other and a parallel activity with cut-out shapes to represent: 'my street', 'my town', 'my county' and 'my country'. With the help of an atlas, groups of children arrange similar sets of teacher-made materials to show the relationships between the component parts of the British Isles. The children also sort teacher-prepared addressed postcards into cardboard-box 'pigeonholes' labelled 'England', 'Scotland', 'Wales' and 'Northern Ireland'. This work is reinforced by the use of a large wall map of the British Isles on which the children, over the course of the following weeks, record places they have visited, where relatives live, places in the news, the location of sporting teams and events, famous landmarks and 'record breakers' (the highest, hottest, wettest, etc. places). At the end of the unit the children are provided with a worksheet on which there are three maps of the British Isles. They have instructions to colour and label Ireland and Great Britain on the first map, the United Kingdom and the Republic of Ireland on the second map and England, Scotland, Wales and Northern Ireland on the third. They also have to write the missing words in a paragraph:

_____, _____ and _____, together with _____ _____, make the United Kindgom.

The teacher goes through each completed worksheet and notes the number of correctly positioned labels on the maps and correct answers in the paragraph completion exercise. She uses a template prepared in advance to score the children's work rapidly and enters their scores in her record book. Later, she talks to children who have labelled their maps incompletely or incorrectly. Perhaps some of them whose understanding seems still insecure play 'country snap' or 'country dominoes' while others simply complete a fair copy of the correct map.

This unit of work, which deals with spatial relationships, includes several types of assessment. There is the initial 'baseline' assessment of asking the children to complete an addressed envelope. There is some real purpose to the activity, so the children do not feel that they are just 'doing something again'. The task enables the teacher to check on any 'lost learning' from previous teaching. It is a simple activity, simply recorded. Understanding that places 'nest' or fit inside each other is rather more complex. Some notes are made on individual children who have difficulty with this idea and these notes may well help to build up a more complete picture of children's learning across the curriculum as a whole. (She may for example find that there are parallel difficulties in the understanding of time, or concepts in science). Her listening and observation alerts her to a potential area of misunderstanding and it is this that provides the rationale for the various arranging and sorting activities. These are presented at several levels of difficulty, depending on her informal appraisal of the children's needs. Lastly, the children are required to undertake a more structured form of test and scores from the marked work are recorded, leading to a further 'prescription' of activity for some children. All this information enables her to report to parents on their child's understanding of spatial relationships and may suggest some small ways in which parents can help at home (such as reinforcing their knowledge of parts of the British Isles by referring to the TV weather maps and asking what the weather will be like in different parts of Great Britain and Ireland).

AN ATLAS SKILL

A class of 7 to 8 year-olds are learning how to use the index and grid code system of their atlas. The teacher explains with a wall map of the British Isles how alphanumeric grid codes work. The children then use a worksheet which has a map of the British Isles with some towns identified and, in a blank table, have to write the grid code for each town. The children complete the table with varying degrees of success. Those who appear not to have grasped the idea yet are formed into a small group for further explanation and practice. Those who complete the table correctly are asked to sort some cards, on which place-names are written, into alphabetical order. The place-names are differentiated by the first letter only of the alphabet (e.g. Aberdeen comes before Bristol). Again, those who are unable to complete the task successfully are given support by further practice, this time using an alphabet strip to help. Others proceed to tasks requiring more demanding sorting of place-names, when for example the second and third letters are the same (e.g. Leeds comes before Liverpool, which comes before London). The most difficult task of the series is to sort place-names with many letters the same and with breaks in words (e.g. Southampton comes before Southend-on-Sea, which comes before South Shields).

The next task is for children to use the index of their atlas to look up a number of towns and to write in a table by the side of each town the name of the river on which it is situated. After this they look up a number of foreign cities and say which country each is in, adding one additional piece of information that the atlas provides about each place (such as its height above sea level, or how large it is, or whether or not it has an airport).

This sequence of teaching is highly structured and is heavily based on teacher-prepared worksheets. These materials have been made by the geography co-ordinator in the school in consultation with colleagues and are used by all the teachers in the school who teach at this level. The children's progress through each activity is similar to that of, for example, an individualized maths scheme. Moving to each subsequent activity depends on previous success. The tasks are carefully graded and the teacher monitors each child's progress through the tasks. The children also record their own progress using a wall chart which has a series of boxes against their names which are to be coloured or ticked. They can either go to the teacher to have their work marked or can check their answers themselves against a master sheet. They can tally their score for each sheet and perhaps complete a graph to show the results. Each child knows exactly where he or she is 'up to' in the scheme.

This type of assessment is fairly rare in primary geography and is generally limited to map skills. Some such skills lend themselves well to the approach, however, and there are some good structured materials available from commercial publishers. These are generally in the form of graded worksheets or activity books to accompany, for example, particular atlases or textbook schemes. Assessment in this case is intimately linked to teaching and provides good evidence of pupil attainment. The teacher can readily demonstrate exactly what each child has achieved but there are some attendant dangers. The approach can rapidly become mechanistic in that worksheet completion may appear to become the purpose of the activity for children and a substitute for quality learning. Much skill is needed also in preparing carefully graded activities that genuinely extend children's thinking at each level.

A LOCALITY IN AN ECONOMICALLY DEVELOPING COUNTRY

A class of 9 to 10 year-olds are studying a locality in an economically developing country. It is a village in India and the core resource is a pack of materials produced by an aid agency, consisting of photographs, maps and a video of 'a day in the life' of a child who lives in the village. The teacher has supplemented these materials with some Indian music on audio tape from the 'world music' section of a local music store, some recipes for Indian food, travel posters and a collection of library books including some children's fiction set in India. The first project activity is a brainstorming task. The children are asked to imagine they wake up in an Indian village. What do they see and hear? They each write down their ideas. These are then pooled and compared in small groups and the most common words and phrases written down on cards for sorting. Then, as a whole-class exercise, the teacher helps the children sort these ideas into categories: 'things we are all sure we would see and hear', 'things we are not all sure about'. The class then talk about the evidence they would need in order to test their ideas. At the end of the session the teacher collects the children's first individual thoughts about life in an Indian village. She pays careful attention to their initial ideas and notices that many are stereotyped (for example, saris, curry, elephants, tigers), some are gross errors or fundamental misunderstandings (wigwams, feathers), while others are strongly negative or pejorative (mud huts, dirty). The pattern of responses gives a broad-brush picture of the range of images held by her class and some clues to their attitudes. She decides as a result to present as positive a view as possible of this locality in order to correct the children's first impressions. Towards the end of the topic work, after the class have seen the video, questioned a parent with travel experience in India, investigated the photographs and compared some case-histories with their own daily lives, the children are asked to write and illustrate an account of waking up in the village. This time their writing is rich and varied. They draw attention to insects, building materials, sounds of breakfast being made and preparations for going to school, and appear to recognize that there are more similarities than differences between their own lives and those of Indian children.

The children's work forms the basis for a display and the teacher keeps a sample of each child's writing and drawing for inclusion in their portfolio. These are stored in the classroom and form a useful basis for discussion on parents' evening about the learning that has taken place. With this material the teacher can brief herself in advance of the meeting and complete her notes on each child's record sheet. Having the work available allows her to illustrate what she has to say about attainment. 'You can see in her picture that Rebecca has drawn lots of things you wouldn't really expect to find in an Indian village. She doesn't yet have an understanding of similarities and differences between places.'

Collecting the information on children's developing attitudes towards distant people and places helps this teacher monitor the effectiveness of her teaching for international understanding. This is difficult to do perhaps at the level of individual children but by collecting information across the class as a whole she is able to obtain a broad overall impression of their attitudinal development.

A THEME: FARMING

A class of 10 to 11 year-olds from an urban school are about to start a project on farming. Their teacher assesses their initial perspectives by asking each child to complete a word association test. 'Write down all the things that come into your mind when I give you the name of this occupation. It's . . . a farmer.' She also asks the children to 'draw a farmer'. These two pieces of evidence yield some interesting results. For the word association test most children mention cows, pigs, sheep, dogs, horses and hens. Tractor is the most popular word, but little other machinery is mentioned, apart from hand tools. Overall, the children appear to have an 'Old Macdonald' image of a farmer's job. This is confirmed by their drawings. All the pictures are of men. Most have beards or moustaches, wear patched, old or dirty clothes, carry sticks and chew straws. Intrigued, the teacher explores their understanding further by drafting a simple 'questionnaire' for the children. It includes items such as:

Can a woman be a farmer?
Does a farmer ever wear a suit?
Do farmers get paid a wage?
Do you think farmers are rich or poor?
Do you think being a farmer is a good or bad job?
Do you think farmers use computers?
How do you think people learn to be farmers?

The 'questionnaire' results were analysed by the children using a simple database and the range of responses discussed. The children then prepared for their visit to a dairy farm in the Yorkshire Dales. They located the farm on maps, compared its size and the height of the land and distance from the nearest towns with places they knew in their own locality. They gathered weather information about the farm's location and discussed how the weather there might be different from that at home. During the visit they had to collect information about the farmer's year and a typical day in the season in which they visited. They also had information to collect about the farm's inputs and outputs.

The teacher had briefed the adults who were to accompany her and the children on the visit about the content of the questionnaire and the children's responses. These, together with a set of prompt cards about the operation of the farm as a system, were to form the basis for their discussions with groups of children during the visit. On the coach on the return journey to school the teacher reviewed with each accompanying adult the learning gains observed. Each adult had been responsible for six children and it was relatively easy to make quick notes on a few children in each group. One adult reported that Andrew had said, 'A system is like, for example, cows go in in October and come out in April. That's a system. The inputs are fertiliser, feed, natural things like rain and soils. The output is slurry, milk, butter in winter and eggs.' When asked 'Was it like a factory?', he replied 'Well, at *Custom Cartons* they make cardboard boxes, at the farm they make butter, milk and eggs.' The teacher later makes a note on Andrew's record sheet that he 'understands that the farm is a system and can give examples'. She recognizes that this level of thinking matches the Level 4 descriptor in the National Curriculum and provides useful evidence about Andrew's progress.

Follow-up work after the visit includes making a map of the farm using a base map and data gathered during the fieldwork. The teacher is particularly keen to see whether at this stage all the children identify the colours and symbols they use with a key and show scale in some meaningful way. The maps are reviewed by the teacher and assessed for content and accuracy. She ticks each child's ability to use key and scale in her record book.

These children are at the end of their time in primary school and the teacher will soon have to make a 'best fit' judgement about their attainment in geography. She has a clear idea about the type of evidence she needs and has briefed those working with the children also to be on the lookout for such evidence. The results of the excursion only produce a small part of the total evidence needed but, by targeting her attention on a small number of children on each occasion, she is able to build up the summative picture she needs over a number of weeks and add it to the map skill data.

SUMMARY

Each of these types of informal diagnostic assessment are an integral part of teaching. They each provide children with an opportunity to demonstrate what they know or can do. They are each non-threatening and potentially enjoyable.

Taken as a whole the procedures are fairly simple and do not demand too much time to complete. They mainly alternate 'broad sweeps' across the class and more detailed, thoughtful, reflection on the work of individual children. They allow some comparison across the year group but aim mostly to target individual children's achievement and progress.

Evidence is also collected which can back up statements when reporting to parents and others.

Assessment is not easy. Each of these teachers are 'starting small' but they will together build up knowledge and experience which will inform their own understanding of the structure of the subject and how work in geography may be differentiated.

NOTE

The work on farming described above is based on an M.Ed. special study by Anne Wilson at the School of Education, University of Leeds, and quoted here with permission.

BIBLIOGRAPHY

Blyth, A. (1990) *Making the Grade for Primary Humanities*, Buckingham: Open University Press.

Blyth, A. and Krause, J. (1995) *Primary Geography: A Developmental Approach*, London: Hodder and Stoughton.

Butt, G., Lambert, D. and Telfer, S. (1995) *Assessment Works: Approaches to Assessment in Geography at Key Stages 1 and 2*, Sheffield: The Geographical Association.

Chapter 25

Teacher assessment in the National Curriculum

David Lambert

INTRODUCTION

'Teacher assessment' is a term that came into use with the introduction of the National Curriculum following the 1988 Education Reform Act. It is a term that had to be invented in order to differentiate, within the national assessment system, between tests and tasks which were to be externally devised and administered in some kind of standardized manner and other internal, continuous assessments which were wholly the responsibility of teachers. In geography, since the 1994 'Dearing Review' of the National Curriculum, the prospect of external tests or 'standard assessment tasks' (SATs) being introduced at KS1, 2 or 3 looks most unlikely. The School Curriculum and Assessment Authority (SCAA) will continue to issue guidance on standards (partly in the form of exemplars of pupils' work) but, this apart, the sole responsibility for assessing pupils against the national statutory criteria (the level descriptions) falls to teachers of geography, using a process of 'teacher assessment'.

Precisely what is meant by 'teacher assessment' (TA), and how to do it, remains ambiguous. Is TA intended to be primarily summative or formative, or can it serve both purposes? As we saw in Chapter 23 this is a key question, for purpose holds sway over how assessment is perceived by both teachers and pupils. The aim of the present chapter is to explore this question in a practical and positive manner. The underlying theme is to find a way to interpret and use TA in order to enhance our understanding of pupil progress and to enable pupils to achieve their best, as well as using it as the means of straightforwardly reporting 'level' achievement of pupils at the appropriate time.

A FRAMEWORK FOR TEACHER ASSESSMENT

Taking the analysis discussed in Chapter 23 as a starting-point, is it possible to identify a framework in which to develop TA policy and practice at school level? As we noted in that discussion there are particular difficulties in organizing and managing assessment which purports to serve more than one purpose at the same time.

However, this may be in part because the traditional principles or assumptions upon which much assessment practice has been based are inflexible and are now found wanting. TA may best be envisioned as an entirely new approach to assessment, a system of authentic processes which could become known as 'educational assessment' (Gipps 1994) with the notion of pupil progress as the central concern. Traditional assumptions have lingered beyond their 'sell-by' date because they are difficult to ignore. But we have now become more sophisticated and ambitious in our understanding of assessment issues. More specifically, Caroline Gipps writes that the 'most challenging task in developing a theory of educational assessment is that of reconceptualizing reliability. Underlying this challenge is a shift in our world view' (Gipps 1994: 167).

What this requires is something like a paradigm shift from a scientific, psychometric model of assessment to an educational model:

> Assessment is not an exact science, and we must stop presenting it as such. This is of course part of the post-modern condition – a suspension of belief in the absolute status of 'scientific' knowledge. The modernist stance suggests that it is possible to be a disinterested observer, while the post-modernist stance indicates that such detachment is not possible: we are social beings who construe the world according to our values and perceptions. The constructivist paradigm does not accept that reality is fixed and independent of the observer; rather reality is constructed by the observer, thus there are multiple constructions of reality. This paradigm would then deny the existence of such a thing as a 'true score'.
>
> (Gipps 1994: 167)

In other words, in relation to developing TA, assessment results are heavily dependent on their context or circumstances, the marker and the motivation and perceptions of the pupils being assessed. This is not to adopt an extreme relativist position of 'anything goes', but it is to question whether it is feasible, or even desirable, to preserve traditionally rigid, objectivist assumptions of realiability. To put the point simply, an educational model of TA is unlikely to be achieved under a departmental assessment system dependent entirely on standardized end-of-module tests.

But can an alternative framework be identified? Such a framework would support the development of TA using constructivist principles like those Gipps outlines, and it would need to be sufficiently robust for a school's reported 'level' judgements to 'mean something' beyond the confines of the particularity of a single school. Table 25.1 summarises what Gipps considers to be 'alternative criteria of quality in educational assessment' (1994: 172). These have been adopted as the guiding principles, or framework, for

Table 25.1 Checklist of quality criteria in Teacher Assessment (TA)

Criterion	*Comment*
Curriculum fidelity	A similar idea to 'validity', but easier to specify as it relates strictly to the statutory National Curriculum (e.g. have the teaching and assessment programmes included opportunities for pupils to engage in active and independent enquiry?)
Comparability	A similar, though less rigid, idea to 'reliability' achieved through consistency of approach by teachers, and common understanding of assessment criteria. The above can be maximized by training, using exemplars, and moderation
Dependability and public credibility	A term which combines notions of validity and reliability (and recognizes their relationship, which is one of tension). Dependable assessment is that which can demonstrate that steps have been taken to maximize curriculum fidelity, and optimize comparability. Assessment that is dependable gains public credibility
Context description	Authentic assessment, having maximum curriculum fidelity, is unlikely to yield scores which are generalizable. On the other hand, it is possible to judge the 'transferability' of an assessment, if we have a detailed description of the context in which it took place. Those undertaking educational assessment should be prepared to offer such description.
Equity	This reflects the aim of good assessment to elicit quality performance from all pupils. This is achieved by providing multiple opportunities and various contexts and circumstances in which pupils can show what they can do.

Source: Gipps 1994

what follows, which is an attempt to describe an educational approach to TA in geography.

THE LEVEL DESCRIPTIONS

Geography in the National Curriculum consists of a single Attainment Target, 'Geography'. Attainment against this target is described by eight level descriptions (LDs), plus a ninth for 'exceptional performance'. The LDs have been designed to apply to all pupils between the ages of 5 and 14 years. It is possible to identify at each level several 'constructs' (those underlying components which make up composite 'attainment' in geography), and in this way they can be said to describe 'progression' in learning. The components are Scale and Place, Themes (physical, human and environmental geography), and Skills and Enquiry.

The point to emphasize is that achievement in geography consists of all the above. While it is tempting to disaggregate the subject into its component parts, especially for the purpose of making assessments, when coming to a summative 'level' judgement of a pupil's attainment the LDs are to be used 'in the round' and as a whole. There is a sense in which this represents a lesson learnt, for the 1991 and original version of the National Curriculum proved unworkable mainly because it effectively forced teachers to 'chase' a very large number (183) of specific so-called 'Statements of Attainment'.

Although the LDs need to remain intact, so that they can be used 'in the round' in the manner intended in their design, most teachers seem to accept that for practical purposes the different components of knowledge, understanding, and skills can be unpacked in the first instance. In effect, we can 'look inside' them (Figure 25.1 provides an example), not to re-invent Statements of Attainment to use as a tool against which to match individual pieces of pupils' work, but to help our interpretation of general progress. On the other hand, just as teachers and examiners use different strategies at GCSE for assessing different aspects of knowledge, understanding and skills, these require different tools of assessment at KS3 too. It is therefore helpful to identify components of the LDs, so that an appropriate variety of assessment opportunities can be provided over the Key Stage which are fit for purpose. Note that the terms chosen in Figure 25.1 and the elaborations offered are a matter of choice; teachers of geography need to discuss these matters with each other in order to come to a shared understanding.

THE COMPONENTS OF LEVEL DESCRIPTIONS

The following sections provide examples of how analysis of LDs can assist the planning of National Curriculum teacher assessment.

change brought about by natural
conditions and human actions which
influence a place, e.g. the development
of a river channel or housing

produce a statement (or
representation) of something
in words, figures, drawings, etc

local, regional, global

where things are, and why
they are there

distribution of place
features, land use, etc, are
how they fit together

Level 4

children need to study places of
differing size and scale rural and
urban differing locations

Pupils show their knowledge, and understanding and skills in
relation to studies of a range of places and themes, at more than
one scale. They begin to describe geographical patterns and to
appreciate the importance of location in understanding places. They
recognize and describe physical and human processes. They begin
to show understanding of how these processes can change the
features of places, and that theses changes affect the lives and
activities of people living there. They describe how people can both
improve and damage the environment. Pupils draw on their
knowledge and understanding to suggest suitable geographical
questions for study. They use a range of geographical skills drawn
from the Key Stage 2 or Key Stage 3 Programme of Study, and
evidence to investigate places and themes. They communicate their
findings using appropriate vocabulary.

characteristics, landscape, etc.

use selectively some of their
previous learning

progressing beyond
knowledge, starting to
describe how things relate
and connect

skills, including IT, need to
become more complex and
integrated as the children
progress

e.g. maps, graphs, photos, field
experience, etc

pupils decide on the enquiry route

through a variety of means verbal,
graphical (e.g. maps and charts),
written, pictorial, annotated field
sketches, IT

Figure 25.1 Looking inside a level description
Source: Butt et al. 1995: 18

	Patterns and places	Location and links between places		Geographical themes
Level 3	Pupils describe and make comparisons between the physical and human features of different localities.	They offer explanations for the locations of some of those features.	They show an awareness that different places may have both similar and different characteristics.	They offer reasons for some of their observations and judgements about places.
Level 4	They begin to describe geographical patterns.	They begin to appreciate the importance of location in understanding places.	They begin to show understanding of how these processes can change the features of places, and that these changes affect the lives and activities of people living there.	They recognize and describe physical and human processes. They describe how people can both improve and damage the environment.
Level 5	They describe and begin to offer explanations for geographical patterns.	Pupils describe ways in which places are linked through movements of goods and people.	They describe how these processes can lead to similarities and differences between places.	They describe and begin to offer explanations for a range of physical and human processes. They offer explanations for the ways in which human activities affect the environment and recognize that people attempt to manage and improve environments.
Level 6	They describe ways in which processes operating at different scales create geographical patterns.	They describe ways in which processes operating at different scales lead to changes in places.		They explain a range of physical and human processes. They describe and offer explanations for different approaches to managing environments and appreciate that different approaches have different effects on people and places.

Level 7	They show how interactions create geographical patterns and contribute to change in patterns.	They show understanding that many factors influence decisions made about places, and use this to explain how places change. They appreciate that peoples' lives and environment in one place are affected by actions and events in other places.	They describe the interactions within and between physical and human processes. They recognize that human actions may have unintended environmental consequences and that change sometimes leads to conflict.

Figure 25.2 Progression in knowledge and understanding of places and themes
Source: Digby and Lambert 1996

Scales of study

Scale is an essential contextual feature to acknowledge and understand in the study of geography. Knowledge recall, understanding and skills represent different elements of learning, but they are sometimes harnessed together in relation to scale. For instance at Level 5 'pupils show their knowledge, understanding and skills in relation to studies of a range of places and themes, at more than one scale.' And at Level 6 'pupils show their knowledge, understanding and skills in relation to studies of a range of places and themes, at various scales.'

If pupils are to achieve the upper levels, it is necessary to provide them with a range of scales of study. This component of the LDs is therefore helpful because it tells the pupil and teacher something about what is different at Level 6 compared to Level 5. This is not to say that the study of a range of scales itself 'switches on' Level 6. Neither does it mean the contrary, that in the unlikely event pupils fail to provide evidence of study through a range of scales, that failure in this *per se* disallows Level 6 to be achieved. It is just one of several components of the composite LD which should be taken into account when considering the summative level of an individual's attainment in geography.

Knowledge and understanding of places

Figure 25.2 shows progression from Levels 3 to 7 for Key Stage 3 for knowledge and understanding of places and themes. The descriptions refer to knowledge and understanding of places in terms of:

- patterns and places;
- location and links between places;
- places and processes.

At Level 3, there is no statement about physical and human process, an aspect which comes in at Level 4 for the first time. 'Locations and links' are separated from studies of the characteristics and uniqueness of places at Level 5; interdependence between places is assessed at Level 6 and above. Once a simple analysis such as this has been done, the LDs should be reassembled and left intact in order to avoid the adoption of the over-simplified notion of 'progress' which the sequence identified in the pre-vious sentence implies, and for which there is as yet virtually no research evidence.

Knowledge and understanding of themes

A similar process to that outlined in the previous section can be applied to knowledge and understanding of themes. For example, Level 4 requires a simple activity about environmental damage and improvement – singular. Level 5 requires 'explanations' about 'human activities' and recognition about 'environments' – all plurals. Again, this is a simple analytical process designed to highlight how one component of the LDs has been configured. It is essential to repack the Levels as whole entities to prevent them from being reduced to lists to be ticked off. This allows LDs to be used holistically as a means to what has been called 'synoptic assessment' (Digby and Lambert 1996), that is, to identify the main features of a general, overall pattern of attainment.

Skills in geography

Figure 25.3 shows the variety of phrases between Levels 3 and 7 describing skills. There are fundamental issues for teachers here. Above Level 3, teachers may find it useful to see strands of enquiry separated into:

- questions for enquiry;
- using skills;
- communicating findings.

A number of discriminators are used in the LDs:

- the degree of help needed for pupils to conduct an enquiry successfully. Level 3 shows that children should be able to take part in an enquiry which is teacher-planned, and where questions are identified for the pupil. At Level 7, independent enquiry is required. The implication for geography teachers is that they need to allow for children to identify

	Questions for enquiry	Using skills	Communicating findings
Level 3	They use skills and sources of evidence to respond to a range of geographical questions.		
Level 4	Pupils draw on their knowledge and understanding to suggest suitable geographical questions for study.	They use a range of geographical skills drawn from the Key Stage 2/3 Programme of Study, and evidence to investigate places and themes.	They communicate their findings using appropriate vocabulary.
Level 5	Pupils identify relevant geographical questions.	Drawing on their knowledge and understanding, they select and use appropriate skills from the Key Stage 2/3 Programme of Study and evidence to help them investigate places and themes.	They reach plausible conclusions and present their findings both graphically and in writing.
Level 6	Drawing on their knowledge and understanding, pupils identify relevant geographical questions and suggest appropriate sequences of investigation.	They select and make effective use of a wide range of skills (from the Key Stage 3 Programme of Study) and evidence in carrying out investigations.	They present conclusions that are consistent with the evidence.
Level 7	With growing independence, pupils draw on their knowledge and understanding to identify geographical questions.	With growing independence, pupils establish a sequence of investigation, and select and use accurately a wide range of skills (from the Key Stage 3 Programme of Study) and evidence.	They are beginning to reach substantiated conclusions.

Figure 25.3 Identifying progression in geographical skills

questions for themselves in order to support (though not guarantee) high-level achievement.

- how far pupils select skills by which to investigate and present information. Level 3 states in relation to using skills 'They use . . . ', whereas Level 5 specifies 'They select and use . . . '. Again there are clear implications for teachers designing lessons and assignments for children.
- the quality of written communication and evidenced conclusions. Extended writing and attention to the evidence become important considerations so that pupils draw conclusions which are 'plausible' (Level 5), 'consistent with the evidence' (Level 6), and 'substantial' (Level 7).

ESTABLISHING A TEACHER ASSESSMENT SCHEME FOR KEY STAGE 3

National Curriculum teacher assessment is not required to be done every week. However, teachers need to do more than attempt to 'best guess' the quality of pupil work at the end of year 9 without a sound knowledge base from which to draw. Such knowledge of pupils' strengths and weaknesses is gained from a mixture of informal and more formal assessment methods. In other words, regular formative assessment work provides over time the required knowledge base upon which more summative judgements can be based, but there is now a clear need for teachers to work more closely with each other on common approaches. The flow diagram in Figure 25.4 attempts to show this in the context of curriculum planning and implementation. The crucial element, one that has never before existed, is the possibility of a feedback loop linking the shared understanding of progress (based on the interpretation of the LDs) to the design of the curriculum and evaluation. This professional process contributes to the achievement of Gipps' first two 'quality criteria', curriculum fidelity and comparability. A vital mechanism within the system is the compilation of 'level portfolios' of pupils' work. The very act of arguing over what can be included to exemplify, say, Level 3, 5 or 7 is considered to be the key to teachers beginning to share an understanding of progress; rapid and easy consensus is thought to be unlikely, but working compromises quite feasible and useful. Portfolios can be reviewed annually.

The practical features of an assessment scheme over the period of three years can be identified as follows:

- it should be developmental and seek to extend the range of levels assessed over the three years;
- it uses a mixture of classroom resources and strategies, plus local enquiry-based work carried on outside the school;
- it uses the LDs 'synoptically', as best-fit guides on which to 'map' the main features of pupils' overall attainments;
- it can also use LDs 'analytically' to help teachers and pupils understand the nature of the next steps they need to take in order to 'make progress' in National Curriculum terms.
- assessing pupils builds up over time, using evidence from single lessons to longer, planned enquiry work and tests.

Much of the above, but particularly the last two points, are of course essential to promoting the principle of equity in the assessment of pupils (see Gipps' 'quality criteria', Table 25.1).

As the flow diagram (Fig. 25.4) reminds us, the LDs have been designed principally with summative assessment in mind. The intention is that teachers identify the 'best' level for each pupil, a process that must involve

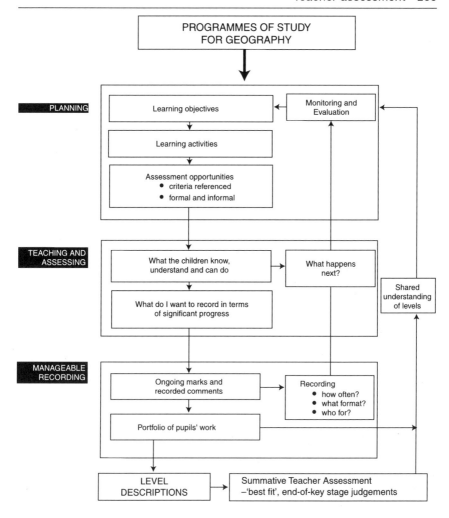

PROGRAMMES OF STUDY
FOR GEOGRAPHY

PLANNING

Learning objectives

Learning activities

Assessment opportunities
• criteria referenced
• formal and informal

Monitoring and
Evaluation

TEACHING AND
ASSESSING

What the children know,
understand and can do

What do I want to record in terms
of significant progress

What happens
next?

Shared
understanding
of levels

MANAGEABLE
RECORDING

Ongoing marks and
recorded comments

Portfolio of pupils' work

Recording
• how often?
• what format?
• who for?

LEVEL
DESCRIPTIONS

Summative Teacher Assessment
–'best fit', end-of-key stage judgements

Figure 25.4 Assessment in the Geography National Curriculum
Source: Butt *et al.* 1995: 11

a detailed knowledge of the range of levels in comparison with the work that pupils have been able to produce over the Key Stage.

Knowledge of the levels, and what they mean in relation to pupils' work, will grow with experience, as indeed it must if TA is to be seen as dependable and is to gain public credibility. It is unlikely that useful experience of this kind can be gained in a solitary way: teachers talking to each other, comparing departmental portfolios of pupils' work and agreeing between themselves what counts as progress through the levels, is the path to take. These exchanges would include, crucially, context descriptions. It would be reassuring to be able to anticipate a network of regional moderators who would be able to broaden such local dialogue, but to date there are no plans to introduce such support, but only the promise of non-statutory KS3 test and task materials from SCAA in 1996, together with exemplars of pupils work.

SUMMARY

'How can I use teacher assessment to support the progress of my pupils?' Assessment takes place as an ongoing activity during teaching, or as a final activity which follows teaching. Pupil performances will not develop unless teachers plan for them and use the LDs as a means of cross-checking schemes of work. In order to review the opportunities given to pupils to perform at higher levels, the following questions might be useful for teachers:

- Do I allow pupils the freedom to pose questions for investigation? Unless I do, I may be placing a ceiling on their performance.
- Do I let them select and choose how they will present information?
- Do I give pupils opportunities to develop arguments and ideas? For pupils to perform convincingly at Level 7, they will need this to meet the requirements for that Level.
- Do I profile pupil achievement? If so, do pupils have an input into the process? Do they understand their strengths and weaknesses? Do they know what to do in order to improve?
- Have I got records of pupils' work? Do I have a means to demonstrate or exemplify departmental standards, such as a departmental portfolio?
- Do I assess pupils in a similar manner to other teachers in the department? Do we all mark work using agreed criteria? Do we moderate each other's work?

REFERENCES

Bennetts, T. (1995) 'Continuity and Progression', *Teaching Geography* 20(2): 75–9.
Butt, G., Lambert, D. and Telfer, S. (1995) *Assessment Works*, Sheffield: Geographical Association.
Digby, B. and Lambert, D. (1996) 'Using level descriptions in the classroom at Key Stage 3', *Teaching Geography* 21(1): 40–3.
Gipps, C. (1994) *Beyond Testing: Towards a Theory of Educational Assessment*, London: Falmer Press.
SCAA (1995) *Consistency in Teacher Assessment: Guidance for Schools*, London: SCAA.

ACKNOWLEDGEMENT

The author wishes to acknowledge the contributions, made in earlier discussions and writings, of Graham Butt, Bob Digby and Steve Telfer.

Chapter 26

Geography and the GCSE

Sheila King

INTRODUCTION

Geography for pupils aged 14 to 16 has undergone numerous and major changes in recent years. The latest revisions were in 1996, but, before discussing the current situation, it is necessary to have a brief understanding of the changes which took place before this date.

THE HISTORIC CONTEXT

Before 1951 pupils were entered for the School Certificate examination which was awarded for performance across a number of subjects. During the 1940s many universities and professions were requesting an examination system which would be more effective in filtering out the type of pupils suited to their needs. At the same time, the Norwood Report (1943) recommended an examination system which would reduce the amount of external examination secondary pupils would have and so, in 1951, a two-tier system, the General Certificate of Education, Ordinary (O) and Advanced (A) levels were introduced.

O level was intended for selective grammar school pupils only, and could be taken on a one-subject basis. The number of grammar school places varied between local education authorities (LEAs) so that in some areas of England and Wales large numbers of 16-year-olds took O level (Westmorland 42 per cent) while others entered only a few (Gateshead 9 per cent) (Daugherty *et al.* 1991: 11). It was also obvious that many secondary modern school pupils had the ability to take O level while at the same time, for a variety of political and social reasons, pressure built up for an examination designed specifically for secondary modern school pupils. Thus, in 1963, a new examination, the Certificate of Secondary Education (CSE), was introduced. O level aimed at the top 20 per cent of pupils while the new CSE aimed at a further 40 per cent.

CSE spawned a variety of syllabuses which often gave great freedom to teachers in syllabus design and assessment. Geography teachers at the time were able to design, teach and assess their own syllabuses with only the moderation process coming from the examination boards. Where both Geography GCE and CSE examinations were offered, many geography teachers had to cope with two very different examination syllabuses within a year group and therefore had to decide whether a pupil was to be entered for CSE or GCE up to two years before the examinations took place. This consequently led to setting in groups, where many CSE pupils saw themselves as failures and gave up trying. To overcome the divisive nature of the examination, many school geography departments 'double-entered' pupils for both CSE and O level. This caused organizational and financial problems for schools as well as an administrative problem for the Schools Council, the body charged to ensure that standards remained uniform and grades comparable.

The 1960s and 1970s saw an increase in the secondary school population, due mainly to the raising of the school leaving age in 1974 but also to a growth in the comprehensivization of schools. Against this background there was continual pressure from schools to merge GCE O level with CSE, and full details of this can be found in Nuttall (1984). In 1970 the Schools Council decided in principle to back such a common examination at 16 plus and from 1976, after feasibility studies and school trials, some common geography syllabuses began to appear.

There was then a ten-year period of further work and political delay so it was not until 1986 that the General Certificate of Secondary Education, GCSE, was finally created. This examination was common to all pupils and was operated under common national criteria which were both general to all subjects and also subject-specific. It was, however, left to the examination boards to devise syllabuses and to attract teachers to use them. This became a time of active marketing by the examination boards with increased opportunities for INSET (in-service education and training) for teachers. Unfortunately the process of syllabus production and dissemination was a protracted one with many syllabuses being released after teachers had started teaching in the Autumn term!

GCSE 1986–1996

Some of the main features of the 'new' GCSE examination which differed from previous examination systems were:

- national criteria developed, both general to all subjects and subject-specific;
- all pupils would study essentially the same syllabus built from the same framework;
- all pupils would take the same examination, but there would be differentiated papers and/or questions to cope with the wide range of ability;

CSE		GCE		GCSE
1		A		A
		B	- - - - - - - -	B
		C	- - - - - - -	C
2	- - - - - - - -	D	- - - - - -	D
3	- - - - - - -	E	- - - - - -	E
4	- - - - - - -	U	- - - - - -	F
5	- - - - - - -		- - - - - -	G
U	- - - - - - -		- - - - - -	U

Figure 26.1 Comparable examination grades

- all pupils were to undertake coursework as part of their work;
- grade criteria used to link levels of pupil competence to specific GCSE grades;
- there would be seven grades, A–G, which were comparable to old CSE and O level grades as shown in Figure 26.1;
- all pupils would get the same type of certificate.

Perhaps the most radical change at GCSE involved the system of setting absolute standards through criterion referencing rather than by traditional norm referencing. Norm-referenced assessments relate levels of performance to the distribution of attainments in a population as a whole and indicate only the differences between candidates' performances. Sir Keith Joseph, Secretary of State for Education in the early 1980s, initiated the development of grade criteria in a speech at the North of England Conference in January 1984. 'We need a reasonable assurance that pupils obtaining a particular grade will know certain things and possess certain skills or have achieved a certain competence.' Criterion referencing decides the tasks, skills and levels of competence (the criteria) which must be mastered in order to be given a grade (the reference). Grade criteria are therefore explicit statements of what a candidate has to achieve to be awarded a particular grade.

The geography specific criteria written in 1986 had a significant impact on geography teachers at the time. They reflected changes in geographical curriculum thinking and assessment practice during the earlier two decades and many syllabuses were brought much more up to date. These changes included:

- approaches based on concepts and key ideas;
- a greater relevance to pupils through the study of economic, social, environmental and political issues;
- enquiry approaches which would encourage environmental sensitivity;
- the recognition of the importance of values, attitudes and perceptions in dealing with issues and enquiries.

(Orrell 1987: 88–92)

In addition, teacher assessment of coursework and a greater emphasis on the fact that fieldwork and coursework should be assessed became a permanent feature of most geography syllabuses.

THE GCSE REVISION

In comparison to the changes in geography education at 16 plus leading up to the mid-1980s, the ten-year period of GCSE 1986–1996 may have seemed a relatively stable time. However, it was not completely without change. In 1991 the National Curriculum Orders for geography were introduced in England and Wales and the old GCSE syllabuses had to be replaced with new ones which would deliver the Key Stage 4 Geography Order. Revised draft criteria were developed in 1991 and published in a modified form in 1993. Subsequently, however, it was decided that Key Stage 4 would no longer be tied to the National Curriculum, and a new set of criteria, both general and subject-specific, was introduced in September 1996 for each subject. These would build on Key Stage 3 and reflect the National Curriculum Orders. Therefore a new set of GCSE syllabuses was written from the new criteria, to be introduced from September 1996.

GCSE AS IT IS TODAY

Geography, ranking seventh, is one of the most popular subjects at GCSE: 295,229 candidates obtained grades A–G in the summer 1995 examination. However, after the Dearing Review of the National Curriculum, the status of Geography at Key Stage 4 has been markedly weakened. Having been compulsory for all pupils from 1995 to 1997, geography is now optional. Teachers must argue the case for geography and sell the merits of the subject to pupils who make their subject choices at the end of Key Stage 3. There is likely to be some movement towards short geography courses, perhaps linked with other subjects and towards humanities GCSEs as well.

There are six different examination groups, made up of former CSE and GCE Boards:

Southern Examining Group (SEG)
University of London and East Anglian Council (ULEAC)
Midlands Examining Group (MEG)

Northern Examinations and Assessment Board (NEAB)
The Welsh Joint Education Committee (WJEC)
The Northern Ireland Schools Examination Committee (NISEC)

Addresses for each board are given in the Appendix at the end of this chapter. On the whole, geography departments have free choice as to which boards and which syllabuses they choose, though for financial or parochial reasons, some LEAs and schools restrict choice.

All GCSE syllabuses must conform to the general criteria for all subjects as well as the subject-specific criteria. SCAA (School Curriculum and Assessment Authority) and ACAD (*Awdurdod Cwricwlwm ac Asesu Cymru*: Curriculum and Assessment Authority for Wales), the Assessment Authorities for England and Wales, are the bodies responsible for approving the syllabuses at GCSE (single subject, short courses and combined subjects) as well as other syllabuses used by pupils up to the age of sixteen. To help them in this task, teachers and other subject experts are nominated by SCAA, ACAC, teacher associations and professional associations, such as The Geographical Association. In addition, the link is kept with the National Curriculum since syllabuses are charged to build on the knowledge, understanding and skills established by the National Curriculum (SCAA/ACAC 1995: 43). There are clear aims on which all geography syllabuses are designed, and these are shown in Figure 26.2.

The main changes from the old to the new GCSE examination can be summarized as follows:

All syllabuses should give pupils opportunities to:

acquire knowledge and understanding of a range of places, environments and geographical patterns at a range of scales from local to global, as well as an understanding of the physical and human processes, including decision-making, which affect their development;

develop a sense of place and an appreciation of the environment, as well as awareness of the ways in which people and environments interact, and of the opportunities, challenges and constraints that face people in different places;

appreciate that the study of geography is dynamic, not only because geographical features, patterns and issues change but also because new ideas and methods lead to new interpretations;

acquire and apply the skills and techniques – including those of mapwork, fieldwork and IT – needed to conduct geographical enquiry.

Figure 26.2 Aims of geography GCSE syllabuses

- The geography criteria emphasize syllabus content as opposed to assessment objectives. The assessment objectives simply state that candidates should demonstrate knowledge, understanding and skills as specified in the content sections of syllabuses. The content section, which forms the greatest part of the criteria, outlines the content requirements, including the balance between human, physical and environmental aspects, themes, scale and variety of place coverage, patterns and inter-relationships, values, attitudes and enquiry skills.
- All syllabuses must now have a 20 to 25 per cent coursework element. This represents a substantial reduction for some syllabuses and is a disappointment for many geography teachers.
- Pupils must now be entered for one or two tiered papers targeted at grades G to C and D to A*.
- An additional grade description, A*, is awarded to candidates who perform at an exceptional level.

CHOOSING A SYLLABUS

It may seem surprising that, with national criteria for GCSE as a whole, and specific ones for geography, syllabuses can differ so much! However, the guidelines are flexible enough to allow for great variety between syllabuses and teachers have to apply considerable thought before making their choice. Undoubtedly there is inertia. Schemes of work, textbooks and other resources, banks of worksheets, activities and teacher expertise which departments build up all mean that change does not come frequently or easily to a department.

Change is probably generated for one or more of the following reasons:

- Dissatisfaction with the existing syllabus.
- This may be due to changing trends in geography education, for example a move to enquiry learning or a people–environment approach. Alternatively, it may be that the population of pupils studying geography has changed, perhaps when the school intake has declined or increased in ability and the existing syllabus does not meet the pupils' needs.
- Arrival of a new head of department or a change in geography teaching staff. Many teachers, having worked with a syllabus which has a particular emphasis, e.g. high coursework assessment, act as agents of change and persuade their new department to change syllabuses.
- Change in national syllabuses at a time when wholesale changes are being made. e.g. 1986 or 1996.

The process of choosing a syllabus is not always easy. Teachers can write to all six examination boards requesting syllabus details and specimen examination papers, but it can be a formidable task to decipher similarities and differences between them. It is not a task to be tackled without a clear checklist of departmental requirements. On the occasions when national changes do occur this task is often helped by articles in the *Times Educational Supplement* or The Geographical Association's *Teaching Geography* which publish summaries. *Teaching Geography* 21(2) is one source of articles comparing the new syllabuses and offering advice on preparing schemes of work, planning new coursework and using IT to support investigations.

Currently, geography teachers have eleven syllabuses from which to make their selection, with each board offering at least two. Essential differences on which choices are likely to be made are:

- The syllabus approach. This can be issue, topic, thematic or concept based. MEG/WJEC's syllabus based on the Avery Hill Project and MEG's syllabus based on the Bristol Project still have their distinctive features.
- The emphasis placed on assessment of knowledge, skills and understanding.
- The level of prescription given in the syllabus.
- The length and style of each of the two papers. While most adopt a structured question and answer approach, some offer decision-making or problem-solving exercises.
- The way differentiation within the tiers is achieved. This essentially involves the incline of difficulty of questions or resources, or is achieved through extended writing.
- Choice of questions. Some syllabuses offer no choice at all whereas others offer much greater choice.
- The emphasis and type of coursework assessment. In most syllabuses, coursework accounts for 25 per cent of the marks but the differences lie in the number and length of enquiries and in whether they are chosen by the teacher or the candidate.

ALTERNATIVE COURSES

Some schools offer a humanities GCSE in addition to or instead of geography. Since history and geography are no longer compulsory subjects at GCSE it is likely that some schools will try to persuade geography departments to link up with other humanities subjects and offer one combined course.

Many schools are now offering short GCSE courses as well as full ones. A short course is equivalent to half a GCSE and can be taken over two years (long and thin) or in one year (short and fat). It may also be possible for schools to offer groups of less able pupils a short course over the normal full GCSE time allocation so that more time is available to achieve success. A geography short course cannot stand on its own, however, and must accompany a half course in another subject, e.g. history, as part of an approved combination.

Teachers also recognize that GCSE is unsuitable for the lowest attaining pupils and some provide their own non-examined courses or opt for a test such as the AEB Basic Test in Geography.

ASSESSMENT AT GCSE

For geography teachers it is probably assessment of GCSE which has changed most in recent years. The balance between terminal examination and teacher-assessed coursework has varied widely but the terminal examination has now been set at 75–80 per cent of the marks (non-modular schemes). The inclusion of teacher-assessed coursework, which has long been approved by the majority of geography teachers, now accounts for 20–25 per cent of the overall marks and must include a geographical investigation which is supported by fieldwork. For many teachers this is a marked and disappointing reduction while for a minority it represents an increase and a new way of working.

Another change for many teachers is the tiering of papers so that pupils have to be entered for *either* the Foundation tier (grades G–C), *or* the Higher tier (grades D–A*). Teachers have to decide which tier each pupil is entered for some months before the examination and, where candidates entered for the Higher tier fail to achieve grade D, they are recorded as 'U' for unclassified. This may mean pupils who perform badly on the day have nothing to show for their two years' work.

As discussed earlier, one of the most radical changes to occur in GCSE was the introduction of criterion-referenced grading, where pupils' grades are awarded according to the set tasks, skills and levels of competence (the criteria) which have been achieved. All GCSE syllabuses must now give descriptions for Grades F, C, and A. An example of the grade C description is given in Figure 26.3. The way in which such descriptions are used for the setting of coursework and examination mark schemes has yet to be seen.

One of the best, though not necessarily easiest, ways of becoming familiar with the examination process is to apply to mark papers or moderate coursework. Boards advertise in *The Times Educational Supplement* and national newspapers and usually have vacancies each year. As well as gaining an understanding of what is required of candidates to achieve high marks, another benefit is an insight into the workings of the whole examination system.

COURSEWORK AND COURSEWORK ASSESSMENT

From 1996, 20–25 per cent of the whole GCSE assessment will have been derived from project-based work using geographical enquiry. Although

Candidates recall accurately information about places and themes, at a range of scales, as required by the syllabus, and show a broad knowledge of location and geographical terminology.

Candidates understand geographical ideas as specified in the syllabus in a variety of physical and human contexts. They understand a range of physical and human processes and their contribution to the geographical patterns, the geographical characteristics of particular places, and the interdependence between places. They understand inter-relationships between people and the environment. They understand the effects of attitudes and values of those involved in geographical issues and in decision-making about the use and management of environments.

Candidates undertake geographical enquiry, identifying questions or issues, suggesting an appropriate sequence of enquiry, collecting appropriate evidence from a variety of primary and secondary sources, using a range of appropriate techniques, reaching a plausible conclusion, communicating the outcomes, and appreciating some of the limitations of the evidence and conclusions.

(SCAA/ACAC 1995: 46)

Figure 26.3 Grade C grade description

previous syllabuses had a lower limit of 20 per cent coursework, there was no upper limit. Some teachers valued the high coursework weightings of several syllabuses, e.g. Avery Hill 40 per cent and NEAB 'B' 55 per cent, which gave opportunities to extend fieldwork and enquiries and to utilize a greater range of assessment techniques to measure the variety of abilities that pupils can display. Undoubtedly some syllabuses require more individualized and challenging enquiries than others and there is some criticism of teacher-led enquiries given to a whole cohort. For example, Orrell questions whether pupils should be obtaining 25 per cent of their marks for a teacher-planned, class exercise based on measurements of a small stretch of stream or high street corner, and resulting in a few bar charts with minimal analysis (Orrell 1995: 137).

Some examples of coursework enquiries – sample questions and hypotheses for class, group or individual enquiries – are outlined below (SEG 1993).

- European Community policies have had a direct effect on local farm practice.
- How might the provision for pedestrians in Town A be improved?
- Economic advantages of extensive coniferous plantations outweigh the loss of ecological balance in Area B.
- What are the environmental conflicts in Area C?
- Employment in Dover has changed since the opening of the Channel Tunnel.
- What factors have led to the development of Zone X as a tourist area?

Finding new coursework enquiries is one of the greatest challenges facing teachers of GCSE. One of the best sources of ideas for new enquiries is *Teaching Geography*, the magazine for secondary school teachers produced quarterly by The Geographical Association. Magazines such as *Axis*, written for school pupils, may also offer ideas. Ideally teachers could swop coursework ideas with others working nearby but, with the demise of LEA-controlled schools and the associated advisory services, such collaborative groups are becoming rarer.

The administration and moderation of coursework within the revised GCSE syllabuses remains one of the less uniform changes. The degree of detailed help within syllabuses varies widely and many boards operate a system of coursework approval followed up by moderators who will act in a counselling capacity.

In addition to the search for projects and enquiries there are a number of other issues raised when considering coursework:

- How much help can be given?
- When should coursework be set, given that most subjects expect some coursework assignments and pupil overload needs to be avoided?
- What should be done when pupils miss coursework through absence?
- How should a department ensure fair and accurate marking?
- Should coursework be retained or given back to pupils?

While official guidelines are issued by the examination boards, the professionalism of teachers is never so important as it is in this area.

CONCLUSIONS

That geography for 14 to 16 year-olds has undergone numerous and rapid changes over the last twenty-five years is unquestionable. In many ways, such as the introduction of teacher-assessed coursework and criterion-referenced grades, these changes have been some of the most innovative and have been adopted for pupils of other ages. The changes have, on the whole, been welcomed by the majority of teachers, and some examination boards have used them to enter into a dialogue with schools to solicit their comments and to act upon them.

In our world of rapid technological advances and associated changes in society, to say nothing of political manipulation, it is unlikely that GCSE will stay in a static state for long. The evolution of the process of assessing pupils at 16 plus is set to continue.

REFERENCES

Daugherty, R., Thomas, B., Elwyn Jones, G. and Davies, S. (1991) *GCSE in Wales*, Cardiff: Welsh Office.

Nuttall, D.L. (1984) 'Doomsday or a new dawn? Prospects for a common system of examining at 16-plus', in P. Broadfoot (ed.) *Selection, Certification and Control*, Lewes: Falmer Press.

Orrell, K. (1987) 'Geography', in T. Horton (ed.) *GCSE: Examining the New System*, London: Harper and Row.

Orrell, K. (1995) 'GCSE geography: What happens next?' in *Teaching Geography* 20(3): 137–8.

School Curriculum and Assessment Authority/Curriculum and Assessment Authority for Wales (1995) *GCSE: Regulations and Criteria*, London and Cardiff: SCAA/CAAW.

SEG (1993) *Syllabuses for 1995 Examinations*, S95/18. Southern Examining Group.

Appendix: addresses of examination boards

Southern Examining Group (SEG)
(and Associated Examining Board (AEB) for Basic Test in Geography)
Stag Hill House
Guildford
Surrey GU2 5XJ

University of London and East Anglian Council (ULEAC)
Stewart House
32 Russell Square
London WC1B 5DN

Midland Examining Group (MEG)
1 Hills Road
Cambridge CB1 2EU

Northern Examinations and Assessment Board (NEAB)
12 Harter Street
Manchester M1 6HL

The Welsh Joint Education Committee (WJEC)
245 Western Avenue
Cardiff CF5 2YX

The Northern Ireland Schools Examination Council (NISEC)
Beechill House
42 Beechill Road
Belfast BT8 4RS

Chapter 27

Student assessment in geography post-16

Graham Butt

The 1990s have witnessed significant changes in post-16 geography and 'geography-related' courses as part of a larger reorganization of the education and assessment system for 14 to 19 year-olds. The two Dearing reports (1994 and 1995) into the National Curriculum and its assessment, and 16–19 qualifications, reopened important debates about the structure and purpose of education and have begun to initiate improvements. By the mid-1990s the Conservative government's realization of the need for greater coherence in the 16–19 curriculum and assessment system was long overdue. Nevertheless, following Dearing's recommendations of 1995, there now appear to be real possibilities for creating a more unified structure. A new National Certificate which would encompass both A levels and vocational qualifications has been suggested, along with a reduction in the number of A level syllabuses, greater flexibility of courses, and a rationalization of the 14,000 academic and vocational qualifications that currently exist for the post-16 student.

An appreciation of the need to create more streamlined and less wasteful post-16 educational options, with a particular emphasis on opening clear vocational pathways for certain students, has been a major outcome of Dearing's work. Clearly, any restructuring of the 14–19 education system affects both geography education and the range of options and choices available to children at 14, 16 and 19.

The reorganization of the Department for Education (DFE) into the Department for Education and Employment (DFEE) in 1995 sent a clear message to teachers, parents, students and employers that in future the government visualized a close relationship between the worlds of education and work. The implications for geography education soon became apparent. Only by being aware of these changes and promoting the contributions that geography, and geography teachers, could make to all children's education would the position and status of the subject remain secure.

In the early 1990s Conservative administrations were keen to define three clear educational routes post-16. The first was the traditional academic route, which had been occupied by A levels (and S levels) since the early 1950s; the second was the vocational route related to education in the workplace. Here, the NVQ (National Vocational Qualification), developed in the mid-1980s, was the keystone. The final route involved the GNVQ (General National Vocational Qualification) which was introduced in 1992 to provide a flexible pathway towards either vocational or academic qualifications. A major objective was to keep student options open for longer and to provide vocational qualifications that had the same esteem as traditional academic ones.

A AND AS LEVELS

In 1988 the Higginson Committee considered the future of A levels, but its suggestion that the majority of students should take five 'leaner and tougher' A level subjects was rejected by the government of the time. However, despite continuing government support for retaining this 'gold standard' examination, criticisms about the high drop-out and failure rates of students, the variations in grading standards between boards, the disparity between examinations in different subjects and the problems of progression from GCSE to A levels, all increased. In addition, the restricted applicability of the examination to the entire range of young people's abilities, and the vexed question of 'falling standards' (see Figure 27.1), presented themselves as perennial issues.

By the mid-1990s the government had begun to shift both its stance and opinion about the continuing dominance of A levels within the post-16 qualifications market. White Papers on *Education and Training for the 21st Century* (1991) and on *Competitiveness* (1994) started to promote the importance of offering viable vocational courses post-16. Dearing's (1995) review of 16–19 qualifications similarly emphasized a change of focus. The value of A levels was recognized, but with almost one-third of 16 to 19 year-olds already studying them they were seen to be at their limits of expansion. The new growth would be in students taking vocational courses.

In the summer of 1995 some 43,426 candidates sat A level geography examinations. This made geography the fifth most popular A level subject, accounting for 6 per cent of the total number of candidate entries. In geography there had been an increase of over a quarter in the numbers sitting the examination since the start of the 1990s, compared to an overall increase in all subject entries of around 13 per cent. Interestingly, AS levels have attracted less significant numbers (less than 1,000 each year for geography AS levels since their inception in 1987, with total figures of just over 50,000 each year for all subjects).

✠ INDEPENDENT

FOUNDED 1986

ONE CANADA SQUARE CANARY WHARF LONDON E14 5DL
TELEPHONE 0171-293 2000 0171-345 2000 FAX 0171-293 2435 / 0171-345 2435

EDITOR: Ian Hargreaves

DEPUTY EDITOR: Martin Jacques MANAGING EDITOR: Colin Hughes
SECTION TWO EDITOR: Charles Leadbeater SATURDAY EDITOR: David Robson
EXECUTIVE NEWS EDITOR: Michael Williams ASSISTANT EDITOR: Simon Kelner

NEWSPAPER PUBLISHING PLC, BOARD OF DIRECTORS:
Liam Healy (Chairman) Sir Gordon Borrie Ben Bradlee Juan Luis Cebrián Brendan Hopkins
David Montgomery Javier Díez de Polanco Cornel Riklin Andreas Whittam Smith

ADVERTISING DIRECTOR: Jeremy Reed

No golden age of A-levels

Once again Britain's 18-year-olds have produced a record result. Once again a higher proportion than ever before have passed their A-levels and achieved top grades. And once again the cry has gone up that standards must be falling.

This is both difficult and dangerous territory. Of course standards matter. Anyone who has ever watched A-level examiners at work would know just how seriously, year on year, they take them. But the evidence that standards are falling is thin. And the idea that we can suddenly go back and compare A-level standards with those of some ancient golden age in the Fifties or Sixties is a myth. Not least there is the motivation of those who believe that the only explanation for more and better passes is that exams are getting easier.

Of course more 18-year-olds are passing A-levels. Back in the Fifties, A-levels were the exam of the élite. Just 3 per cent took them. Today 40 per cent do. They are a mass exam offering entry to a welcome and increasingly mass system of higher education. Even so, 17 per cent fail and another 13 per cent drop out of the A-level course.

And the world has changed in other ways. Even if the scripts existed, it would be impossible to go back and compare today's A-levels with those of the Sixties. In those days, Venn diagrams were part of additional maths at O-level. These days, six- and seven-year-olds learn them in primary school. In the early Sixties, the way in which DNA works was just creeping on to the A-level syllabus. Now it is one of the early parts of the A-level course.

In the Fifties, it is true that no one took A-levels in business studies. But the A-levels of the Fifties were equipping an élite for highly academic courses in a tiny university sector in a country where most jobs were still blue-collar. Today we hope to be equipping a nation to compete in a white-collar world of business, services and industry where computers control the lathes and where the skills of how to look up knowledge and apply it are at least as important as the skills of memory and recall. Of course examinations have changed.

The argument that more children cannot possibly be doing better reflects exactly the same élitist view of human nature which believed in the Fifties that there was only a certain fixed "pool" of intelligence. It was that view which maintained that only 20 per cent of children could be bright enough to go to grammar school because there were in fact only 20 per cent of places available in grammar schools. And it is the same view which led Kingsley Amis to pronounce of university expansion that "more will mean worse" – shortly before the Robbins report demonstrated that the so-called "pool" of intelligence was in fact a great lake.

A-levels should not be a competition that a set number have to fail but a set of standards – which will inevitably evolve upwards in terms of knowledge and content over time – that we want people to achieve.

Which is not an argument for complacency. Rigour is required, year on year, to ensure standards do not fall as the content and subject matter of A-levels evolve. But schools and their examinations should be windows to the future, not fogged mirrors reflecting a golden age that never was.

A/AS LEVEL CORES

In March 1992 the then Secondary Examination and Assessment Council (SEAC) produced a small leaflet for schools and examination boards which outlined new principles for the future design of A and AS level courses and examinations. These were to be largely externally assessed through 'terminal' examinations rather than through coursework, which was fixed at a maximum of 20 per cent of the final mark awarded. This imposed a coursework *reduction* on some existing A level geography syllabuses, whose examination boards saw these new restrictions as placing an unnecessary limitation on curriculum development by reversing the trend towards providing greater coursework entitlements for students. This change sat somewhat incongruously with one of the intentions of the new A and AS levels, namely to create a smoother transfer from GCSE courses which, in many cases, had recently increased their coursework provision.

In an attempt to create a more uniform standard of subject coverage by different examination boards, the idea of creating 'subject cores' was reintroduced by SEAC in the early 1990s. Essentially this meant that each examination board would design its subject syllabuses around an agreed 'core' of subject knowledge, skills, techniques, abilities and understanding. Although the idea is rational, and appeared a sensible first step towards standardizing national examinations such as the A/AS levels, it did create some problems with respect to geography. Reaching agreement on the content for the core and optional sections initially proved difficult, as did the creation of assessment activities to test the broad range of skills, knowledge and understanding of geography candidates at this level. In December 1993 the School Curriculum and Assessment Authority (SCAA), which had recently replaced SEAC following a merger with the National Curriculum Council (NCC), announced its finalized geography core, representing one-third of the content of each geography A level (or two-thirds of an AS level). The majority of examination boards saw the geography core as providing a suitable foundation on which to design their new syllabuses for 1995.

In essence the core requires students to develop a range of geographical skills and to gain an understanding of a people–environment theme at a range of different spatial scales. There is a mandatory study of physical and human environments and investigative work based upon the collection of both primary and secondary data. (At AS level primary data collection is not mandatory in the core, but can be included within the optional sections of the syllabus.)

Figure 27.1 (left) 'No golden age of A-levels'
Source: *The Independent*, 18 August 1995

A/AS LEVEL MODULES

At the same time as subject cores were being developed in 1993, SEAC was consulting widely on the possibilities of modularizing A and AS levels. One of the major advantages of successful modularization would be the possibility of transfering 'credits' (gained by passing modules) between academic and vocational courses. If such transfers could be successfully achieved there would be immense possibilities for the creation of a flexible 14–19 curriculum. Students would not suffer as a result of undue specialization at an early stage and could increasingly gear their education according to their needs. However, the difficulties of creating a viable and equitable system of credit accumulation and transfer have always appeared to be major stumbling blocks.

Interestingly, examination boards strongly favoured producing modular A levels for geography in 1995 (see Table 27.1) using the rules set by SCAA for a minimum of 15 per cent of marks to be awarded for each end-of-module examination, and at least 30 per cent for 'terminal' examinations. Boards were allowed to choose between assessing modules at the end of the two-year course, or at predetermined times within the course. This potentially creates two difficulties; first, that of boards administering a possibly huge combination of modules at different times throughout an A level course, and, second, regarding the 'maturation' of candidates during the course. The latter point refers to the way in which candidates develop their knowledge, understanding and skills as courses progress, such that by the time they take their terminal examinations they should be more proficient in each. Candidates' performance on modules assessed at, or near, the end of a course should therefore be better than those assessed at an early stage.

Not all subjects lend themselves readily to modularization. Geography, with its reliance on a sound holistic appreciation of its content, may suffer if it is haphazardly reduced into a series of loosely connected modules that have little overarching connection. The danger of an over-enthusiastic desire for a means of credit accumulation replacing the educational necessity to study a coherent discipline may not be over.

Dearing (1995) has highlighted his wish for there to be a strong connection between modularization at A/AS level and credit accumulation and transfer to GNVQ. This is perhaps the key to the future success of any long term academic–vocational link and the creation of a greater parity of esteem between the two systems.

Promotion of both core skills and modularization within A/AS level and GNVQ courses increasingly bring these qualifications closer together. What is still required is a simple way of comparing and rewarding academic and vocational achievement. The vision of successful modularization leading to a 'new world' of credit accumulation and transfer between such

Table 27.1 A/AS approved syllabuses (as of 30 June 1995)

Board	Syllabus	Assessment route(s)	Coursework
AEB	A Level (0626)	Modular or linear	0 or 20%
	AS (0988)	Linear	0%
NEAB	A Level	Modular or linear	0 or 16.7%
	AS	Modular or linear	0%
OCSEB	A Level (9630)	Modular**	20%
	AS (8370)	Linear	20%
UCLES	A Level (9518)	Modular	16.7%
	AS (8558)	Modular	6.7%
UCLES	A Level (9050)	Linear	4* or 20%
ULEAC	A Level Syl A (9201)	Modular**	15%
	AS Syl A (8201)	Modular**	15%
ULEAC	A Level Syl B (9211)	Modular**	20%
	AS Syl B (8211)	Modular**	20%
UODLE***	A Level (9945)	Modular**	18%
	AS (9945)	Modular**	18%
WJEC	A Level	Modular or linear	16.7%
	AS	Modular or linear	3.3%

Source: SCAA 1995

* A report of an enquiry is required as part of the assessment of a written paper component

** All modules may be assessed at the end of the course

*** Approved subject to the submission of satisfactory specimen assessment materials

ABBREVIATIONS:

AEB   The Associated Examining Board
NEAB   Northern Examinations and Assessment Board
OCSEB Oxford and Cambridge Schools Examination Board
UCLES University of Cambridge Local Examinations Syndicate
ULEAC University of London Examinations and Assessment Council
UODLE University of Oxford Delegacy of Local Examinations
WJEC   Welsh Joint Education Committee

courses is coming into focus, but, as yet, may simply be an illusion. If modularization does not work, and there are already concerns about modularity within A/AS levels reducing standards, the academic–vocational link probably will not either (Butt and Lambert 1993).

In conclusion, the position of A/AS levels in geography, and every other subject, appears secure for the near future. Dearing's (1995) reference to A levels still being 'effective for the purpose for which they are designed', i.e. predominantly academic selection between students aged 18 or 19 for the purpose of university entrance selection, appears to fortify their status.

AS LEVELS

Designed to be of a similar standard to A levels, but requiring half the teaching and studying time, AS levels have not been a spectacular success since their introduction in 1987. Their lack of popularity is linked to a range of perceived difficulties. Schools and colleges have found timetabling and resourcing the courses difficult and have been concerned about the qualification's acceptability to higher education institutions and the world of work. This has partly resulted in parents, employers and students being reluctant to commit themselves to AS level qualifications. Future changes may necessitate AS levels having a similar breadth to A levels, but less depth, in effect, more clearly representing an intermediate qualification between GCSE and A level.

GNVQs AND NVQs

From the early 1990s the Conservative government wished to strengthen the vocational options open to 14 to 19 year-olds and provide a viable alternative to the dominance of the academic pathway occupied by A and AS levels. Mindful of the increasing numbers of students 'staying on' at the age of 16, the further development of vocational courses seemed essential. Additionally, extending vocational courses 'downwards' to 14-year-olds would widen their educational options rather than restricting them. This had a particular influence on geography, which had once again become an optional subject in Key Stage 4 following the first Dearing (1994) review. Not only was competition to be faced from other optional subjects, but also from new 'part 1' vocational GNVQs which would also contend for the 40 per cent of the school curriculum that was no longer deemed 'compulsory'.

The first stage in this process was to unify a confusing plethora of different vocational qualifications into two new qualifications: the NVQ and GNVQ. The NVQ is essentially a work-based, vocational qualification whereas the GNVQ is mainly taken in schools and colleges and can be geared either to vocational or to academic routes (see Table 27.2).

By 1993 the government was clear that GNVQs should develop into a mainstream qualification for young people, catering for as much as half the 16–19 age-group, and that they should exist on a par with academic qualifications. This created something of a dilemma for geography teachers, and teachers in other disciplines, concerning the status of vocational

Table 27.2 Comparisons between A/AS levels, GNVQs and NVQs

A/AS level	GNVQ	NVQ
Academic.	Broadly vocational (work-related).	Specific to occupation (work).
Studied mainly at school or college.	Studied mainly at school or college.	Studied mainly at work.
Attainment-based.	Attainment-based.	Competence-based.
Centred on knowledge, understanding and skills.	Centred on knowledge, understanding, skills and principles.	Centred on performance.
Assessment narrowly based. Each subject has a core of content prescribed.	Assessment broadly based, including core skills.	Assessment of work-based competence.
Terminal examinations.	No terminal examinations.	
Modular structure to many courses with separate modular exams. Externally set, marked and administered.	Some written tests, externally set, marked and administered.	No terminal examinations. Performance assessed in the workplace.
Course work.	Portfolios of work.	
Graded.	Graded (including merits and distinctions).	Pass/fail assessment. Can do/cannot do criteria.
Usually a two-year time limit.	No time limit on completion.	No time limit on completion.

Source: after Hyland 1995

courses. If parity of esteem was secured what would be the effects on geographical education? The questions this raises are crucial ones. In which domain of education do we want the discipline of geography to be strongly represented? Should geography be pursued solely as an academic subject, and perhaps run the risk of losing its post-16 foothold altogether? Or should it promote a more vocationally orientated approach, and possibly endanger its academic future and 'respectability'?

What is perhaps clear is that few geographers want their subject simply to become a purveyor of map-reading skills, or disembodied knowledge of where places are. We have a broader contribution of skills, knowledge and understanding to make towards the education of young people.

Being a vocational qualification a GNVQ in geography *per se* does not, and will not, exist. However, there are various geographical elements in

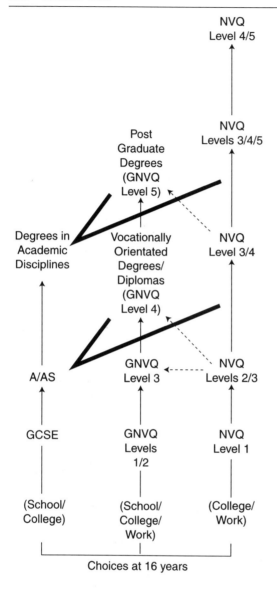

Figure 27.2 National Qualifications Framework
Source: *The NVQ Monitor*, Summer 1995, London: NCVQ

courses such as Leisure and Tourism, Manufacturing, and Land-based and Environmental Industries which geography teachers have been asked to deliver within their schools and colleges. The additional funding from the DFEE associated with GNVQ students has been an obvious attraction to many of these institutions.

60 per cent of young people should achieve 2 A levels, an advanced GNVQ or NVQ level 3 by the age of 21.

85 per cent of young people should achieve 5 GCSEs at grade C or above, or an intermediate GNVQ or an NVQ at level 2 by the age of 19.

75 per cent of young people should achieve level 2 competence in communication, numeracy and IT by the age of 19, and 35 per cent should achieve level 3 competence in these core skills by the age of 21.

Figure 27.3 National targets for education and training by 2000
Source: White Paper *Competitiveness – Forging Ahead* May 1994, CM2867 (proposed by the National Advisory Council for Education and Training Targets)

At first glance the structures of GNVQ courses are complex, but they do have a logical order and composition. Figure 27.2 indicates the nature of these courses and their approximate comparability to academic qualifications. For many students the prospects of returning to school after either failing, or receiving unsatisfactory, GCSE results to study for retakes has proved less attractive than starting a new vocationally based course such as the GNVQ.

There is evidence that 'GNVQs have developed more rapidly than anyone expected, and more rapidly than government targets which were widely regarded as over-optimistic' (Wright 1995). The initial period has been fraught with difficulties with regard to assessment, record-keeping, rigour, guidance and standards, each of which has been widely reported (Smithers 1993; OFSTED 1993, 1994; Utley 1994; CBI Report 1994; Hyland 1995). As yet, the acceptability of GNVQs to a range of university degrees is also unclear, as are the plans for many universities to establish their own higher level vocational degrees (Targett and Tysome 1994).

By the end of this century, under current plans (see Figure. 27.3), some three-quarters of all young people should take some form of vocational qualification (Smithers 1995). Indeed, by the middle of the 1990s some 250,000 students had already started GNVQs, a figure equivalent to one-third of those studying for A levels. The widespread introduction of GNVQs naturally has implications for staff retraining, revising workloads and updating systems of resourcing, administration, assessment and record-keeping. In many schools and colleges the need for geography teachers to have gained some relevant vocational experience has also become pressing. This led some observers to advise geography departments to be cautious about taking on large-scale GNVQ commitments too hastily (Marvell 1994; Butt 1994).

CONCLUSIONS

Daugherty outlines three obstructions to the development of assessment policies for 16 to 19 year-olds in England and Wales which together, he believes, 'exercise a powerful and malign influence'. The first concerns the faith that written examinations *on their own* can offer a valid basis for assessing attainment; the second is the belief that by merely putting together the pieces of an assessment system one can create a coherent and complete assessment package; while the third is the conviction that criterion referencing will easily form the basis for a national assessment system, rather than being 'the first step in designing a credible, workable, system' (Daugherty 1995). In crude terms, the first 'obstruction' typifies the A level examination, the second represents the need for both A level and GNVQ to benefit from clear planning, while the third relates to the assessment of GNVQs. As Daugherty concludes, 'If the A level and GNVQ approaches are to co-exist and, taken together, to serve the needs of all students, some clear thinking is required in respect of assessment as well as curriculum'.

The age-old problem of vocational courses being seen by many as the fate of the academically less able, thus ensuring the continuation of an academic–vocational divide, has not been lessened (and indeed may have been worsened) by the over-hasty introduction of the GNVQ. Establishing equality of esteem and comparability of standards will not be easy; only two years after their introduction it became increasingly apparent that 'base GNVQs [were] losing the alchemical struggle to become golden A levels' (*THES* 'Opinion' 4 November 1994). However, as Dearing (1995) himself has pointed out, it takes at least ten years for a new qualification to become well known and understood by the community at large.

The immediate hurdle for post-16 courses appears to be in unifying assessment systems created for different purposes, which have different structures and different methods of assessment. Knowledge-based A levels, including those for geography, contain up to six modules and are assessed across five grades; process-based GNVQs contain twelve units and have three grades; while the practical NVQs have variable unit numbers and no grades whatsoever! Only after a more comparable assessment and accreditation system is devised will thorny issues like credit transfer and accumulation be resolved.

Geography educationalists have traditionally been keen to introduce innovative courses for the post-16 student, as previously witnessed by the Schools Council 14–18 Bristol Project and the 16–19 Project. The recent past has also seen geographers involved with Industry Years, working with local and national industries, in TECs, and with The Geographical Association's Geography Schools Industry Project (GSIP). Geography has been marketed as being applicable to the world of work, where its skills, knowledge and understanding can be of direct relevance. But how far should we go in developing this utilitarian and vocational function?

The danger may be that if we do not embrace vocationalism to some extent, and 'marginalise geography as a narrowly "academic subject"' (Butt and Lambert 1993), it may lose its curriculum foothold completely. Nonetheless, the continuing need for children to experience coherent, exciting and relevant geography courses up to, and beyond the option choices at 14 is essential. If they do not, the maintenance of a base of GCSE, A/AS level geography students, 'geography-related' GNVQs, and eventually degree entrance geographers will become problematic.

REFERENCES

Butt, G. (1994) 'Geography, vocational education and assessment', *Teaching Geography* 19(4): 182–3.

Butt, G. and Lambert, D. (1993) 'Modules, cores and the new A/AS levels', *Teaching Geography* 18(4): 180–1.

Confederation of British Industry (1994) *Quality Assured: CBI review of NVQs and SVQs*, London: CBI.

Daugherty, R. (1995) 'To pastures new', *The Times Educational Supplement*, 8 September: 23.

Dearing, R. (1994) *The National Curriculum and its Assessment: Final Report*, London: School Curriculum and Assessment Authority.

Dearing, R. (1995) *Review of 16–19 Qualifications: Interim Report*, London: School Curriculum and Assessment Authority.

Hyland, T. (1995) *A Critical Study of GNVQs*, Warwick University: Continuing Education Research Centre.

Marvell, A. (1994) 'Should your school geography department consider GNVQ Leisure and Tourism?', *Teaching Geography* 19(4): 175–6.

OFSTED (1993) *GNVQs in Schools*, London: HMSO.

OFSTED (1994) *GNVQs in Schools*, London: HMSO.

School Curriculum and Assessment Authority (1995) *A/AS Geography: Approved Syllabuses*, London: SCAA.

Smithers, A. (1993) *All Our Futures: Britain's Education Revolution*, London: Channel 4 Dispatches Report.

Smithers, A. (1995) 'A quiet revolution in post-16 education', The *Independent*, Education Section, 20 March.

Targett, S. and Tysome, T. (1994) Vocational degrees delay, *The Times Higher Education Supplement*, 24 June.

Utley, A. (1994) 'Teething troubles plague GNVQs', *The Times Higher Education Supplement*, 24 June.

Wright, P. (1995) *Vocational Qualifications and Standards in Focus*, London: Higher Education Quality Council.

Index

active learning 94, 159; games 51, 113; role-play 45, 51, 100, 108, 113, 137; simulations 45, 51, 113, 140

Advanced (A) Level 3, 35, 51, 52, 55, 83, 109, 243, 298–309; assessment 260; fieldwork 193; introduction of 287; progression in 197

aims: of education 27, 52, 181; of geographical education 8–9, 27, 187; geographical instruction 137

assessment: criterion referencing 118, 289; formal 256; formative 3, 29, 256, 258, 267; in GCSE 294–6; informal 29, 273; KS3 284; KS4 26, 29, 298–309; of local area 220; models of 276; monitoring progress 28, 29; National Curriculum 20, 25, 276-86; norm referencing 256, 266, 289; objectives 29–30; in the primary school 266–74; pupil 1, 3, 61, 67, 141, 254–65; purposes of 60, 257; student 298–309; summative 3, 29, 61, 144, 284; teacher 3, 29, 258, 276–86; see also examination(s)

Attainment Target(s) 19, 25, 26, 41, 69, 82, 99, 118, 278

bias 3, 112; cultural 181; ethnocentric 180–8; gender 117–28; race 117–28
Bloom, B.S. 40
Bruner, J. 35, 43
Bullock Report 154
bullying 100

Chomsky, N. 154
citizenship 10, 19, 99, 102, 108, 117, 233, 241, 249; education for 2, 93–104, 119, 128, 242

cognitive: acceleration 143–53; development 168: theories of 176–7;
coherence 2, 11, 298
community understanding 2, 99–103
course development 35–48
critical: agents 181; approaches 247; geography 117, 241–52; pupils 47; review of textbooks 180; thinking 94, 112, 114; theory 245–8; thought 30; tradition 242; questions 94
cross-curricular 12: concerns 80–92, 93–104; co-ordination and collaboration 86–8; themes 2, 93–104, 105–14, 119, 139, 245
curriculum: balance 11, 16, 22, 57, 94, 119; change 52–3, 69; coherence 59– 68; Cymreig 137; development 35–48; development and equal opportunities 118–19; integration 11; KS4 26; place of geography in 7–14; planning 35–48, 70, 133, 144; primary 8, 10; secondary 8, 10; whole 25, 117, 119, 190
Curriculum Council for Wales (CCW) 96, 102, 224
Curriculum and Assessment Authority for Wales (ACAD) 291

Dearing 18, 22, 23; Report 25, 26, 30, 93, 298; Review 21–2, 83, 103, 107, 244, 276, 299, 304
development 118; education 2, 124, 105–11, 245; geography 123–5; and the National Curriculum 110, 124
Dewey, J. 9
differentiation 69–79, 146, 195

early years of schooling 9, 59
Earth science 80–92

Economic and Industrial Understanding (EIU) 2, 93–104, 119
Education Reform Act (ERA) 2, 25, 41, 64, 118, 244, 276
empowerment 94, 113, 243; education for 181–2
England 1, 93, 110, 133, 143. 203, 241, 287, 290
environment(s) 10, 28, 49, 53, 54, 55, 56, 105–14, 118, 119, 138, 249, 301
Environmental Education (EE) 2, 19, 94, 119, 189, 105–16, 245
environmental geography 19
enquiry 140; in GCSE 295; geographical 25, 44–6, 53, 54, 83–6, 90, 137, 193; and IT 205–6; learning 19, 218; skills 30; questions for 225
equal opportunities 2, 69, 117–29; and resources 125–8
Europe 117, 191, 231–2, 248; Eurocentric 182, 185; European bias 180; European dimension 231–40
examination(s) 287–8; A level 299, 302; boards 41, 81, 301–2, 290–1; see also assessment
experience: first hand 10, 219–30, 232; geographical 9

Field Studies Council 191
fieldwork 27; alternative approaches to 190; importance of 10; and IT 198– 9; planning 193–8; progression 197–8; teaching and learning strategies 191–3; value and purpose of 189–90

games 51, 113, 122–3; see also active learning
GCSE 3, 21, 26, 35, 41, 83, 143, 151, 287–97; aims of 291; assessment 294–6; choosing a syllabus 292; criteria 56, 118; and differentiation 76; fieldwork 193; grades 144; historical context of 287–90; maps 174; national criteria 55; progression 197; syllabus content and assessment 29, 278
Geikie, Archibald 7–8, 49
gender 117–28, 186, 219; differences in geographical learning 120–3; and resources 125-8

Geographic Information Systems (GIS) 203, 214–16
Geographical Association (GA) 7, 15–17, 29, 49, 191, 197, 207, 239, 250, 291, 293
GNVQ 3, 26, 98, 299–309
graphicacy 163, 169; skills 27, 30; see also maps
group work 45; 122–3; 158–9

Hadow Report 9, 218
Herbertson, A.J. 7, 49
Her Majesty's Inspectorate 218
historical: context of GCSE 287– 90; roots of geography 7–8, 49–50, 242–4

Information Technology (IT) 29, 67, 139, 202–17, 239
In-Service Education and Training (INSET) 67, 288
interdisciplinary: approach 12; enquiry 11
International Geographic Union 128
issues 27; based approach 11–13; controversial 21, 117; environmental 3, 19, 28, 56, 60, 106, 107, 193, 207; geographical 21

key stage(s) 1, 16, 23, 25-29, 38, 55, 83–4, 118, 139, 195, 234; and CCTHs 96, 98, 101, 108, 110–11; and differentiation 70; and Earth science 89; and geographical skills 203–4; KS4 assessment 290, 304; and locality 219–30; progression in 61–8
knowledge 41, 45, 59, 171, 226; and the CCTHs 100, 110–11; critical 247; of environment and development problems 111–14; geographical 16, 21; locational 23, 168; objective 181; personal 218; of place 19, 187, 219, 267–9, 281–2; positivist 246; progression of 281; representation of 180, 187; and SATs 276; social construction of 181; of themes 282

language: geographical terms 164–6; groupwork and 158–9; and learning 154–67; map 169, 171; reading 163–4; talk 155–8; use of 45, 154; writing 159–63

league tables 41
less able pupils 11–12
level descriptors 22, 266, 278–83
local: community 219–30, 250; locality, study of 10–11; locality in an economically developing country 270–1

Mackinder, Halford 7–8, 49
maps 27, 29, 220; cognitive development through 175–7; communication through 168–79; community 229; digital data 203; and gender 120; language 169, 171; mental maps 27, 174; projections 232; properties of 170–3; purpose of 173–5; scale 27, 171; skills 170, 175, 177, 270
metacognition 147, 177
Modules, A/AS level 302–4
motivation: pupil 11, 12; teacher 140

National Curriculum 1, 11,12, 25–30, 35–48, 55, 80, 83, 88, 118, 169, 182–5, 193; and assessment 266; CCTHs 93–104, 105–16; development of 15–23; differentiation in the 69, 76; and educational reform 243–4; English Orders 56, 187, 218, 290; European dimension in 231–2; fairness in 260–1; framework 259; overprescription 119; and recording 262–4; requirements 133, 137, 219; teacher assessment in 276–86; Welsh Orders 56, 108, 290
National Curriculum Council (NCC) 25, 87, 96, 119, 301
New Technologies 202, 214–17, 250
Norwood Report 10, 287

objectives 195; model of planning 39–43
Office for Standards in Education (OFSTED) 22, 41, 46–7, 143, 152, 234, 235, 244, 250

Piaget, J. 136, 151, 154, 176
place 241; experience of 190; geographical places in NC 25, 26, 27; of geography in the school curriculum 7–14; knowledge of place 119
Plowden Report 10
post-16 23, 56, 298–309
primary: assessment in 266–74; education 8–9, 231–40, 266; geography 23; pupil 101; school(s) 3, 9–11, 25, 55, 64–7, 136, 232, 235, 239; teachers 232, 266
programme of study 25, 26, 27, 45, 70, 133
progression 59–68; in Earth science 89; between GCSE and A level 299; in mapwork 168; in the National Curriculum 61–8; principles of 59– 61
progressive 245; ideologies 8; methods 8; practice 7–11

questions: and answers 155–8; and differentiation 78; for developing values 119; for equal opportunities 125; geographical 27, 44–5, 53, 112; key 45, 55

race 117, 186; racism 100, 242; racist 8, 117–28, 180
remote sensing 214–15
resources 46, 71, 90, 139, 237; for equal opportunities 125–8
role-playing 45, 51, 100, 108, 113, 137; see also active learning
Royal Geographical Society (RGS) 7, 11, 49, 191

satellite imagery 29, 163
Schools Council 36, 52, 55
Schools Curriculum and Assessment Authority (SCAA) 25, 26, 29, 55, 260, 276, 286, 291, 302
secondary: development of 7–14; school(s) 3, 10; 25, 55, 64–7, 81, 136, 202, 239, 288; students 101; teachers 7, 23, 143
Secondary Examination and Assessment Council (SEAC) 301
scope of geography 49–58
simulations 45, 51, 113, 140; see also active learning
skills 301; action 114; aesthetic 193; assessment 260; atlas skills 269; core 302; critical thinking skills 112, 114;